Cornelius Friesendorf

The Military and Law Enforcement in Peace Operations

Geneva Centre for the
Democratic Control of Armed Forces
(DCAF)

LIT

Cornelius Friesendorf

The Military and Law Enforcement in Peace Operations

Lessons from Bosnia-Herzegovina and Kosovo

LIT

Gedruckt auf alterungsbeständigem Werkdruckpapier entsprechend
ANSI Z3948 DIN ISO 9706

Bibliographic information published by the Deutsche Nationalbibliothek
The Deutsche Nationalbibliothek lists this publication in the Deutsche Nationalbibliografie; detailed bibliographic data are available in the Internet at http://dnb.d-nb.de.

ISBN 978-3-643-80043-5

A catalogue record for this book is available from the British Library

Krotenthallergasse 10/8
A-1080 Wien
Tel. +43 (0) 1-409 56 61
Fax +43 (0) 1-409 56 97
e-Mail: wien@lit-verlag.at
http://www.lit-verlag.at

LIT VERLAG Dr. W. Hopf
Berlin 2010
Fresnostr. 2
D-48159 Münster
Tel. +49 (0) 2 51-620 320
Fax +49 (0) 2 51-922 60 99
e-Mail: lit@lit-verlag.de
http://www.lit-verlag.de

Distribution:
In Germany: LIT Verlag Fresnostr. 2, D-48159 Münster
Tel. +49 (0) 2 51-620 32 22, Fax +49 (0) 2 51-922 60 99, e-Mail: vertrieb@lit-verlag.de

In Austria: Medienlogistik Pichler-ÖBZ GmbH & Co KG
IZ-NÖ, Süd, Straße 1, Objekt 34, A-2355 Wiener Neudorf
Tel. +43 (0) 22 36-63 53 52 90, Fax +43 (0) 22 36-63 53 52 43, e-Mail: mlo@medien-logistik.at

In Switzerland: B + M Buch- und Medienvertriebs AG
Hochstr. 357, CH-8200 Schaffhausen
Tel. +41 (0) 52-643 54 30, Fax +41 (0) 52-643 54 35, e-Mail: order@buch-medien.ch

In the UK by: Global Book Marketing, 99B Wallis Rd, London, E9 5LN
Phone: +44 (0) 20 8533 5800 – Fax: +44 (0) 1600 775 663
http://www.centralbooks.co.uk/html

In North America by:

Transaction Publishers
New Brunswick (U.S.A.) and London (U.K.)

Transaction Publishers
Rutgers University
35 Berrue Circle
Piscataway, NJ 08854

Phone: +1 (732) 445 - 2280
Fax: + 1 (732) 445 - 3138
for orders (U. S. only):
toll free (888) 999 - 6778
e-mail: orders@transactionpub.com

Contents

About This Book *vii*
Acknowledgements *ix*
Abbreviations *xi*

1 **Introduction** 1

2 **The Military, Law Enforcement and Peace Operations** 9

Post-Conflict Security Gaps and International Military Forces 14
Conceptualising Military Involvement in Post-Conflict Law Enforcement 20
Conditions for Military Law Enforcement Support 28

3 **Bosnia-Herzegovina** 33

IFOR 33
SFOR 39
The EU Takes Over 55
The Tricky Question of Effectivenes 72

4 **Kosovo** 89

NATO Enters Kosovo 89
NATO in an International Protectorate 98
NATO and Serious Crime in Kosovo Before and After Independence 104

5 Conclusion: Improving Military Support to Law Enforcement 143

Case Study Findings 145

Improving Military Contributions to Post-Conflict Law Enforcement 150

Beyond the Balkans 158

Final Thoughts 161

References 165

About the Author 193

About DCAF 195

About This Book

For post-conflict stabilisation and peacebuilding efforts to have a chance of success, security gaps need to be closed. Domestic law enforcement agencies tend to be too weak or unreliable after war to enforce the law and fight serious crime. As a consequence, operations against organised crime, the arrest of suspected war criminals and the protection of minorities depend on international intervention forces. Much attention has been paid to domestic police reform and the problems of deploying international civilian police. This book examines the under-explored role of international military missions in post-conflict law enforcement, with a focus on serious crime.

The military is under pressure to fill security gaps. Yet military involvement in crime-fighting is problematic practically (soldiers are generally not trained and equipped for it), politically (crime-fighting is seen as military mission creep) and normatively (it undermines the delineation of military and policing functions). Military support of law enforcement poses a major dilemma in peace operations. Decision-makers continue to struggle with this dilemma in an ad-hoc fashion, while scholars have so far provided few empirical accounts. This book focuses on post-war Bosnia-Herzegovina (BiH) and Kosovo. It argues that the pros of military involvement in law enforcement outweigh the cons, given the continuing lack of strong police forces, the criminalised nature of contemporary wars and the negative influence of spoilers on stabilisation and peacebuilding efforts. Military support of the fight against serious crime is not sufficient for these efforts to succeed, but it is necessary.

This book has three objectives. It describes the role of NATO and EU military missions in law enforcement in BiH and Kosovo from the 1990s through early 2009, thus filling an empirical knowledge gap. By formulating a strategy for military involvement in law enforcement, the book also makes a normative contribution to the debate on peace operations. Drawing on, among other sources, interviews in these two 'international protectorates', the book shows that military support of the fight against serious crime has lacked effectiveness, efficiency and legitimacy, examples of success notwithstanding. Third, the book adds conceptual value to the debate on peace operations, by drawing on security governance, Security Sector Reform and Security Sector Governance. These concepts help to understand the military role in post-conflict law enforcement and to guide improved efforts.

Acknowledgements

Earlier drafts of this book were presented at the University of Belgrade, the Centre for Civil-Military Relations (CCMR) in Belgrade, the University of Munich, the University of Konstanz, the Belgrade Centre for Human Rights, the University of Geneva and the 2009 Annual Convention of the International Studies Association in New York City. Conference participants provided valuable feedback. The first case study draws on an article co-authored with my good friend and colleague Susan Penksa (in International Peacekeeping 15:5). Special thanks go to the CCMR and the Centre for Security Studies in Sarajevo for hosting me so kindly in 2007 and 2008. I am also grateful to the interviewees (who are cited anonymously), as well as the Volkswagen Foundation, which financed my fieldwork in Southeast Europe between 2006 and 2008.

For discussions, contacts and information I thank Dejan Anastasijević, Peter Andreas, Richard Barszczewski, Wolfgang Benedek, Hans Born, Max Bornefeld-Ettmann, Benjamin S. Buckland, Christoph Buehler, Biljana Đorđević, Petrus C. van Duyne, Tobias Flessenkemper, Friedrich Christian Haas, Alice Hills, Holger Kasch, Fedor Keredzin, Alexandre Lambert, Theodore Leggett, Sanja Mihajlović, Garren Mulloy, David Nosworthy, Markus Orgis, Lulzim Peci, Susan E. Penksa, Sammi Sandawi, Albrecht Schnabel, Fred Schreier, Ursula C. Schroeder, Darko Stančić, Peter Vanhoutte, Victoria Walker, Aidan Wills and especially Heiner Hänggi, Beverly Youmans and two anonymous reviewers.

Any errors and shortcomings in this book are my responsibility. It must also be noted that many of those who helped me in researching and writing this book disagree with some of the findings.

Cornelius Friesendorf
Frankfurt am Main, November 2009

Abbreviations

ANP	Afghan National Police
BBP	Border and Boundary Police
BiH	Bosnia and Herzegovina
BND	Bundesnachrichtendienst (German Federal Intelligence Service)
CIA	Central Intelligence Agency
CIMIC	Civil-Military Cooperation
CIU	Criminal Intelligence Unit
CIVPOL	Civilian Police
COM KFOR	Commander of KFOR
CRC	Crowd and Riot Control
DDR	Disarmament, Demobilisation and Reintegration
ESDP	European Security and Defence Policy
EU	European Union
EUFOR	European Union Force
EULEX	European Union Rule of Law Mission in Kosovo
EUPM	European Union Police Force
GSG 9	Grenzschutzgruppe 9
HUMINT	Human Intelligence
ICG	International Crisis Group
ICTY	International Criminal Tribunal for the Former Yugoslavia
IFOR	Implementation Force
IPTF	International Police Task Force
IPU	Integrated Police Unit
ISR	Intelligence, Surveillance and Reconnaissance
JFC	Joint Force Command
JIOC	Joint Intelligence Operations Center
KFOR	Kosovo Force
KLA/UÇK	Kosovo Liberation Army/Ushtria Çlirimtare e Kosovës
KOCB	Kosovo Organised Crime Bureau
KPC	Kosovo Protection Corps
KPS	Kosovo Police Service
KSF	Kosovo Stability Force
KSK	Kommando Spezialkräfte (Special Forces Command)
LMT	Liaison and Monitoring Team
LOT	Liaison and Observation Team

MNB	Multinational Brigade
MND	Multinational Division
MSU	Multinational Specialised Unit
MTF	Multinational Task Force
MUP	Ministarstvo Unutrasnjih Poslova/(Police of the) Ministry of Interior
NAC	North Atlantic Council
NATO	North Atlantic Treaty Organization
NGO	Non-governmental Organisation
NIC	National Intelligence Cell
OHR	Office of the High Representative
OSCE	Organization for Security and Cooperation in Europe
PIFWC	Person Indicted for War Crimes
PISG	Provisional Institutions for Self-Government
PMSC	Private Military and Security Company
PRT	Provincial Reconstruction Team
RoE	Rules of Engagement
RS	Republika Srpska
SACEUR	Supreme Allied Commander Europe
SALW	Small Arms and Light Weapons
SAS	Special Air Services
SFOR	Stabilisation Force
SIPA	State Information and Protection Agency/State Investigation and Protection Agency
SPU	Special Police Unit
SRSG	Special Representative of the (UN) Secretary-General
SSG	Security Sector Governance
SSR	Security Sector Reform
SSU	Special Support Unit
STOP	Special Trafficking Operations Programme
SWAT	Special Weapons and Tactics
UN	United Nations
UNHCR	United Nations High Commissioner for Refugees
UNMIBH	United Nations Mission in Bosnia and Herzegovina
UNMIK	United Nations Interim Administration Mission in Kosovo
UNODC	United Nations Office on Drugs and Crime
US	United States

Chapter 1

Introduction

When war ends law enforcement is needed. War criminals must be arrested, organised crime checked, and attacks on minorities and refugees prevented or punished. If those committing serious crime are given free rein to violate laws and human rights with impunity, efforts to stabilise war-torn countries are bound to fail. Law enforcement is necessary for post-conflict stabilisation and peacebuilding.

This book focuses on the role of the military and highlights a major dilemma. Military involvement in law enforcement is needed to fill security gaps.[1] Domestic security forces tend to be weak or compromised after war, and international civilian police (CIVPOL) forces usually arrive late and in insufficient numbers. Moreover, conditions in post-war countries may draw the military into the law enforcement realm.

Yet military involvement in law enforcement is problematic. Soldiers are trained to confront, and kill if necessary, organised enemies. But when arresting members of organised crime networks and seizing their assets, it is crucial to secure the chain of evidence. When a rioting mob pelts security forces or returning refugees with stones, opening indiscriminate fire at the rioters would be inappropriate. Military forces often do not possess the training and equipment to conduct law enforcement tasks. Not least for this reason, the evolution of democracy has gone hand in hand with the separation of military from policing tasks. Employing the military for law enforcement undermines the international message that post-conflict states should respect the norms associated with modern, democratic statehood.

Moreover, many decision-makers invoke the danger of mission creep. During the 2000 United States (US) Presidential Campaign, Condoleezza Rice, then-foreign policy adviser to George W. Bush, said: "We don't need to have the 82nd Airborne escorting kids to kindergarten."[2] Many argue that engaging soldiers in non-core military activities undermines troop morale and preparedness for warfare, and increases the risk of military casualties.

This book contributes to the debate on peace operations in three ways. First, by describing military involvement in post-war law enforcement in two concrete cases, the book fills an empirical knowledge gap. The empirical question to which this book attempts to find an (incomplete and tentative) answer is: To what extent have NATO and European Union (EU) military missions in Bosnia-Herzegovina (BiH) and Kosovo participated in the fight against serious crime?

Many authors have noted that after the Cold War, soldiers have been drawn into operations against crime, terrorism and other 'homeland security' issues.[3] Authors have also focused on the involvement of international military forces in law enforcement operations abroad, particularly as part of the US 'war on drugs'.[4] Further, some authors have examined the rise of constabulary forces in international affairs and underlined their advantages vis-à-vis the police and regular military forces.[5] Blurred military and policing functions are both a cause and a consequence of the blurring of internal and external security.[6]

The rule of law is a major political and scholarly topic as well. Over recent decades, numerous rule of law programmes have been exported to developing, transitional and post-conflict countries. As part of the debate on post-conflict intervention and peacebuilding, much attention has been paid to the role of spoilers of peace processes such as organised crime groups,[7] post-conflict Security Sector Reform (SSR) efforts,[8] especially police reform,[9] and the deployment of CIVPOL.[10] Furthermore, much interest has been paid to issues of civil-military relations after conflict, such as military support of economic reconstruction.[11] While authors have also examined the military-police interface in peace operations,[12] few studies reveal the empirical details of military involvement in post-conflict law enforcement.[13] By taking a close look at dynamics not only on the diplomatic, strategic and doctrinal levels, but also on the operational and tactical levels, this study sheds light on militarised law enforcement after war.

In addition to making an empirical contribution, this book is policy-relevant and proposes an ideal-type strategy for coping with the dilemma of involving military forces in post-conflict law enforcement. The question here is: To what extent should the military become involved in the fight against serious crime? It is argued that when CIVPOL and domestic security forces are weak, international military forces should do things done by the police in more stable settings.[14] However, the military should hand over law enforcement responsibilities to the police as soon as possible. Thereafter, viable police-military networks are needed to enforce the law. Moreover, when becoming involved in law enforcement, soldiers must avoid any excessive use of force and respect standard judicial principles.

This book fills a conceptual gap as well. It shows that the concepts of security governance, Security Sector Governance (SSG) and SSR help to understand the military role in post-conflict law enforcement and serve as normative guidance for improving this role. The question here is: How can the police/military interface in peace operations be conceptualised?

Several caveats and limits of this study must be mentioned. First, the book does not provide a systematic explanation for why soldiers engage in law enforcement.[15] Doing so would require a close look at decision-making and institutional learning by international organisations and governments.[16] However, the book does refer to factors such as the fear of military mission creep (to explain military reluctance of becoming mired in 'policing' tasks); the role of entrepreneurial decision-makers and new crime-fighting discourses (to explain military activism); and problems of multilateral military coalitions, military training and military equipment (to explain unsystematic military law enforcement).

Focusing on the cases of post-Dayton BiH (hereafter also referred to as Bosnia) and post-war Kosovo, this book examines efforts of NATO and EU military forces against serious crime. A dilemma means that there is no perfect choice between two options – a decision either way has disadvantages. However, one course of action may still be better than the other. Serious crime in post-war Bosnia and Kosovo has presented the military with a major dilemma.

Second, measuring organised crime and the impact of counter-efforts is notoriously difficult. A lack of available and reliable information on serious crime, the secretive nature of law enforcement and intelligence operations,[17] and the large number of actors and programmes make it difficult to study policy impact. Yet, available data and information suggest that the military has only partially been successful. If organised crime thrives, if suspected war criminals are not caught and vulnerable individuals and groups are attacked despite the presence of peacekeepers, law enforcement is not high on the military agenda. If the military does engage in law enforcement, even haphazardly, post-conflict security governance is flawed.

Third, the notions of law enforcement, rule of law, serious crime and organised crime are controversial.[18] Crime is not simply out there. Instead, the criminalisation of specific activities reflects culturally and temporarily contingent collective perceptions, as well as the prejudices and priorities of powerful individuals and institutions.[19] This book defines serious crime as criminalised acts that destabilise reconstruction and peacebuilding efforts.[20] These are war crimes committed during war, attacks on minorities and returning refugees after war and organised crime activities, especially the smuggling and trafficking of people and goods. Conventional crime such as burglary or murder not committed for political reasons is not discussed in depth (despite the seriousness for those affected).

Forth, this book does discuss CIVPOL and domestic law enforcement agencies, showing how their weaknesses have facilitated military involvement in law enforcement. However, police and border guard agencies are studied only with regard to their links to the military. This study also does not discuss domestic military forces, or the role of international military forces in national defence reform.

A fifth caveat pertains to methodology and sources. This study draws on primary documents, secondary literature, media materials and interviews with military and civilian officials; most of the interviews were conducted in the Balkans in 2007 and 2008. Governance, especially in 'international protectorates', is about asymmetric power relations, perceptions and adaptive responses to situations that arise suddenly. Hence, arrangements on the ground often play out differently than are envisaged and documented by headquarters. To reveal the frictions, contradictions and ad-hocracy of governance, this study has complemented research conducted in capitals and at the headquarter level with fieldwork done on the operational and tactical levels. In other words, the aim of the study is to shed light on the implementation of governance on the ground. Interviews were necessary since information and data available in print, such as in official documents, is limited or unreliable. This is due to secrecy provisions, a lack of systematic documentation of activities and lessons learned and the fact that those committing serious crime usually operate clandestinely.

The downside is that many interviews must be conducted informally, without the presence of those who habitually talk to external observers, such as heads of missions and press officers. The format of background talks allows interlocutors to express themselves relatively freely. Yet most interlocutors interviewed for this book insisted on anonymity (this book does not reveal the identity even of those who would not mind being quoted by name). The condition of anonymity requires much faith on the part of the reader in the sincerity of the author to select interview partners who are well-informed and whose views are not merely odd minority views. This book draws on interviews with around two hundred representatives of international and domestic governmental institutions, international organisations and civil society organisations. Interview partners range from senior decision-makers to 'foot soldiers'. Many of their statements have been paraphrased for this book. However, several interview partners are quoted verbatim. This was done in cases where paraphrasing would change not only the letter but also the spirit of a statement. In these cases, the author has paid special attention to ensuring that the quotes represent a more general view, to avoid distorting reality. The quotes, even though anonymised, hopefully enhance authenticity.

Terminological clarifications are warranted, too. Here the term 'military forces' refers to forces under military command. They include regular military forces, special forces and constabulary forces. By discussing constabulary forces as part of the military, it is not implied that they are more a part of the military than the police – they are in between. But in Bosnia and Kosovo most constabulary forces have been deployed under military command. Hence, here they are considered as military actors.

The term 'law enforcement' designates efforts to apprehend the perpetrators of serious crime or to prevent such crime. Using the generic term law enforcement avoids the circularity of labelling something a policing or military task and then criticizing the involvement of the military in tasks defined as police prerogatives. Although law enforcement is arguably more an internal security issue, and thus a police task, the arrest of suspected war criminals and other post-war challenges may require military assets.[21] Thus, while it is acknowledged that the police are best prepared for law enforcement, there is room for military involvement too.

This book is based on several assumptions. First, it is assumed that conflict prevention is better, morally and financially, than having to intervene in war-torn countries.[22] Better conflict prevention would help avoid the dilemma of employing the military in post-conflict law enforcement in the first place.

Second, crime-fighting is not sufficient for stabilising post-war countries.[23] Coercive security sector actors can only do so much;[24] coercion, even if applied appropriately, does not create jobs or bring people together after war. Concerted political, economic and social efforts are needed to reverse the high likelihood of a reversion to conflict.[25] Moreover, improving military law enforcement capabilities is no substitute for deploying more and better CIVPOL. This book acknowledges that adapting the military to law enforcement is risky since it may alleviate the pressure on policymakers to invest in prevention, CIVPOL deployment and SSR. Moreover, coercive responses against criminalised activities can alienate the citizens who depend on "tricks of everyday" life for survival after war.[26]

The third assumption pertains to local ownership. Law enforcement should be the task of domestic security forces, especially the police, and not the task of international police or military forces. But when domestic police forces are biased or simply not there, 'internationals' must take over.

Fourth, the distinction between internal security tasks for which the police is responsible, and external security which is safeguarded by the military, should be resuscitated to the extent possible. The Westphalian Model, negative consequences such as security dilemmas notwithstanding, is preferable to neo-medieval overlapping security functions. Suggesting ways of improving the effectiveness and efficiency of military involvement in law enforcement is not the same as pleading for a further erosion of Westphalian norms. Ideally, domestic police forces should enforce the law. If that is not possible, CIVPOL should become involved, with an executive mandate if necessary. But due to the shortcomings of civilian policing, the role of the military in law enforcement must be thought through to stabilise war-torn societies and to save human lives.

Militarised law enforcement thus involves trade-offs and negative consequences. But this is the nature of dilemmas. Without law enforcement 'soft' strategy elements will fail. Development hinges on security (and vice versa) and fighting serious crime is essential for fostering security. Adapting the military to post-conflict law enforcement is a necessary evil.[27] Not giving the military a role in this field is worse than transforming soldiers into law enforcers.

Chapter 2 lays out the conceptual framework. It first shows that military and policing tasks have become increasingly blurred since the end of the Cold War. It then discusses the problem of post-war security gaps. Subsequently, the chapter helps to conceptualise the involvement of international military forces in post-conflict law enforcement, referring to Security Governance, SSG and SSR. Lastly, it formulates conditions that impact on the military's ability to support law enforcement in war-torn countries.

Chapters 3 and 4 discuss the fight against serious crime in Bosnia and Kosovo, applying the heuristic framework developed in chapter 2. The cases reveal that military reticence to enforce laws has allowed 'spoilers' of stabilisation efforts to become entrenched and to violate human rights with impunity. Yet operational activism by NATO and EU forces has been problematic, too. From a functional point of view, the military scored merely tactical victories. From a normative point of view, military activism has blurred distinctions between military and policing functions, undermining a central SSR principle touted by the 'international community'.[28] Bosnia and Kosovo also underline the difficulty of constructing military-police networks. It took until late 2005 to find a modus operandi in Bosnia. In Kosovo, military and police tasks were still without proper delineation by early 2009.

The conclusion provides a summary of the empirical findings. Drawing on these findings, it then develops an ideal-type strategy for military involvement in post-conflict law enforcement. Subsequently, the discussion is extended to other cases. Despite their idiosyncrasies, both Bosnia and Kosovo illustrate problems of military law enforcement in general.

This book posits that closing public security gaps is a major challenge in military operations, whether multilateral or unilateral ones, and whether major combat operations have ended or not. Improving post-conflict law enforcement is not very difficult in practical terms. Preparing for and engaging in law enforcement should become part of military transformation more largely; deploying more constabulary forces and using them appropriately would help fight serious crime. Using the military for law enforcement will further erode Westphalian norms and alter military cultures. But the persistent lack of political will to deploy more CIVPOL, and the failure to put rhetorical commitments to conflict prevention into practice,[29] make the need to increase the spectrum of military tasks inevitable. Proper training and force planning can mitigate the negative externalities of broadening the scope of military activities.

Notes

1 On security gaps, see Oakley, Dziedzic and Goldberg 1998.
2 Quoted in: Michael R. Gordon, Bush Would Stop U.S. Peacekeeping in Balkan Fights, in: New York Times, 21 October 2000: 1A.
3 Clarke 2006; Kraska 2001; Andreas and Price 2001.
4 Friesendorf 2007.
5 Perito 2004; Hills 1998; Lutterbeck 2004; Armitage and Moisan 2005; Larsen 2002.
6 Bigo 2001; Lutterbeck 2005.
7 Cockayne and Pfister 2008; Teran 2007; Marucelj 2005.
8 Schnabel and Ehrhart 2005.
9 Marenin 2005.
10 Hansen 2002.
11 Sedra 2005.
12 See Hills 2001; Penksa 2006; Holt and Berkman 2006.
13 Exceptions include Sharp 1997/1998; Perito 2004; Perito 2008; Zaalberg 2006; Lyck 2008; Oakley, Dziedzic and Goldberg 1998.
14 For a similar argument, see Jones et al. 2005: 225; Marten 2007.
15 For an explanation of EUFOR's operational activism in Bosnia, see Friesendorf and Penksa 2008.
16 These issues are examined in Penksa 2006.

[17] Ascertaining who collects what intelligence, and how intelligence is shared among which actors, is a difficult undertaking since security actors, especially the military, generally do not discuss operational matters. While some works examine the interface between intelligence and law enforcement agencies (see, for example, Baker 1994/1995), there is hardly any literature on links between military intelligence and law enforcement (an exception is Vetter 1995). This book does not purport to fill this gap, as this would have required more interviews with members of military intelligence cells. However, the case studies do discuss problems of intelligence gathering and sharing.

[18] On the 'rule of law', see Carothers 2005 and Mani 1998. On organized crime, see Van Duyne et al. 2004.

[19] See Andreas and Nadelmann 2006.

[20] See also Rausch 2006.

[21] See Hills 2001: 83.

[22] International Commission 2001.

[23] Hazen 2007. On the challenges of peacebuilding more generally, see Paris 2004.

[24] For definitions of the security sector, see Hänggi 2003: 10; OECD 2007: 22.

[25] See Collier et al. 2003.

[26] Pugh 2007: 4.

[27] I owe the idea to use this term here to Albrecht Schnabel.

[28] The term international community implies a high degree of homogeneity among the actors constituting this community. In practice, this homogeneity is largely absent.

[29] On the reasons for the lack of conflict prevention, see Schnabel 2002: 20.

Chapter 2

The Military, Law Enforcement and Peace Operations

The 1648 Treaty of Westphalia was supposed to end perennial warfare by prescribing the norm of state sovereignty as a principle governing international relations. The creation of modern states went hand in hand with the creation of modern armed forces.[1] The state was to protect the security of its citizens by militarily safeguarding the national territory and population against threats from abroad. Westphalia set the foundation for the division of labour between the police (responsible for internal security) and the military (responsible for defending countries against foreign attack).

It took long for this division of labour to evolve since it depended on, in addition to state creation, another process: democratisation. Distinguishing between policing and military functions reflects a search for effectiveness and the understanding that citizens deserve protection from undue state repression, and that the police, due to their training and equipment, are the most appropriate instrument for interacting with citizens. The distinction between military and policing functions is at the core of the modern *Rechtsstaat*.[2]

When democracy is weak the military tends to be active domestically. In the second half of the 20th century, in many countries freed from colonial rule, the military quelled internal dissent. Military juntas in Latin America and elsewhere furthered the security of the state/the ruling elite, not the security of citizens. Military involvement in internal security operations was a symptom of weak democracy as well as an impediment to democratisation.[3]

Yet many states did distinguish between military and policing tasks during the second half of the 20th century.[4] NATO member states created huge armed forces against the perceived Communist threat and militarised the border between the two blocks. Yet governments generally refrained from using the military in law enforcement operations. Germany, for example, due to the country's history of all-powerful security forces accountable only to the Nazi government, confined the military to external security functions to ensure democratic control of armed forces. Even the creation of paramilitary police forces proved politically controversial. Only in the later 1970s, after a wave of terrorist attacks, were such forces created.

In other countries, there has been more overlap between policing and military work. The British armed forces, after moving into Northern Ireland in 1969, became involved in law enforcement operations. This involvement culminated in Bloody Sunday, with British troops killing numerous civilians in 1972 on the streets of Belfast. In 1976, the police assumed primacy over law enforcement.[5] But blurred lines between terrorism, insurgency, crime and street protest enabled joint and partly overlapping activities of armed forces, police and intelligence services. Defining what is police and what is military work is even more difficult in countries that possess police forces with military status. In Italy, the Carabinieri play an important role in the fight against the Mafia and other organised crime groups. In Spain, the Guardia Civil is one of the main protagonists in the fight against ETA terrorists. In France, the Gendarmerie collects counter-terrorist intelligence and makes arrests. Such examples notwithstanding, the use of the military in internal security operations has been circumscribed in many countries during the Cold War.

The end of the Cold War catalyzed into a reshuffling of security forces. The democratisation of former Communist countries imposed new limits on how the military could be used; establishing civilian control over the military was a sine qua non of the transition to democracy. The military was to be better controlled, among other measures, by strengthening parliamentary control over defence expenditure, demilitarising borders and curtailing the power of paramilitary forces. Norm-setting efforts such as the 1994 Code of Conduct of the Organization for Security and Cooperation in Europe (OSCE) have been vital in this regard.[6]

One of the assumptions underlying efforts to establish democratic control of armed forces has been the distinction between internal security, for which the police should be responsible, and external security, the prerogative of the military. Democracies exporting their norms and practices have pushed ex-authoritarian states to distinguish between policing and military tasks. As one SSR expert writes, "in principle it is undesirable that the military should be involved in civilian law enforcement".[7] Similarly, a handbook for SSR practitioners states that the military "should only be used in highly exceptional and well defined circumstances (for example, during a state of emergency); either under the direction of the police or in joint command of operation".[8] The OSCE Code of Conduct allows for more leverage. But the Code also expresses unease about military involvement in internal security matters by stating that states "will ensure that any decision to assign its armed forces to internal security missions is arrived at in conformity with constitutional procedures."[9]

While the end of the Cold War provided a window of opportunity to demilitarise states and societies, it also had the opposite effects: it blurred distinctions between internal and external security, and policing and military work. This trend has posed risks to civilian control and oversight of the military (by politicising the military), and to citizens facing soldiers not trained for law enforcement tasks.[10]

One of the main factors spurning this trend has been the increasingly transnational nature of security problems, as well as the corresponding need for transnational responses. Criminalised activities were conducted across borders even during the Cold War. Indeed, many forms of smuggling and trafficking are possible only when there are borders and concomitant economic incentives such as tax differentials. Moreover, terrorists and other violent non-state groups violated national sovereignty long before the end of the Cold War.

But the end of the Cold War accelerated these trends. The collapse of the Berlin Wall, as well as advances in communication and transport technologies, enabled an increased exchange of people, goods, services and money across borders. While most exchanges were legal, the transition of the 1990s also benefited criminal entrepreneurs. These entrepreneurs smuggled and trafficked people and goods across borders, made money and gained political clout in criminalised 'new wars', busted international sanctions against rogue regimes[11] and sold the weapons and military know-how of ex-Communist countries.

Thus, whereas the Cold War was dominated by state-based military threats, post-Cold War international security has been dominated by risks such as organised crime, terrorism, climate change, failed states and financial crises. These risks are more diffuse than threats, as it is difficult to clearly identify hostile actors, their potential to inflict damage and their intentions.[12] The diffuse, asymmetric and transnational nature of security risks puts a question mark behind traditional security postures. In contrast to state-based military threats, risks do not threaten specific territories or borders. Instead, they alter the fabric of societies (as is the case with drugs) and make critical infrastructures vulnerable (as is the case with terrorism). While risks often manifest themselves locally as internal security problems, their source is partly abroad and thus an external security matter. The line of defence is now seen as beyond the border, requiring integrated internal and external security instruments.

Partly in response to these new security parameters security actors have changed. One significant change has been the internationalisation of police forces. The Westphalian model, according to which the police operates internally, historically has been more ideal-type than reality. The 19th century, for example, saw close cooperation among European and US police, with agents exchanging information and travelling to other countries to aid in the arrest of 'their' criminals.[13] During the 20th century various states sent police abroad. This was the case with repressive regimes that had 'political' police forces at their disposal. But democratic countries did so as well with the US taking the lead. Mainly as part of the 'war on drugs', the US government set up police liaison programmes with US law enforcement agents operating around the world.[14]

The end of the Cold War has boosted international policing again with the US in the lead. The perceived threat of organised crime led US law enforcement agencies to further increase their presence abroad. The attacks on New York and Washington on 11 September 2001 not only invited US military action but also catalyzed into more global policing. Terrorism underlines the difficulty of delineating internal from external security. Countries other than the US, such as Germany, have expanded their international policing presence as well. Moreover, the interior ministries of many states who are responsible for overseeing policing have created external affairs departments. The world's most highly institutionalised law enforcement network is within the EU. While EU member states are still reluctant to supranationalise policing competencies, they have gone far with regard to joint strategy planning, joint operations and the exchange of information and intelligence.

Police forces have become militarised as well. While some police forces and border guards have shed their militarised past, others have been increasingly using military equipment and tactics. The US-Mexican border has seen significant militarisation since the 1990s.[15] A similar process can be observed along the Schengen external border. Austria, for example, has regularly deployed troops along its eastern border against illegal migrants.

Police forces operating far away from borders have also been militarised. Most countries now possess specialised police forces such as Special Weapons and Tactics (SWAT) teams. These forces use military equipment and tactics against terrorists, hijackers and bank robbers. In the US numerous police departments have created paramilitary squads.[16] Special police forces can operate domestically as well as internationally. For instance, the *Grenzschutzgruppe 9* (GSG 9), created after the attacks on the Munich summer Olympic games in 1972, famously liberated plane passengers taken hostage by Palestinian terrorists in 1977 in Somalia. Paramilitary policing tactics and equipment are also used against low-level targets, such as football hooligans.

Further, militarised law enforcement becomes evident when looking at the role of constabulary forces. Many countries have forces that can operate under military or civilian command. Their structure, equipment and functions vary depending on the country and whether there is war or peace. Constabulary forces include a variety of specialists including counter-terrorism experts, snipers and parachutists. Their means comprise, among others, batons and shields, heavy machine guns and helicopters. These means are used for counter-terrorism, crowd and riot control (CRC), traffic control and operations against organised crime. Constabulary forces reject the descriptor 'paramilitary' and emphasise that they are police forces under military command. However, their military structure, their training for internal security operations and their equipment all underline their hybrid status. They embody the blurred distinction between internal and external security, and policing and military roles.

Further, the military itself is affected by new security postures.[17] Military involvement in non-traditional military tasks includes disaster relief at home and abroad. Moreover, and central to this book, the military has increasingly provided law enforcement support. Generally troops do not have the power of arrest, but instead deter wrongdoers or back up police forces. In France the 'vigipirate' scheme, intended to deter terrorists, has deployed soldiers to public places. In the US, National Guard troops have guarded subway stations and streets to thwart terrorist attacks. In Switzerland troops stand in front of diplomatic premises and have backed up the police at major events such as the Davos World Economic Forum and the 2008 European football championship. The government of Silvio Berlusconi in summer 2008 militarised the streets of Italy in order to counter irregular migration and other perceived security threats. The German military used Tornado jets in 2007 to take pictures of demonstrators' camps at the G-8 meeting in Heiligendamm.

Militarised law enforcement also manifests itself as police training by the military. Such training is problematic since it may lead to militarised policing and concomitant problems such as human rights abuses. A notorious example is the School of the Americas where Latin American police and other security forces, some of which committed human rights violations, received training from US security forces, including the military.[18]

Blurring the line between military and policing tasks has clashed with the SSR norm of separating the military from the police. SSR is intended to create a security sector that provides security to the state and to citizens in an effective and efficient way. Moreover, security must be provided in a framework of democratic governance.[19] All too often and in many parts of the world a malfunctioning security sector has hampered development, democratisation and conflict resolution.

Several elements are needed to ensure the effective, efficient and legitimate delivery of security. One of these is a clear division of labour among security agencies. When responsibilities are blurred it becomes more difficult to exert democratic control, and there is a risk that human security and respect for human rights will fall victim to turf battles, the abrogation of responsibility and inappropriate measures taken by security forces. The 'policisation' of the military, as well as the militarisation of the police, is therefore a troubling development from an SSR perspective.

The trend towards blurred boundaries between military and policing tasks – in war-torn countries as well as in stable democracies – has triggered debates over the appropriateness of using military force for internal security missions. These debates indicate that the norm circumscribing the internal use of military forces is still salient. However, the fact that troops have been, and continue to be, deployed also reveals the volatility of the norm. In Europe and North America, the military function to protect against external attack has been complemented and partially substituted by internal security missions, as well as the participation in peace operations[20] – where militarised law enforcement is particularly pronounced. The next section explains why.

Post-Conflict Security Gaps and International Military Forces

There are no blueprints for reconstructing war-torn countries. All international actors involved, including forces under military command, struggle to define their role. Post-conflict intervention has often been conducted in an ad-hoc, uncoordinated fashion and inappropriate strategies and tactics have been applied. For instance, the international drive to rapidly privatise state-owned assets has exacerbated poverty and exclusion and facilitated fraud.[21] Worse, some members of international military and civilian missions who were supposed to protect and reconstruct have colluded with criminals and violated human rights.

Security gaps have been a main challenge to intervention in war-torn countries. Agencies that enforce laws and maintain public order efficiently, effectively and democratically are usually absent after war. US administrators in post-World War II Germany struggled with the existence of murder, looting and petty crime. Moreover, domestic police and criminal justice agencies were tainted by political policing and other pathologies of Nazism. A combination of (albeit imperfect) vetting by the Allies and military support of law enforcement helped rid German institutions of some of the worst perpetrators of injustice and to end post-war chaos.[22]

The task of stabilising Germany was formidable, but it was made easier by the fact that World War II, in large part, had been a confrontation between countries' military forces. Guaranteeing democratic public order is more difficult after civil war. Intervention forces may face security forces that have sided with 'their' group and that therefore do not enforce the law impartially. This was the case in Bosnia. Or, domestic security forces withdraw or are expelled by international intervention forces. This was the case in Kosovo and East Timor. Statutory security forces can also be disbanded, as happened in Iraq.

Over recent decades, the number of interstate wars has seen a sharp decline, while intrastate wars have become the dominant type of warfare. Traditional warfare was dominated by regular soldiers and the death of soldiers. Intrastate wars are dominated by a mix of ethnic, religious and – arguably most importantly – economic motives. In so-called new wars, paramilitaries, rag-tag militias, marauding troops, thugs and criminals feature prominently.[23] While attacks against the 'other' side are often justified in political, religious, or ethnic terms, in reality, contemporary combatants try to assume control over lucrative smuggling routes or attack civilians to steal their fridges, cars, or land.[24] The criminalised nature of contemporary warfare means that civilians are the first victims. Internal warfare also undermines public security after the end of combat. Security forces are tainted by human rights violations and are involved in crime. When security forces cooperate with criminals, or when they fail to treat citizens impartially, law enforcement suffers. Moreover, war profiteers usually have much economic and political clout after war. The criminal legacies of 'new wars' are hard to break.[25]

The most logical way of addressing this problem is to deploy international CIVPOL officers. Since the 1990s, post-conflict policing has seen a boom. CIVPOL officers may advise, restructure, provide intelligence to domestic police forces and even engage in executive policing. Up until the mid-1990s, international actors had few experiences with multilateral policing. Traditional peacekeeping was focused on military aspects of conflict and post-conflict stabilisation, hence on maintaining the status quo. Peace operations, in contrast, are intended to manage change, requiring different postures of intervening actors.[26]

Due to the growing number of operations in environments without viable state institutions, international administrators have begun to pay attention to public security and the 'rule of law'. The United Nation's (UN's) representative in Kosovo, Bernard Kouchner, stated that peacekeeping missions "need to arrive with a law-and-order kit composed of trained police, judges and prosecutors and a set of security laws".[27] Similarly, Paddy Ashdown, after years of serving as High Representative in Bosnia, said that criminals posed the greatest threat to stability and that the rule of law, instead of early elections, should have been the international priority.[28]

However, problems linger on. There is still a lack of political will to muster the financial and personnel resources needed for international policing.[29] By summer 2009 the staff of the EU police mission in Afghanistan was still far from reaching the ceiling agreed on by the EU.[30] Moreover, international actors lack the knowledge to implement effective policing programmes, due to coordination problems, because recommendations are not read, and some who write the recommendations are inexperienced.[31] Further, police agencies have not provided sufficient career incentives to officers for participating in missions (in contrast to soldiers, police officers cannot be ordered to participate in a peace operation).[32]

Given that commitments to make available more and better CIVPOL are largely rhetorical, and given the problems of domestic law enforcement agencies, the posture of international military forces becomes crucial. Soldiers are the first to enter a war-torn country in large numbers, and later dwarf the presence of police officers, development experts and staff of non-governmental organisations (NGOs). After 'new wars', hostilities do not automatically end: paramilitaries and criminal gangs continue to roam the countryside; many citizens hold weapons; landmines are ubiquitous; and domestic security forces, if present at all, cannot be trusted. Civilian agencies can therefore not operate freely.

The most pressing need after war is to prevent a resumption of hostilities through disarming the combatants, enforcing the withdrawal of heavy weapons and separating the enemy forces. Moreover, if the military does not protect aid convoys, dismantle illegal road blocks and repair vital infrastructure, civilian agencies cannot operate. Moreover, civilians are often dependent on information and intelligence collected by the military, which after all possesses superior technical capabilities and cross-border contacts.[33] Because "there is no one else to do the job",[34] the military becomes involved in a variety of tasks, including law enforcement. Peace operations have accelerated the constabularisation of military forces, requiring them to use a minimum of force in environments in which there is neither war nor peace and in which military involvement is not about military victory.[35] In the words of Georg Ehrhart and Albrecht Schnabel:

> Traditional functions of national defense and deterrence give way to, or are complemented with, capacities to engage in conflict prevention, peace enforcement, peacekeeping and the restoration of security and order. In this context, the main goal of military activities is not the defeat and elimination of an adversary, but the creation of a safe environment for a comprehensive and inclusive post-conflict political and social order.[36]

Many policymakers and analysts acknowledge that the military may have to step in to fill security gaps.[37] However, the military is a "reluctant recruit"[38]. Commanders and ministers of defence adamantly reiterate that soldiers are not policemen and that law enforcement is a policing task. As Robert Perito writes, "military forces are unwilling to tackle situations that involve controlling civil disturbances and law enforcement."[39] This stance has significantly contributed to the opening-up of public security gaps and thus undermined post-conflict stabilisation and peacebuilding by allowing spoilers to become politically and socially entrenched and by undermining public faith in international peace operations.[40]

The US has contributed the most troops to international peace missions due to its global military and political reach. But the US has been deeply marked by the Somalia debacle. In October 1993 US special forces tried to capture the wanted militia leader and self-proclaimed Somali president Mohamed Aidid in Mogadishu. Eighteen US soldiers were killed and over seventy injured in a drawn-out battle with Aidid supporters (hundreds of Somalis died as well). A shocked US public saw the bodies of US soldiers being dragged through the streets of Mogadishu. In some cases, the US successfully used a mix of intelligence, military and police capabilities, such as it did during the successful hunt for Colombian drug lord Pablo Escobar in 1992-1993. But the shock of Somalia was stronger, bringing the Vietnam-induced fear of mission creep to the fore. Vietnam stood for the indefinite deployment of increasing numbers of troops to a remote quagmire. Similar to Vietnam, Somalia showed that asymmetric conflict strategies can offset superior US military capacities. Somalia underscored the belief, as laid out in the Weinberger-Powell doctrine, that the US should deploy military force only when the political objectives are clear, when the exit strategy is properly defined and when the US can use overwhelming force to secure a clear victory. This had been the case during the 1991 Gulf War. But in Bosnia, with Mogadishu on their minds, US officials refrained from intervening. Colin Powell, then Chairman of the Joint Chiefs of Staff, compared the US stance towards Iraq and Bosnia by saying: "We do deserts, we don't do mountains."[41]

John Mueller argues that internal, criminalised wars are waged by relatively small numbers of thugs who are no match for disciplined armies. He thus calls for more political will to conduct "policing wars".[42] Yet this is a type of warfare the US has shied away from.

US fears of entrapment have also influenced US stabilisation policies after war. In Bosnia, as the US deployed tens of thousands of troops, military objectives such as the separation of enemy forces were quickly achieved. But little progress was made in implementing civilian aspects of the Dayton Peace Agreement. The US is not the only reluctant post-war law enforcer. The upholding of the warrior ethos, force protection requirements, a lack of familiarity with law enforcement and the search for a quick military exit have led, and continue to lead, all countries to eschew law enforcement abroad.

The British army emphasises the distinction between military and policing work.[43] British soldiers are often said to excel at counter-insurgency and at supporting police. Experiences in colonies and in Northern Ireland have led the British army to devolve significant decision-making powers to low-level officers and non-commissioned officers and to cooperate closely with civilian agencies. Moreover, Britain has less stringent force protection requirements than the US: British troops tend to wear soft caps and carry their weapons on their backs much earlier than US troops. However, this does not make British soldiers policemen. In Northern Ireland, the remit of the British military differs from the one of law enforcement agencies, especially the Royal Ulster Constabulary.

Military forces in the Euro-Atlantic area have undergone significant restructuring since the end of the Cold War. They have been downsized and professionalised; several countries have abolished compulsory conscription and created volunteer forces. The Revolution in Military Affairs has changed the nature of warfare (enabling NATO to wage an all-aerial war against Serbia). Moreover, armed forces have been geared towards tasks variously labelled as counter-insurgency, complex emergencies, limited intervention (such as the evacuation of embassy personnel), 'operations other than war', low-intensity conflict and also law enforcement.[44] The attacks of 9/11 have accelerated military transformation.[45] Supporting the 'war on terror' is now one of the main missions of the US armed forces, which has included invading countries seen as sponsoring terrorism, lending equipment to other US agencies and gathering intelligence. Even non-military agencies conduct military missions. Thus, in 2002 the Central Intelligence Agency (CIA) reportedly fired a missile at a presumed senior Al Qaeda operative travelling in a convoy in Yemen.[46]

Still, the military remains reluctant to engage in law enforcement. This reluctance is particularly pronounced in peace operations, due to the risks for soldiers and the related fear of mission creep. Many military officers who have commanded peace operations acknowledge that the military may have to lend support to law enforcement.[47] Military support of rule of law activities is even discussed in a 2007 counter-insurgency manual of the U.S. Army.[48] Many would share the view of a senior officer of the US National Guard who writes that the military "has come to appreciate that often soldiers must be prepared to assume police duties until a regular police unit can be established."[49] However, many within the military, as well as their civilian superiors, are cautious. The view that the military has become interested in internal security matters to avert budget cuts understates the wariness to engage in internal security matters.[50]

This aversion notwithstanding, the military has been under pressure to aid the implementation of civilian stabilisation elements. Over the 1990s it became increasingly evident that military reluctance to support law enforcement had added to the problems of weak police forces. Such pressure has had consequences: While instances in which the military has directly performed police work are rather rare,[51] the need to fill security gaps has meant that some form of military mission creep has been the rule rather than the exception in peace operations[52] – although the military tends to deny this. As Dag Hammerskjöld said, peacekeeping is not a soldier's job, but only a soldier can do it. Law enforcement is not a soldier's job either. But history has shown that often only a soldier can do it.

Those who have called for more military flexibility include representatives of governments, international organisations and NGOs, as well as scholars advocating human security. Proponents of a proactive military stance acknowledge the limits of military intervention and the practical and normative risks involved. But military task expansion is increasingly seen as preferable to the opening up of security gaps and the committing of crimes with impunity. Pressure on the military is also due to the fact that some tasks may require military assets and tactics. In stable settings police SWAT teams may be able to arrest wanted criminals. But in hostile environments, a military approach may be warranted. For example, snatch teams may use fast combat helicopters flying at low altitudes to arrest suspected war criminals who are being protected by parts of the local population.

Military law enforcement is problematic. Doctrine and training prepare the military for fighting war. Arresting citizens, seizing assets and controlling riots are different matters. Also, the military does not want to perform police work because the military is the "coercive resource of last resort and cannot be seen to fail."[53] Yet failure is inherent in policing; wars end, but policing does not.[54] Also, blurring the distinction between military and policing work can undermine attempts to make security agencies democratically accountable. Still, this book argues that the benefits of military encroachment on civilian turf outweigh the costs.

While pressure has moved the military closer into the law enforcement realm, military and civilian decision-makers have been reluctant to expand the military portfolio. Moreover, the drive towards military law enforcement has been slowed down by practical and normative concerns. Given these contradictions, military engagement in post-conflict law enforcement has been haphazard. Before examining two cases of unsystematic law enforcement, the role of the military in the fight against serious crime must be conceptualised.

Conceptualising Military Involvement in Post-Conflict Law Enforcement

One way of conceptualising military support of law enforcement is through the prism of civil-military cooperation (CIMIC).[55] During the Cold War many states considered CIMIC an important aspect of military activity. Colonial counter-insurgency campaigns and Cold War proxy wars depended on the ability of the military to win the hearts and minds of the local population. The military therefore helped to build bridges, dig wells and distribute food by using their own military CIMIC officers or by supporting civilian agencies.

The end of the Cold War placed new demands on CIMIC due to an increase in wars victimising civilians, the availability of military assets and a growing number of peace operations.[56] In these environments their badges no longer protected humanitarian aid workers from attack; indeed, insurgents and criminals increasingly began to deliberately target humanitarians. Aid workers thus became reliant on military protection.[57] Also, the military became directly involved. After the US toppled the Taliban regime in Afghanistan, international military forces dug wells, rebuilt dams and schools, and delivered supplies to needy communities, often cooperating alongside civilians as part of Provincial Reconstruction Teams. In the southern Philippines, providing medical support to destitute people has helped US Special Forces to make tactical progress in the 'war on terror'.[58] The military uses CIMIC to deprive insurgents and terrorists of popular support and to obtain information and intelligence.

Humanitarians are wary of the use of aid for military purposes and, more generally, of closely cooperating with the military.[59] When people no longer distinguish between the military and humanitarians, the latter may no longer be seen as impartial and, as a consequence, may live more dangerously. Such fears are exacerbated by the tendency of the military to regard CIMIC operations as instruments for furthering military objectives. The notion of CIMIC has become part and parcel of the post-modern military,[60] which is supposed to interact closely with civilians and assume civilian functions, if necessary. A soldier nowadays "is not only a fighter but also a peacekeeper, policeman, diplomat, social worker and Peace Corps worker".[61]

The notion of CIMIC does not shed much light on military law enforcement contributions. It is a malleable notion used to describe "all contacts between civilian and military actors in [peace operations]; or to describe efforts by the military to engage in humanitarian aid or development assistance; or simply as a new kind of civil-military relationship to achieve a common goal".[62] There is no common definition of CIMIC, and existing definitions tend to treat the interface between the military and civilian law enforcement and criminal justice institutions in vague terms; CIMIC refers first and foremost to relations between the military and institutions, both state and non-state, in the humanitarian and reconstruction sectors.[63] Also, the notion of civil-military relations fails to grasp relations between security sector actors on the national and international levels. Furthermore, the notion conveys agnosticism regarding the need to reform the security sector in order to promote the efficient, effective and legitimate deliverance of security to the state and to citizens.

A better way of conceptualising military support of crime-fighting is by drawing on the three interrelated concepts of security governance, SSG and SSR. As shown below, these concepts take into account the relationships among security sector actors on the national and international levels. Moreover, these concepts – especially when applied normatively and not merely analytically – stress the task of improving the performance of security sector actors and optimising linkages among such actors. Lastly, these concepts also leave conceptual space for para-state and non-state actors.

Security Governance and the Military

Over recent years security governance has become a popular research concept. Its meaning is contentious as is the case with related concepts such as governance and global governance.[64] Governance denotes a shift from hierarchic to polycentric policymaking. Globalisation has enhanced the complexity of policy issues and challenged the ability of governments to formulate and implement decisions. As a result, policy networks have sprung up on levels ranging from the local to the international and supranational. The role of governments within these networks varies. They dominate 'governance by government', but are less prominent in 'governance with governance' and can, indeed, be absent, as in 'governance without government'.[65]

Even when governments make their presence felt governance systems are rarely dominated by a single actor. A hallmark of governance, as opposed to traditional government, is the presence of international organisations and private actors engaged in policy formulation and implementation at the national and international levels. Thus, at the core of governance is the "absence of a central political authority"[66]. Decisions agreed upon by the actors constituting governance systems are often non-binding, but they can be binding too.

A key characteristic of security governance is the shift from hierarchic to polycentric policymaking in international security. The rise of security governance, both as practice and as analytical tool, reflects the paradigmatic shift away from state-based threats towards diffuse risks partly caused, or mitigated, by non-state actors.

For a security governance system to be both effective and legitimate several conditions must be fulfilled. First, since states cannot manage transnational risks on their own states should cooperate with one another across borders. Yet security governance is about a special kind of cooperation. States can no longer act as monolithic entities (if they ever did); instead, they must "disaggregate into their functionally different units"[67], such as police agencies, the military, prosecutorial offices and development experts.[68] These units forge close relations with their foreign counterparts, creating policy networks that flexibly reach across borders.

Second, policy networks increasingly include international organisations, NGOs and private businesses.[69] Para-state and non-state actors have significant material capacities, know-how and reach. Addressing complex security risks obliges governments to co-opt these actors. The growing relevance of international organisations and non-state actors is not least a consequence of the deliberate outsourcing of functions that used to be state prerogatives. This is evidenced by the astounding number of private contractors in Iraq and Afghanistan, and by the practice of EU member states to require transport companies to check migrants' documents and filter those who are allowed to migrate from those not eligible. In post-conflict stabilisation and peacebuilding private companies have been asked to invest in the economy and also to work alongside states, international organisations and NGOs.

Security governance systems thus have a networked structure.[70] Decentralised, complex governance networks have complemented and in some areas substituted hierarchical, linear government structures. The nodes constituting networks share an interest in a specific issue area and interact with one another in institutionalised, but more commonly in informal and voluntary, ways.[71] Networks generally lack a centre of gravity and have built-in redundancies that make them resilient against attack. They are difficult to steer, however. Striking the right balance between chaotic multi-actor constellations on the one hand, and coherent policy formulation and implementation on the other hand, is tricky.

The third condition of success is that security governance systems must reflect the nature of the problem that is to be solved.[72] Human trafficking is not only a problem of organised crime but is also a problem of poverty and discrimination. To address these socio-economic root causes counter-trafficking governance systems must incorporate actors who are able to offer positive incentives in the fields of development, migration and gender. Similarly, coercive instruments are insufficient for fighting organised crime in peace operations. Leaders of organised crime groups often swim like fish in the water, benefiting from a lack of jobs for citizens who can therefore be employed as drug mules, bodyguards, prostitutes, and street vendors of contraband goods. To deprive organised crime leaders and other armed non-state actors of their support base, peacebuilders must address economic malaise and compete for legitimacy with non-state armed actors.[73] Hence, security governance must be strategic and holistic.[74]

These three characteristics are needed to ensure effective and efficient security governance. When governmental agencies are unable to innovate, learn from past mistakes and cooperate with foreign counterparts, they will not make strides. When states try to go it alone, without drawing on the resources of international organisations and non-state actors, they will fail. Even global military and political hegemony are insufficient to rebuild states or fight crime and terrorism, as the US has experienced in Iraq. During the Cold War many conflicts were internationalised.[75] Yet under conditions of globalisation any conflict is international: Weapons are smuggled into conflict zones from abroad; resources from conflict zones are sold abroad; and the Internet allows non-state armed actors to recruit. Successful counter-efforts must therefore draw in a variety of actors operating across the globe.

Yet security governance is not only about effectiveness and efficiency, but is also about legitimacy. A governance system may target terrorists, smugglers, traffickers and war criminals. But without legitimacy success will be short-lived. When efforts against armed non-state actors violate democratic principles these efforts undermine the normative structure upon which long-term success depends (see Guantanamo or Abu Ghraib). Terrorists, smugglers and traffickers are said to master transnational, networked forms of cooperation. Many therefore argue that states must also counter these "dark networks".[76] In other words, "it takes networks to fight networks".[77]

Yet while transnational law enforcement networks may be more effective and efficient than bureaucratic government hierarchies, they are also less transparent. Informal exchanges among security practitioners may speed up things but also undermine oversight by parliaments, the media, and NGOs. Waging "netwars" can clash with legitimacy and accountability.[78] Non-state armed actors do not play by the rules but licit actors have to.

Post-conflict stabilisation and peacebuilding efforts are a prime example of the need for security governance. After war a host of international actors moves into post-conflict countries. Some even may officially assume governmental functions. This is the case in 'protectorates' (which this book focuses on) where international actors have executive powers. Sovereignty may also be shared de facto in cases where governments of post-conflict countries are too weak to exercise full sovereignty. Creating effective, efficient and legitimate post-conflict security governance is difficult, not least because the priorities, skills, mandates and worldviews of international actors diverge a lot. For example, the potpourri of common and civil law approaches in international protectorates reflects the power and traditions of the most powerful governments. Generally coordination between donor governments, international organisations and NGOs has been weak.[79]

The military is a key contributor to post-conflict security governance. Most obviously, international military forces contribute by preventing a renewed outbreak of war by deterring or co-opting armed actors and thus creating the conditions necessary for fighting serious crime. The security governance nature of peace operations becomes clear when looking at force structures: National military forces usually operate under a multinational umbrella. Military functions may include patrolling streets, controlling no-fly zones and disarming those violating ceasefires or peace agreements. Regarding networking, the military needs to cooperate with other international actors. For fighting crime the police and criminal justice actors are the prime partners. But the military must also team up with actors whose remit is not coercive such as governmental development agencies or human rights NGOs. Peace operations forge unlikely coalitions between soldiers and organisations generally sceptical of soldiering.

Security Sector Governance and the Military

Security governance pertains to the formulation and implementation of security policy on the international level. SSG, in contrast, refers to the governance of the security sector on a national level.[80] In this sense, SSG can be regarded as a subtype of security governance, i.e., governance that becomes manifest on the state level.

As used in this book, SSG has a normative dimension. If applied merely analytically, there would not be a difference between SSG in a failed state such as Somalia and in a stable democracy. After all, in both types of polity there are security sector actors that are linked to one another in some way or another. But for the present purpose and in line with most writings, SSG arrangements are evaluated through the prism of democratic norms. Only when the security sector on the state level adheres to principles of 'good governance', such as the ability of citizens to seek redress against human rights abuses committed by security forces, is it appropriate to speak of a properly functioning SSG system. In other words, relations between security sector actors should protect citizens against the illegitimate use of force by state actors and the use of force by non-state actors. To ensure democratic SSG, SSR is needed; SSR is a means for enhancing the effectiveness, efficiency and – crucially – legitimacy of SSG.

Who are the actors of an SSG system in a war-torn country? There is no standard definition of the security sector. A narrow definition would include core security actors such as the police and military, but would not include NGOs or the media.[81] The narrowest definition would not even include the judiciary, but would focus on 'power ministries' such as the Ministry of Interior and Defence and their respective agencies. For post-conflict countries, the security sector should be defined broadly,[82] and include private domestic actors such as NGOs.

In a stable democracy, or even in an authoritarian state where international actors have a limited presence, domestic actors play the main role. By contrast, in war-torn countries, and especially in protectorates, 'internationals' formulate and implement policies and therefore form part of an SSG system. SSR intends to maintain, or re-establish, governance systems that ensure a state monopoly over the legitimate use of force. In war-torn countries this is often not possible, at least in the initial stage after international intervention, as the domestic security sector is usually in disarray or does not deliver security in an effective and impartial manner. Where there is no state to speak of or where state agencies do not employ force in democratic ways, international and domestic public actors should jointly hold a public monopoly on the legitimate use of force.[83] The emphasis is on public actors: only actors endowed with legitimacy can employ force in a democratic way. To be sure, non-statutory security actors such as Private Military and Security Companies (PMSC) have been increasingly challenging the Westphalian model whereby state actors are the only wielders of force.

Thus, SSG in war-torn countries comprises all security sector actors, both international and domestic, that have an impact on security in a country.[84] These may be public actors, agencies with close ties to states, or purely private actors. With regard to international actors, an SSG system in a war-torn country comprises representatives of donor states, especially powerful ones; international executive institutions in protectorates; agencies of donor states such as the military, police and criminal justice agencies; international organisations; non-statutory security forces such as PMSC; international NGOs and other non-statutory civil society actors; international private businesses; and the international news media reporting on security issues. With regard to domestic actors, the security sector includes ministries and their security and justice agencies; security management and oversight bodies such as parliamentary committees that hold security agencies accountable; non-statutory security and civil society organisations; businesses; and the domestic news media. A post-conflict security sector may also include paramilitary groups, illegal intelligence agencies, warlords and other remnants of war.

International military coalitions are often at the centre of post-conflict SSG. By preventing renewed combat through tight control of domestic security forces, these military coalitions create the conditions required for a counter-crime SSG system to work. Also, SSG aims at ensuring that international and domestic military forces act coherently and that democratic oversight mechanisms are in place. Civilian institutions should ensure accountability of both international and domestic military forces. This includes prosecuting soldiers guilty of wrong-doing,[85] as well as allowing international organisations, NGOs and the media to scrutinise military activities. Close military-police relations are needed to fight serious crime after war. But when civilian law enforcement agencies cannot function as intermediates, international military forces may establish close, direct ties with prosecutors, judges, tax authorities and other crime-fighters.

Security Sector Reform and the Military

SSR is essential for stabilising post-conflict countries. SSR is closely related to SSG, with the former enhancing the latter. While SSG focuses on relations between security sector actors, SSR stresses activities undertaken to create a stable and democratic security sector. When the security sector is unstable and undemocratic, war is likely to re-erupt and human rights abuses are likely to continue. The aim of SSR is to make state institutions primarily subservient to citizens, not the other way around. The concept of human security is thus at the core of SSR.[86]

SSR activities in post-conflict countries include establishing mechanisms to ensure civilian control of the military, demilitarisation of the police and reform of judicial institutions. SSR is also closely related to, and partially dependent on, the disarmament, demobilisation and reintegration (DDR) of former combatants; the control of small arms and light weapons (SALW); de-mining; the vetting of members of security services: and transitional justice.[87] SSR can be pursued in various formats, ranging from foreign donors lending their advice to endowing 'internationals' with executive competencies.

By preventing renewed fighting and by supporting SSR-related activities such as DDR, international military coalitions create the precondition for SSR, which cannot proceed as long as the fighting continues. Former combatants often do not disband, hand in their weapons or dismantle checkpoints voluntarily; they need to be coerced into doing so. Only international military forces have the means to credibly threaten the use of force in case of non-compliance. International military coalitions may also engage in defence reform: through train-and-equip programmes, they may prepare the domestic military for joining international organisations (especially NATO) or for participating in peace operations abroad. They may also promote the rights of armed forces personnel.[88]

More directly, the military can support crime-fighting by propping up domestic law enforcement institutions. It may, for example, offer training and equipment. Soldiers may also use their often superior logistical capacities to feed the police crime-related information and intelligence. However, the military has to treat its support of the police carefully. As the two case studies in this book show, a lack of military activism in the law enforcement realm is problematic functionally since the police often do not have the means to enforce laws. Yet military activism is problematic as well. Functionally, the military has trouble achieving sustainable results. Normatively, military involvement in law enforcement undermines the SSR norm of delineating military from policing functions. The conclusion elucidates this dilemma further and makes recommendations for how to cope with it. Before turning to the case studies, the factors that have a bearing on the ability of security sector actors to fight crime, and on the military's law enforcement stance more narrowly, must be discussed.

Conditions for Military Law Enforcement Support

The security governance, SSG and SSR concepts help guide military involvement in post-conflict law enforcement. This book argues that security gaps must be filled as quickly as possible by the military, if necessary. Civilian agencies should have primacy over law enforcement but the military must become involved if necessary. When they are involved, the military should calibrate the use of force and respect standard judicial principles. Viable military-police networks are essential for the effective, efficient and legitimate fight against serious crime. As the country becomes safer and the police become stronger, the military should phase out law enforcement tasks.

Whether this strategy can be pursued hinges on a number of conditions. Table 1 summarises the arguably most important conditions in the post-conflict country as well as the ability and will of 'locals' and 'internationals' to enforce laws that prohibit serious crime.

When levels of violence are high and threats against international personnel are frequent, it is difficult even for robust police units to operate. Against well-organised opponents of international intervention such as insurgents, militias, criminal gangs, and regular security forces, the police can do little. The same holds true when basic infrastructure, such as roads and power plants, has been destroyed. Effective and impartial law enforce-

Table 1. Conditions Influencing Prospects of Crime-Fighting After War

Post-war conditions	• Levels of violence • Availability of basic infrastructure • Legal framework
Capacities of 'locals'	• Presence and strength of domestic police and criminal justice sector • Levels of corruption and collusion • Unity and war-time record of security forces
Capacities of 'internationals'	• Political will, adaptation and learning • Presence and strength of international police and criminal justice sector • Deployment of constabulary forces • Training and equipment of troops • Appropriate mandates and commonality of purpose • Gathering and sharing of information and intelligence • Interpersonal relationships

ment suffers as well when the legal framework enabling action against serious crime is deficient.

Furthermore, domestic political and law enforcement institutions influence law enforcement outcomes. Local ownership of crime fighting becomes difficult when law enforcement institutions are absent or weak, or when corruption and criminal collusion are rampant. Also, when statutory security forces are divided and when their members have violated human rights during war, they are likely to use force in a partial way.

The fight against serious crime depends on international actors as well. To deploy strong security forces that are able to fight serious crime, international organisations and donor states need to have political will and be able to adapt to changing circumstances and learn from past mistakes.[89] Giving primacy for law enforcement and criminal justice to civilian institutions requires the timely deployment, right number, competency, and integrity of CIVPOL forces, as well as of international prosecutors, judges, and correction personnel. The early deployment and proper use of constabulary forces matters as well.[90] In addition, 'normal' military forces must be trained and equipped to fight serious crime; and they need appropriate mandates.

Commonality of purpose and action is essential but difficult to achieve when dozens of countries contribute troops, and when governments impose caveats on the use of 'their' troops that turn force commanders into managers with little decision-making power. The gathering of information and intelligence is essential, too. It hinges on, among other things, technical capacities and individual will. Individual perceptions and actions have a major impact on the implementation of security governance, SSG and SSR. If military officers do not share information and intelligence, interpret military mandates' flexibly and establish good relations with civilian agencies, the fight against serious crime suffers.

The following two chapters apply the heuristic framework outlined above to the cases of post-war Bosnia and to post-war Kosovo. The cases show that the partial absence of the conditions stated above has led to unsystematic crime-fighting and to haphazard military support to law enforcement.

Notes

1. Tilly 1985.
2. Haltiner and Kümmel 2008: 11.
3. In many undemocratic countries (such as the Soviet Union), political police forces, accountable only to governments, have tended to be widely employed, too.
4. Democracy, as a system where citizens rule over their own affairs, comes in various forms. The now dominant model, with free elections at its core, is not the only one imaginable.
5. Hills 2001.
6. OSCE 1994.
7. Born 2003: 54.
8. OECD 2007: 164.
9. OSCE 1994: Paragraph 36.
10. Born, Haltiner and Malešič 2004: 17.
11. Andreas 2005.
12. Daase 2002.
13. Andreas and Nadelmann 2006.
14. Nadelmann 1993.
15. Andreas 2000.

16 See Kraska 2001; Andreas and Price 2001.
17 See Forster 2006.
18 Gill 2004.
19 Hänggi 2009.
20 Haltiner and Kümmel 2008: 12.
21 Pugh 2005.
22 Zaalberg 2006; Crane 2005.
23 Kaldor 2005; Münkler 2005. On the controversy over 'new wars', see Duyvesteyn and Angstrom 2005.
24 Mueller 2004.
25 Pugh and Cooper 2004; Andreas 2004.
26 Aoi, de Coning and Thakur 2007: 5.
27 Quoted in: Zaalberg 2006: 338.
28 Ashdown 2007: 71-78, 222-224.
29 Smith, Holt, and Durch 2007: xiv.
30 Interviews with security practitioners, Kabul, July 2009. To be sure, the number of staff had risen, as compared to 2008. See Judy Dempsey, Europe Lagging in Effort to Train Afghan Police, in: International Herald Tribune, 28 May 2008.
31 Peake and Marenin 2008.
32 Mobekk 2005: 24.
33 Zentrum für Internationale Friedenseinsätze 2003: 96.
34 Bronson 2002.
35 Janowitz 1960: Chapter 20; Born, Haltiner and Malešič 2004: 16; Mandel 2007.
36 Ehrhart and Schnabel 2004: 10.
37 See, for example, Jones et al. 2005: 225; Martens 2007.
38 Zirnite 1997.
39 Perito 2004: 5.
40 On spoilers, see Stedman 1997. Spoilers play an ambiguous role after war. They may organize attacks against minorities and international personnel. But they may also provide jobs or reign in other radicals, due to the lust for political power or for economic motives, thus supporting international stabilization efforts.
41 See Reluctant Warrior, in: The Observer, 30 September 2001, available at http://www.guardian.co.uk/world/2001/sep/30/usa.afghanistan (download 10 August 2009).
42 Mueller 2004. See also van Creveld 1991: 225.
43 Hills 2001: 86-90.
44 Cousens 1998; Kaldor and Salmon 2006: 22.
45 See Gates 2009.
46 See Baer 2003.
47 See, for example, Smith 2006: 380-381.
48 U.S. Army 2007: 360-361.
49 Stark 2004: 2.
50 This view is espoused, among others, by Bigo 2001: 108. See also Farrell and Terriff 2002.
51 Hills 2001. 81.
52 International Commission 2001: 59.
53 Hills 2001: 81.

54 Mueller 2004: 22.
55 One could also conceptualize such support as Civil-Military Cooperation (CMCO), a term that may better capture inter-institutional cooperation. From this perspective, CIMIC would be part of CMCO, with the former denoting military support to reconstruction or humanitarian aid (I thank Max Bornefeld-Ettman for his comments on this point). However, for reasons of convenience this book uses the more established term CIMIC.
56 Pugh 2001.
57 See Weiss 1995; Weiss 1999; Refugee Policy Group 1998.
58 Kaplan 2005: 153-154.
59 See Gordon 2007; Pugh 1998; Pugh 2000; Abiew 2003; Zaalberg 2006: 277, 283, 401.
60 See Moskos, Williams and Segal 2000.
61 Schnabel and Ehrhart 2005: 3.
62 Ehrhart 2007: 13. See also Ank 2007; Gordon 2007.
63 This has been noted by Penksa (forthcoming).
64 See Ba and Hoffmann 2005.
65 See Czempiel and Rosenau 1992; Daase and Engert 2008; Zürn 1998.
66 Krahmann 2003: 11.
67 Slaughter 2004.
68 On security governance in the field of international police cooperation, see Andreas and Nadelmann 2006.
69 See Caparini 2006; Hall and Biersteker 2002.
70 Krahmann 2005.
71 Eilstrup-Sangiovanni 2005: 7; Krahmann 2005: 25.
72 On the nature of problematic situations, see George 2000: 75.
73 For a list and discussion of armed non-state actors, see Schneckener 2006.
74 Williams and Baudin-O'Hayon 2003: 142.
75 See Nordstrom 2004.
76 Raab and Milward 2003.
77 Arquilla and Ronfeldt 2001: 15.
78 Kenney 2007: 261, note 15.
79 Brzoska and Heinemann-Grüder 2004: 137.
80 Hänggi 2003: 8.
81 OECD 2007: 22.
82 See Hänggi 2003: 10.
83 See Wulf 2007.
84 Bryden, Donais and Hänggi 2005: 3.
85 The immunity of 'internationals' from prosecution by domestic courts has proven problematic, as in many cases courts of the countries where the accused come from have not taken action. This problem is particularly acute with regard to members of PMSCs that have operated in a legal vacuum.
86 Krause 2007.
87 See Bryden and Hänggi 2005; on transitional justice, see Mobekk 2006.
88 Born and Leigh 2008.
89 On institutional learning, see Kenney 2007.
90 Fukuyama 2006: 235.

Chapter 3

Bosnia-Herzegovina

The war in Bosnia was Europe's worst conflict since World War II. Around 100,000 people were killed, and many more were wounded. 'Ethnic cleansing' displaced 2.3 million of Bosnia's 4.4 million citizens.[1] Economic devastation was tremendous, too. By the time the General Framework Agreement for Peace in Bosnia and Herzegovina (referred to as Dayton) ended the fighting in late 1995, Bosnia was destroyed.

Many journalists and scholars have written about the war and international involvement after Dayton. Much attention has been paid to NATO's Implementation Force (IFOR) and its successor mission, the Stabilisation Force (SFOR), with criticism levelled against NATO for its failure to support crime-fighting. This case study builds on these works. Moreover, drawing on interviews and personal observations in Bosnia, it adds new insights on counter-crime efforts over recent years. While IFOR and SFOR are well covered in the literature, few works discuss the role of the European Union Force (EUFOR), the successor mission of SFOR.

This chapter chronologically traces military support provided to the fight against serious crime after Dayton. It shows that both military activism and passivity has been costly, in terms of human lives and legitimacy. Yet the Bosnian case also shows that NATO and the EU have improved over time.

IFOR

IFOR was the first peace operation deployed by NATO and constituted a major test for the alliance. The troops entered Bosnia in January 1996 and, a little later, had reached strength of around 60,000. This was the most powerful peacekeeping force ever, in terms of troop strength and equipment. NATO's decision to deploy heavily armed infantry and airpower means such as helicopter gunships was motivated by the presence of around 400,000 former combatants, many of whom, especially on the Serbian side, were hostile to NATO. Bosnia was no longer at war, but there was no real peace either.

Regular armed forces proved less of a challenge than paramilitary gangs still roaming the country and 'police officers' clad in fatigues and wielding Kalashnikovs. The most notorious group was the Ministarstvo Unutrasnjih Poslova (MUP, [Special Police of the Ministry of Interior]). Carrying long-barreled rifles, grenades and other weapons, the MUP of the Republika Srpska (RS) tried to consolidate 'ethnic cleansing' by hindering the return of refugees and displaced persons to their properties in the RS.[2] Moving into Bosnia, NATO quickly managed to compel former combatants to cease hostilities and withdraw into their respective zones, and to control the movements of heavy weapons. NATO implemented the military aspects of Dayton within six months. This was astonishing. However, some sources of instability were not clearly within the remit of the military.

The Bosnian war had been a criminalised war. Mary Kaldor and others who distinguish traditional, Clausewitzian warfare from 'new wars' find much evidence for their thesis in the Balkan wars of the 1990s, especially the one in Bosnia.[3] Bosnia was a paradise for war profiteers. Smugglers and traffickers benefited from international sanctions imposed on the Balkans. Paramilitaries such as 'Arkan's Tigers' became rich by chasing away and killing civilians and stealing their belongings. They became folk heroes in the process, despite the cowardice of many of their acts and the fact that most paramilitaries were common criminals, not fanatical nationalists.[4] The Bosnian war attracted numerous 'internationals' as well, including soldiers, NGO workers and journalists. The large international presence, particularly in Sarajevo, fuelled black marketeering.[5] The war thus forged a new entrepreneurial class that marginalised older elites.[6]

Many war profiteers did not stop smuggling and trafficking after the war. Bosnia exemplifies criminal state capture, since some of those conducting illicit businesses during the war had political and economic clout after Dayton. In Bosnia, "criminal capital accumulated during a criminalized war has been converted to political capital after the war."[7] Serious crime thus persisted after the war, with civilians, as before, being the main victims. During the war, profiteers had portrayed looting and killing as patriotism. Now, they continued to exploit and exacerbate ethnic divisions in order to secure, and increase, their fortunes – nationalism was an "ideological camouflage for their racketeering activities."[8] The 'new war' pattern in which violence against civilians and the interests of criminals are two sides of the same coin persisted even after Dayton.

Few of those who had been forcibly displaced heeded the calls to return home from states that had absorbed large numbers of refugees (many were simply sent back). Often, there was no home to return to. Even if there were, other people were occupying houses, or return was too risky. Those opposed to a democratic, multi-ethnic Bosnia knew that their military options were none against NATO. They thus operated in areas for which the military did not feel responsible and over which civilian actors were too weak to assert authority.[9]

As Noel Malcom writes, the "real problems, during the one year in which President Clinton had pledged to keep his soldiers [in Bosnia], would concern the security of ordinary life in the back streets of eastern Bosnian towns; and these were problem with which Western troops with tanks and heavy artillery were ill-equipped to deal."[10] IFOR was obligated to ensure the implementation of the military requirements in the Dayton agreement (Annex I), not the civilian ones.[11] The language of the Dayton agreement (e.g., article IV) was vague with regard to military support to civilian implementation, as observed by Jane Sharp: "It's helping, it's assisting, it's observing, it's monitoring; it's not really mandating and doing."[12] Even more problematically, Dayton was relatively unspecific on crucial issues related to the fight against serious crime, such as customs and border services and also the reform of intelligence agencies – shortcomings that have crippled counter-crime efforts ever since.[13]

IFOR could help civilian agencies but only if it wanted to. Commanders generally chose not to: With few exceptions, IFOR did not take action against those involved in organised crime and inter-ethnic crime, as well as those who had committed crimes during war. Even in areas with a high density of NATO soldiers, little was done to ensuring freedom of movement and protecting returning refugees, e.g. by removing illegal checkpoints, clearing mines, or disarming Bosnian police officers. IFOR was willing to provide 'area security' but said it was not responsible for the security of individuals.[14] In the words of a Dutch analyst:

> Although peacekeeping was often still considered 'not a job for soldiers', the military [after the earlier disasters in Somalia, Rwanda and Bosnia] became convinced they could succeed as long as they were allowed to do peacekeeping on their own terms, which meant going in with the capacity to enforce the peace and a clearly defined objective that was strictly limited to the military sphere. While crucial experiences from previous years were incorporated into the mission, particularly those related to the possible use of force, others were consciously ignored. IFOR turned out to be a giant leap forward in strictly military terms, but it was a big step backward in terms of civil-military cooperation. Moreover, the clock was turned back on military involvement in public security-related tasks.[15]

This became obvious early on in the mission. In spring 1996 seven Sarajevo municipalities controlled by Bosnian Serbs were to be transferred to the Federation government.[16] Many Serbs did not want to live in what they regarded as a Muslim-dominated city and decided to leave. Yet there were also Serbs, possibly up to 30,000, who did not oppose the concept of a multi-ethnic society (indeed, many Serbs had helped to defend Sarajevo against their fellow Serbs). Many of these were forced to leave by thuggish militias under the control of the Bosnian Serb leadership in Pale. As the exodus of between 70,000 and 100,000 Serbs from Sarajevo began, many buildings evacuated by their owners were destroyed (wires were pulled out of walls and plumbing fixtures were taken away) and/or booby-trapped. IFOR troops stood by and did not employ their own firefighting equipment, refused to protect the outdated equipment used by the Bosniaks and ignored pleas from the Office of the High Representative (OHR) to arrest rioters and pleas from civilians to be protected against attack. The reputational consequences for NATO were enormous.

An IFOR spokesperson, justifying the military's stance, said: "IFOR is not a police force and will not undertake police functions."[17] IFOR's initial RoE prevented the mission from using minimal force to protect civilians. As a Swedish soldier recalls, "I was allowed to do more as a civilian on the streets of Stockholm to prevent a crime from taking place than I was as an IFOR soldier on patrol in the Balkans."[18] IFOR eschewed taking responsibility even against those clearly posing a threat to stability and freedom of movement. Especially IFOR's failure to control the paramilitary MUP police, especially the MUP of the RS, was "an outright evasion of NATO's responsibilities".[19] As a consequence, inter-ethnic violence continued.[20]

IFOR also did not regard the arrest of suspected war criminals as within its remit. In February 1996, the IFOR Commander, US Admiral Leighton Smith, set the tone when he – incorrectly – asserted on Bosnian Serb TV that IFOR had "no right to arrest anyone".[21] In October 1996, the new IFOR Commander, US Admiral Joe Lopez, said at a NATO meeting in Heidelberg that he saw "no military value in arresting indicted war criminals."[22] Some IFOR contingents helped to locate Persons Indicted for War Crimes (PIFWCs).[23] Yet such action was not institutionalised within the NATO mission. IFOR even emphasised that it would not dispatch more patrols to areas where suspects lived. To the frustration of the prosecutors of the International Criminal Tribunal for the Former Yugoslavia (ICTY) in The Hague, IFOR (and the first SFOR rotations) on several occasions actively avoided contact with suspects, knowing of their whereabouts.[24]

Military reluctance to arrest war criminals partly originated in the failure of the Contact Group (the group of states that had tried to stop the war) during and after Dayton to specify ICTY arrest procedures.[25] Obviously, a lack of political pressure and clear mandates influenced the interpretation of mandates by military commanders on the ground.

IFOR was a US-dominated mission. The EU, despite much huffing and puffing, had failed to stop the war. In the later phase of the war and at the time of Dayton, the US exercised leadership. The stance of its troops left no doubt that any aggression against IFOR would meet a response different than the feeble one of the war-time United Nations Protection Force (UNPROFOR), which had not even been able to protect its own personnel. Yet US military and civilian leaders were marked by Mogadishu. This translated into an emphasis on force protection and military objectives, and a marked unwillingness to let the UN or even NATO allies encroach on US strategies and tactics. US commanders refused to do anything that smacked of policing. The practice whereby US troops would leave their fortified camps only in heavily armed convoys prevented the troops from closely interacting with civilian agencies and ordinary citizens. NATO had learned lessons for force protection from the UN, but its Balkan operations suffered from the failure to understand that complex peace operations required replacing the principle of neutrality with the principle of impartiality, with the latter implying a much more proactive approach against anyone threatening peace and security.[26]

In the first two years after Dayton the peace was fragile. IFOR and, in the early stage, SFOR felt they were in a war-like environment.[27] Consequently, NATO focused on what it regarded as core military activities and on force protection, regarding Bosnian security forces, especially those dominated by Bosnian Serbs, as the opponent. This stance impeded crime fighting, and lingered on even as security conditions improved. Bosnia was divided into three sectors under the command of the US, France and the UK, respectively. The intensity of crime-fighting varied across sectors. Yet given US military hegemony, the US stance left a large imprint on the mission as a whole.

In addition to the US preoccupation with force protection and the use of overwhelming power to deter hostilities, law enforcement also suffered from a lack of police capacities. Bosnian police forces were factionalised and continued to abuse human rights; they had to be coerced into removing checkpoints and giving up their weapons. The deployment of international police officers was fraught with problems (setting the course for other policing missions over the following years in various parts of the world).

Dayton proscribed the creation of the United Nations International Police Task Force (IPTF). Due to a convergence of European government and Pentagon preferences, the IPTF was given a weak mandate.[28] This left a "huge gap in the Bosnia food chain", as US General Wesley Clark, military advisor at Dayton, remarked to Richard Holbrooke, one of the architects of the Dayton agreement.[29]

IPFT officers were unarmed and did not have executive powers.[30] They were there merely to monitor, advise and train Bosnian law enforcement institutions (at a later stage, the IPTF was given the right to recommend the dismissal of unsuitable police officers). Paradoxically, the IPTF depended on cooperation from Bosnian institutions, yet such cooperation was not a given.[31] For protection, the IPTF relied on IFOR, yet it had no authority over IFOR. The IPTF was a large mission, at its peak numbering almost 2,000 officials. Yet it took too long to reach this level. In the crucial immediate post-war period, the IPTF was barely visible. Also, being unarmed and poorly equipped in a partially still hostile environment narrowed IPTF officers' tactical options, as became clear early on: During the Serb exodus from Sarajevo, the IPTF had neither the right nor the power to intervene. Bosnian citizens knew they could not count on the IPTF to protect them against abusive police officers and ordinary thugs. IPTF's credibility was further undermined by the fact that some of its members lacked the most basic policing competences, such as driving skills. There are numerous accounts of IPTF incompetence and even criminal collusion.[32]

The IPTF, like the UN as a whole, was not allowed to give any instructions to NATO. The US government was weary of the UN's failure in Bosnia and Somalia, and was even sceptical about the 1994 intervention in Haiti.[33] The Republican-dominated Congress exerted much pressure on the Clinton administration to limit US exposure to UN politics. The result was the creation of a dual command system whereby the UN was overseeing the implementation of the civilian aspects of Dayton while NATO was responsible for the military aspects. Responsibilities for the grey area activity of fighting serious crime were left undefined.

The travails of the IPTF reflected a weakness of civilian agencies more generally. The first High Representative, Carl Bildt, lacked the most basic means to promote peacebuilding. He told the first IFOR commander, Admiral Leighton Smith, who showed little patience with civilian matters: "Admiral, you had a year to plan for this operation, a huge staff and the requisite infrastructure to get you into the theater, set up, and supported. I started out with a cell phone in a parking lot a few weeks before we were to begin operations."[34] More importantly, initially the High Representative had no coordination powers vis-à-vis international institutions and no enforcement powers vis-à-vis Bosnian actors. And the institution had no authority over NATO, but instead depended on the military's goodwill. Given the weakness of civilian institutions and the restrained posture of the military, there was a big security gap.

SFOR

The change from IFOR to SFOR in late 1996 did not immediately fill the security gap. SFOR was a smaller mission than IFOR, counting 35,000 soldiers. Similar to its predecessor, SFOR was dominated by the US, even though European influence increased over the years. Clinton was under strong pressure from Congress, which was weary of horizontal mission creep, to withdraw US troops from Bosnia. However, arguing that a quick exit could result in a new war, Clinton accepted incurring domestic political costs.[35] NATO's military presence had been scheduled to last one year. The shift from IFOR to SFOR revealed that this tight schedule was unrealistic. Over the following years, the mandate to deploy troops was renewed time and again.

Some progress was being made towards peace. In fall 1996 general elections were held, with the support of NATO, which distributed and collected ballots and provided security. International community representatives touted the elections as evidence of democratisation. However, most observers nowadays argue that the elections were held much too early and in a climate of fear, resulting in an astounding victory of nationalist parties mired in corruption and thriving on threats and fears.[36] On the economic front, some infrastructure was repaired.

Yet in general, political, economic and social recovery was feeble. The lack of military support of law enforcement persisted as well. Many senior SFOR commanders argued that 'policing' was not covered by the military missions' mandate.[37] But this view was more informed by the fear of body bags and the attempt to cling to traditional military roles than it was by a close look at the Dayton mandate and military doctrines. Neither the mandate nor doctrines prevented the military from fighting serious crime.[38]

From mid-1997 NATO's mission was no longer to end the war, but to build peace. The military now shed some of its intransigence. This was due to public pressure on SFOR to protect returnees and to arrest suspected war criminals. Changes on the top decision-making level were important, too.[39] In the US, the hawkish Madeleine Albright replaced the cautious Warren

Christopher as Secretary of State and also came to dominate over the cautious Defense Secretary William Cohen. In Britain, Prime Minister Tony Blair committed himself to defending human rights. At NATO, the new Secretary-General Javier Solana told the new NATO Supreme Allied Commander Europe (SACEUR), US General Wesley Clark, that Clark "must actively help the civilians to succeed" in Bosnia.[40] The team Solana-Clark was crucial for expanding the scope of military tasks in Bosnia, with Clark being willing to involve "the military in police work", as he later wrote in his memoirs.[41]

In Bosnia, changes occurred as well. The new High Representative, Carlos Westendorp, was given the power to rule as de-facto governor. A conference in 1997 in Bonn reinforced the powers of the High Representative by granting the office holder the right to dismiss Bosnian officials who were seen as failing to comply with the international reform agenda (the High Representative answers to the 55 governments and organisations constituting the Peace Implementation Council). Over the following years, the High Representatives made extensive use of these powers.[42] Parallel and partly in response to these developments, many SFOR officers came to realise the negative consequences of narrowly interpreting a "safe and secure environment". The military thus became more proactive, even as SFOR commanders, for instance US General Eric Shinseki, retained their cautious attitude. Interpretation mattered a lot, as SFOR continuously had to decide whether ordinary crimes, including the stockpiling of weapons, violated the Dayton agreement, thus meriting military intervention.[43]

Enhanced military activism manifested itself in various ways. SFOR, especially its CIMIC teams, supported an increasing number of reconstruction projects, even those not of immediate military importance.[44] Bosnian citizens benefited because their water systems, power infrastructure and roads were repaired. The military benefited as well. By helping the population it could gather information and intelligence and thus protect itself against attack. SFOR also helped to supervise elections and resettle refugees.

SFOR equally became less tolerant of war-mongering. In 1997 it seized TV installations used by Radovan Karadžić's men for propaganda purposes. This was an important sign of support for Karadžić's former ally and now rival, Biljana Plavšić, who received the support of the West and of SFOR. However, SFOR was still reluctant to fight serious crime. Only by the early 2000s did threat perceptions enable more systematic crime-fighting support. Even then, the military's posture remained incoherent.[45] While SFOR did expand its portfolio, crime-fighting efforts were haphazard.

One way in which SFOR supported policing was through the use of more military police.[46] Yet the main assets were constabulary forces. By 1998 NATO had come to realise that many important security tasks were beyond the remit of traditional military units. It thus deployed, in August of that year, Multinational Specialised Units (MSU). 386 officers, or around 75 percent of the unit, were Italian Carabinieri.[47] Yet there were also troops from other countries, including the non-NATO and non-EU members Argentina, Romania and Slovenia. These countries often used their constabulary forces at home, e.g., against football hooligans. Their deployment to Bosnia reflected the need to calibrate the use of force to defuse dangerous situations and to deter, or take on, mobs.

Italy was the framework nation for the MSU. According to an Italian official, the MSU were an Italian idea.[48] But it is more likely that the impetus came from the US.[49] Congress and Defense Secretary William Cohen were keen to withdraw US troops and to better share the burden of stabilising Bosnia with European countries. But withdrawal was not feasible as long as public security was not ensured. The US thus pushed its European partners to deploy in-between forces – which the US did not have and which would fill the gap between SFOR and the IPTF. The main task of the MSU was to ensure public order. However, SFOR often failed to exploit the full potential of the MSU, as shown below.

SFOR and Suspected War Criminals

The arrest of suspected war criminals was at the core of the debate over the role of SFOR. The Dayton agreement gave the main responsibility to Bosnian institutions, who agreed to cooperate with the ICTY. However, cooperation was not properly defined,[50] and Bosnian officials were unlikely to carry out arrests. After all, those indicted were in senior positions or had sufficient political clout to escape prosecution. Moreover, the police, still politicised, were unwilling to arrest 'war heroes'. Or, they lacked the means to challenge well-armed and financed figures. Many suspects swam like fish in the water, receiving protection from a network of informers and funding from criminal activities.

Much depended on NATO, given that Bosnian institutions were unreliable and that neither the ICTY nor the IPTF possessed the means and mandates to enforce the capture of suspects. Arresting suspected war criminals hinged not only on the collection of timely and accurate intelligence, but also on military capabilities such as surveillance equipment, weapons and helicopters that could quickly deploy snatch teams.

Yet NATO took the position that war criminals would only be arrested if SFOR came across them in the course of their duties; SFOR would not actively search for those indicted. This stance was motivated by the fear of casualties (Mogadishu) and embarrassment in case of failure. It is unlikely that two sides meet who do not want to meet, as remarked in 1998 by Louise Arbour, Chief Prosecutor of the ICTY.[51] NATO's policy thus reduced the chances of arrest to a minimum. One senior UN official at the time describes a visit of NATO's North Atlantic Council (NAC) to Sarajevo in April 1997 as follows:

> As part of his presentation to the NAC Carl Bildt showed on a large-screen display a map of Pale that showed Karadžić's house and the times and route he normally took when traveling to his office or to meetings. Security was not especially heavy around the Serb leader and it would not have been so very difficult for NATO to stop him and attempt an arrest. With the Somali experience poisoning NATO's attitude, however, the presentation on this issue did not make General Joulwan [NATO SACEUR] very happy. The NAC Ambassadors present simply took notes and said little.[52]

In August 1997, the Chairman of the US Joint Chiefs of Staff, General John Shalikashvili, said that US troops would not participate in the arrest of war criminals.[53] Without US leadership progress in this area would be haphazard. France was even accused of protecting war criminals.[54] According to a former UN official, the commander of the British SFOR contingent, upon learning about Karadžić's movements, called London to receive permission to arrest the indicted war criminal. Yet after talking to his superiors and receiving a negative answer, the commander told the UN official: "We're not police, we're soldiers, so this isn't our job. It's up to the RS [Republika Srpska] police to arrest Karadžić."[55]

Yet SFOR, over time, did demonstrate more flexibility. On 10 July 1997, shortly after a NATO summit, British Special Air Services troops arrested indicted war criminal Milan Kovacević in Prijedor, a town dominated by hardline Serbs (another person resisting arrest was killed in a shoot-out).[56] The incident indicated that international actors now paid more attention to war crimes issues, setting a crucial precedent. It also revealed that approaches for dealing with suspected war criminals differed across the different military sectors. British forces (due to their experiences in former colonies and especially in Northern Ireland) were more willing and more capable of undertaking grey-area missions than other countries, and they were more willing to incur the risk of casualties.[57]

Now, war criminals were no longer safe. Snatch operations were often staged by special military forces flown into the country for single operations. Dutch Special Forces, for example, in December 1997, arrested two Bosnian Croats accused of having committed crimes against Muslims. Even Germany, despite its post-World War II reluctance to engage in foreign military operations, deployed its new Kommando Spezialkräfte (KSK, Special Forces Command), with snatch operations occurring in June 1998, August 1999 and October 2000 (during the last operation, three soldiers were severely injured after the suspect blew himself up with a hand grenade).[58] Publicly, Javier Solana continued to endorse the policy whereby troops would arrest suspects only if they encountered them during their normal activities. This policy was reflected in continuing caution by troops on the ground.[59] Yet special forces and intelligence agencies did conduct numerous covert operations.[60]

NATO also shed its reluctance to dismantle illegal checkpoints and arrest Bosnian police officers. PIFWCs depended on police support. The power of Karadžić after Dayton, in addition to Serb television and black-marketeering, rested on the police.[61] By May 1997, NATO finally decided to systematically escort IPTF officers attempting to remove illegal checkpoints, inspect local police stations and disarm police officers who had been dismissed.[62] NATO also cajoled the police into compliance with Dayton by supporting police officers who were not loyal to Karadžić. Even though especially US and French commanders remained reluctant to take away the weapons and identity cards of police officers manning checkpoints,[63] NATO's greater assertiveness, especially when directed against MUP police,[64] helped to marginalise suspected war criminals and made life safer in Bosnia.

A more systematic use of the MSU similarly helped to increase pressure on war crimes indictees. Initially, making arrests was not part of the MSU mandate,[65] depriving NATO of a valuable asset. Over time, however, this restriction was loosened. In the early 2000s, the MSU began to support the ICTY. The MSU main contingent would secure an area and guard against violent crowd reactions while the MSU SWAT team would arrest the suspect. The MSU was also active when investigations were conducted by ICTY operatives. In spring 2002, for instance, MSU officers in civilian cloths observed events from nearby cafés as ICTY investigators searched local police stations and other sites.[66]

However, up until the end of its mandate, SFOR remained a reluctant recruit in the fight against those who had committed atrocities. This reluctance undermined the credibility of the mission in the eyes of

Bosnians,[67] as well as the fight against organised crime (see further below), since many suspected war criminals or their supporters were involved in lucrative illegal activities.[68] Military caution reflected, and was fed by, a lack of political will among powerful NATO member states to arrest war criminals. The fear of casualties trumped concerns about the impact of inaction on stability in Bosnia and on the credibility of NATO.[69]

Generating political will to arrest suspected war criminals was not helped by calls to hold NATO personnel accountable for arrest operations undertaken in legally problematic ways. Several of those captured and transferred to The Hague claimed that SFOR had used illegal means. Both the ICTY prosecutors and SFOR tried to fend off the efforts of the accused and their defence lawyers, as well as the Court itself, to make SFOR reveal the details of arrest procedures (including the names of individuals involved) and to attend hearings in The Hague. In one instance, the Trial Chamber even issued a subpoena requiring the SFOR commander to testify.[70] By indicating that it was willing to jeopardise the security of military operations, the ICTY may have been trying to safeguard human rights, yet at the cost of antagonising SFOR.[71]

SFOR and Crowd and Riot Control

Inappropriate responses to CRC became evident many times. In numerous instances, refugees and minority groups were attacked, eliciting little response from SFOR. On 10 February 1997, for example, Bosnian Croats, including police officers, fired into a crowd of Muslims who peacefully wanted to visit grave sites in West Mostar. One Bosniak was killed and 21 wounded.[72] Only a few unarmed IPTF officers were present. SFOR did not back up the IPTF, later arguing that it had been informed too late. After the demonstration, as armed men took up positions to observe a bridge linking East and West Mostar, Spanish SFOR troops did not intervene either.

On 28 August 1997, supporters of Radovan Karadžić (and Mocilo Krajisnik as well as other members of Karadžić's entourage) violently demonstrated in Brčko.[73] In this "rent-a-crowd" incident, demonstrators, who were paid up to 100 Deutschmark each,[74] opposed the attempt of Karadžić-rival Biljana Plavšić to expand her influence and take over police stations manned by officers loyal to Karadžić. Demonstrators destroyed UN and OHR vehicles and attacked international personnel, including US SFOR soldiers. These had been given authority to use their weapons to disperse crowds. But they were unwilling to do so against demonstrators armed with bricks and clubs, even as some soldiers were injured by demonstrators.[75]

SFOR improvised and managed to evacuate IPTF officials who were trapped by the mob. Nearby, heavily-armed US troops defended a bridge across the river Sava for nearly twelve hours against a mob that included women and children and also dangerous males. As the troops did not want to use their weapons, they had to rely on their fists and rifle butts to prevent the crowd from storming the bridge. Only when a Molotov cocktail was thrown at a US Army vehicle did the troops fire tear gas – the first use of teargas in Bosnia.[76]

These incidents, as well as many others, showed that the military was insufficiently prepared for CRC. "Tanks, armored personnel carriers, and helicopter gunships were of little use against hostile mobs of women and children providing cover for drunken, club-wielding thugs who threw stones and Molotov cocktails."[77] The military's lack of preparation for CRC posed problems for IPTF officers who were trying to reform the police, as well as for Bosnian officials under threat from those opposed to peace.

Yet the main victims of mobs were vulnerable people such as displaced persons trying to return home. "Arson was the weapon of choice of all of the parties in the defense on an ethnically cleansed Bosnia, but the offenders frequently resorted to assault and murder."[78] In the early years of the mission, SFOR did not regard the protection of vulnerable people as part of their mandate. As a consequence, after several years into Dayton, few displaced persons had returned home, not least because the risk of attack was real. On 16 April 1998, for instance, an elderly Serb couple who had just returned to the municipality of Drvar was murdered, just one incident among many against returning Serbs in this region.[79] Following an international attempt to dismiss politicians and Drvar's police chief from office, on 24 April disciplined Bosnian Croat rioters attacked buildings and assaulted Bosnian and international officials and Serb returnees. Canadian SFOR troops failed to intervene, due to restrictive national RoE. This incident, and many other ones, corroborates the charge that NATO discouraged return instead of protecting returnees.[80]

A lack of political will to become involved in law enforcement went hand in hand with inappropriate RoE. German SFOR troops, a few years into Dayton, had no shields, batons, nor training for CRC. This was despite the agreement that each national contingent should have CRC capabilities in its respective sector.[81] Some adjustments were made. Following the Brčko incident described above, US troops received non-lethal weapons.[82] Yet new equipment did not alleviate the fact that soldiers were not trained in CRC.

Rampaging mobs in Bosnia revealed the need for capabilities SFOR hitherto did not possess. Especially the riots in Brčko in August 1997 provided a catalyst for the creation of the MSU.[83] NATO came to understand that the failure to deal with mobs destabilised Bosnia. The MSU offered the required CRC capabilities. However, the deployment of the MSU was fraught with problems. National contingent commanders were reluctant to draw on MSU support because they saw this as an encroachment on their turf. Theoretically, the MSU was the only component of SFOR that could operate theatre-wide, across the entire national territory. Yet in practice, commanders of what commonly was know as "The Three Kingdoms" (the three Multinational Divisions [MND] North, Southwest and Southeast under the respective command of the US, UK and France)[84] wanted to control all military activities in their areas of responsibility. The reluctance of MND commanders to allow MSU operations in their respective sector hampered the ability of the MSU "to conduct mobile patrols, provide a security presence, or gather information. The MSU requests to conduct operations across MND boundaries were often misdirected or lost in the SFOR chain of command."[85]

A related problem was that commanders of regular troops did not understand constabulary forces. US officers, for instance, saw the MSU as part of the strategic reserve of SFOR, a unit that could be called in when the IPTF and Bosnian police forces were overwhelmed by rioters. The MSU, in contrast, was keen on extensive patrolling to gather information before situations would boil over; it wanted to use basic policing skills to prevent conflicts, instead of being confined to a reactive role.[86] Given these divergent preferences, no proper doctrine was devised that would govern the relationship between SFOR and its MSU component. For many years, the MSU remained primarily a reactive force.

Colonel Vincenzo Coppola, the MSU executive officer, also quickly found out during his preparatory briefings in spring 1998 that IPTF officers from Britain, the US and Germany, who held the senior posts in the UN police mission, were equally unfamiliar with constabulary forces. In fact, the IPTF was reluctant to accept constabulary operations. At a time when the IPTF made efforts to train the Bosnian police forces in CRC, they feared competition from the MSU and more inter-organisational complexity. IPTF officers also thought that Bosnian citizens would not be able to distinguish between MSU and IPTF officers which would increase risks for the IPTF. Last, the IPTF found that MSU deployment undermined democratic community policing and sent the wrong message to Bosnia. Due to these concerns, institutional links between the IPTF and the MSU were reduced to an absolute minimum – a single officer assigned to each headquarter.[87] In one case (involving the murder of a teenage Muslim girl in the Serb-dominated town of Zvornik) the IPTF commissioner complained about MSU involvement in the investigation, forcing the MSU to complete the investigation covertly.[88]

To make matters worse for the MSU, even some countries that had constabulary forces were reluctant to deploy them to Bosnia. According to the commander of a French SFOR contingent, Wesley Clark, in his capacity as SACEUR, pushed for including more French Gendarmes into SFOR. Yet the French government declined the invitation, arguing that Gendarmes should not be deployed to countries in which there was no law and order.[89] The Netherlands, Spain and Portugal refused to contribute troops to the MSU as well.[90]

A lack of CRC capacities showed in various ways. The commander cited above requested tear gas for CRC, but his French military superiors did not grant his wish on the grounds that his troops were not supposed to get involved in policing. Yet avoiding policing situations was impossible, and the presence of more Gendarmes would have helped the commander. For instance, he instructed his soldiers to shoot at anyone lighting a Molotov cocktail, assuming that such cocktails are lethal under all circumstances. Yet then Gendarmes told him that Molotov cocktails do not explode on a plastic shield. The commander's limited ability to benefit from the experience and equipment of the Gendarmerie thus increased the risk of uncontrolled escalation. A further problem was the commander's concern that he or his troops would be prosecuted if demonstrators were killed. Only after a military judge came to visit Bosnia, and the commander explained the challenges of CRC in Bosnia, were such concerns alleviated, although not entirely.[91]

Given these constraints, it is not surprising that the MSU was underutilised; often its members were used for guarding buildings and protecting VIPs. In October 1998, MSU members were deployed for CRC for the first time when the troops cleared a road block that had been erected by Croat displaced persons in southern Bosnia.[92] However, the violence surrounding the incident resulted, according to Robert Perito, from wrong orders given to the Italian MSU platoon leader (a captain) by a Spanish SFOR superior (a major).[93]

Following this incident, NATO developed the Blue Box/Green Box concept. This doctrine stipulated that when public order was threatened, the on-site MSU commander would command his own unit as well as other forces present (the Blue Box). Forces that came from outside the Area of Responsibility where the disturbance occurred would be under the command of the most senior MND officer present (the Green Box), and would support the MSU. This arrangement reflected the desire of the military to clearly distinguish police work (Blue Box activities) from military work (Green Box activities).[94] Yet it had the advantage of giving more tactical freedom to constabularies to deal with unrest, including the freedom to decide to use force or not, and to choose the means for quelling riots.

This arrangement proved successful several times. In spring 1999 in Brčko, the MSU prevented new violent demonstrations in the town centre, which became a Blue Box. In this and other instances, the MSU, through the presence of MSU officers in full riot gear and by collecting information on public attitudes, reduced the risk of violence.[95] According to one study, by 2000 the MSU had been able "to resolve 261 of 263 'interventions' without the use of force through a combination of deterrence, dissuasion, and negotiation."[96]

Generally, however, SFOR continued to lack the will to protect civilians. As late as April 2000, the US Army was still refusing to open an SFOR station in Srebrenica, the site of the worst massacre in Europe since World War II. Bosnian Serbs living in the town, having been displaced themselves, prevented the return of Muslims. Even the Muslim mayor, who had been elected by absentee ballot, did not dare to live in the town for fear of attack on his life.[97] The lack of coercive capabilities is also indicated by a report of the International Crisis Group (ICG) published in spring 2000. Examining the need to counter obstructionist Croat networks in Herzegovina under the condition of a reticent SFOR, the ICG proposed the formation of elite armed IPTF units, while not even mentioning the MSU.[98]

Even when SFOR decided to take action, it struggled to ensure public security. The most dramatic events occurred on 6 April 2001.[99] The OHR sent auditors from a US firm to confiscate documents from several branches of the Mostar-based Hercegovačka Banka. The bank was allegedly controlled by shady nationalist Croat networks and served to launder money obtained partially through smuggling and trafficking, to redirect money from international organisations and to administer funds of the nationalist HDZ party – all of this in order to finance the illegal Croat republic of 'Herceg-Bosna'.[100]

For security, the auditors were accompanied by a small number of MSU officers (the operation's Blue Box contingent). Once the auditors and the Carabinieri had taken over the bank branches, a mob quickly assembled. Eventually rioters stormed the banks using death threats and beating and injuring auditors, Carabinieri and other international personnel. The rioters managed to retrieve the confiscated documents. In the town of Grude, the auditors and MSU officers were held at gunpoint for twelve hours. As the bank buildings were being stormed, the MSU radioed SFOR units (the operation's Green Box contingent). But French and Spanish troops failed to rescue those trapped inside the bank buildings, presumably because they feared a larger escalation if they tried to force their way through roadblocks and hostile crowds. Eleven of the twenty nine international and Bosnian personnel injured during the events were MSU officers. By the time SFOR came back ten days later to surround the bank headquarters with armoured personnel carriers, all the documents and records had disappeared.

In this and other cases contingency planning was flawed. One reason was a lack of intelligence capacities which had been cut significantly.[101] Better intelligence would probably have led SFOR to expect more than, as its commander later said, "inquisitive citizens".[102] Another reason was that by 2001 MSU platoons were still in short supply.[103] The lack of pre-planning, intelligence and constabularies showed again on 7 May 2001. That day a Bosnian Serb mob, supported by thousands of onlookers, violently interrupted a ceremony initiating the rebuilding of the Ferhadija mosque in Banja Luka which had been blown up in 1993. The rampage went on for hours, with foreign and domestic dignitaries and civilians being attacked and buildings and cars destroyed. RS riot police did not intervene; instead, officers were seen shaking hands with demonstrators.[104] Nor did SFOR, which had deployed helicopters, armoured vehicles and tanks, intervene. Two days earlier Bosnian Serbs violently protested against the inauguration of the Osman Pasha mosque in Trebinje, a town in southeastern Herzegovina. As in Banja Luka, neither domestic nor international security forces intervened.[105]

Many observers argue that the Hercegovačka Banka riots were a catalyst for improving CRC capabilities. Indeed, SFOR commanders now better understood the MSU. Moreover, the MSU were now allowed to train and work with both the IPTF and Bosnian police forces.[106] Among other activities, SFOR supported the UN Mission in Bosnia in the training of entity police officers in CRC.[107] There is thus evidence of a more systematic use of constabulary forces in CRC, in particular, and greater attention is paid to public security by the military in general.

Yet this positive assessment warrants caveats. Well into the new millennium, military action depended on the interpretation of mandates and what constitutes a safe and secure environment by MND commanders. One IPTF officer said in November 2001: "The last general was helpful; this one is less so."[108] It must also be noted that after 2001 CRC became less of a challenge in Bosnia than before. While there were isolated attacks on minorities, the intimidation of, and attacks against and also by, displaced persons, began to wane. Concomitantly, Bosnia saw a significant return of displaced persons to their home communities from 2000 onward.[109] Also, raids on sites where suspected war criminals were hiding or where crime was perpetrated drew less public anger, reducing operational risks. After 2001, military CRC capabilities were not subjected to extreme tests.

SFOR and Organised Crime

After Dayton, the criminal legacy of the war lingered on, with Bosnia remaining a haven for organised crime. Many organised crime activities were beyond the remit of SFOR. For example, the Sarajevo airport was used as a hub for smuggling people (many of them from Iran and Turkey) into Bosnia and then from there to Western Europe.[110] Only after the EU had pressurised Bosnia to impose visa restrictions was irregular migration reduced. Yet in those areas where SFOR could have made a difference, it did too little. This was partly a problem of mandates. The MSU were not allowed to conduct criminal investigations unless asked to do so by the Commander of SFOR. Yet SFOR commanders largely failed to draw on the crime-fighting expertise of the Carabinieri. As intelligence-gathering initially was not included in the MSU mandate, the MSU G-2 (military intelligence) staff did not "gather, collate, and analyze the wealth of information that MSU patrols routinely collect."[111] This significantly curtailed the ability of the MSU to contribute to law enforcement. To further complicate matters, Italian law prohibited the Carabinieri from investigating crimes or enforcing the law unless they were under the authority of the Interior Ministry. But in Bosnia the Carabinieri served under the Ministry of Defence.[112]

Furthermore, SFOR continued to be a reluctant partner of the IPTF. SFOR had substantial intelligence-gathering capabilities, and better communication between SFOR and the IPTF would have helped the latter to fight crime. SFOR could have also interrupted many criminal activities that were occurring under the eyes of its soldiers. SFOR patrols at or near border crossing points often had no difficulty observing the smuggling and trafficking of goods and people. Yet a lack of training and guidance from SFOR commanders prevented soldiers from intervening. One consequence was that human traffickers bringing foreign women into Bosnia easily passed SFOR checkpoints.

SFOR also inadvertently fostered crime. Near Brčko, along the Zone of Separation between RS and the Federation, the Pentagon in 1996 had funded the creation of 'Arizona market', in the hope of uniting former enemies by enabling them to trade with one another. The area quickly evolved into a major crime zone. Criminal groups controlling the market sold goods including contraband cigarettes, stolen cars and counterfeit CDs. The Bosnian government accrued losses in the form of unpaid taxes worth $30 million per year.[113]

One of the features of the market was the 'sale' of women like chattel for a few hundred dollars.[114] Here and elsewhere in Bosnia, many of the clients giving money to pimps and brothel owners (more often than giving it directly to the prostitutes) were 'internationals', including SFOR soldiers and IPTF officers.[115] Private military contractors working for DynCorp were also deeply involved in the abuse of women. When a whistleblower alerted the authorities to this fact, she lost her job.[116] While BiH citizens were estimated to constitute 70 percent of those buying commercial sex, 70 percent of the profits came from 'internationals',[117] since the latter had to pay more due to their higher disposable income. As in other parts of the world to which young, often single, men were sent,[118] military deployment to Bosnia coincided with a boom in prostitution, including forced prostitution, in that country. Human trafficking in Bosnia, up until 2002-2003, was a large, transnational industry with many of the trafficked women coming from as far away as Moldova and Ukraine.[119]

Some 'internationals' may have hoped that the sex industry would pump foreign money into the Bosnian economy. Yet brothel owners (who often received protection from the police[120]) usually did not pay taxes, and they invested in luxury goods.[121] More importantly, by visiting brothels, foreign clients exacerbated human rights violations, as conditions in some of the brothels resembled conditions in the infamous rape camps during the war. Customers also funded organised crime groups and undermined international credibility – Bosnian citizens did not fail to notice tacit or overt collusion between 'internationals' and local criminals. By contributing to human trafficking, NATO personnel undermined stabilisation efforts, the outcome of which determined whether troop withdrawal was feasible.[122]

Generally, international counter-crime efforts lacked forcefulness. The myopia and indifference towards the illicit economy is shown by the fact that despite clear evidence that the Arizona market was a hub for criminal entrepreneurs, it took many years to control and regulate that market. SFOR, even when action carried no risk, often did not provide support. In one instance in 1999, SFOR did not respond to UN requests to provide escort security to victims of trafficking who were to be repatriated to their country of origin and were believed to be under threat from traffickers.[123] SFOR's reluctance to support the fight against organised crime partly resulted from the mission's unease when it came to sharing intelligence with civilian actors, especially the police. In 1999, for instance, the SFOR commander "refused to show crucial intelligence on illegal funding for radical Bosnian-Croat politicians to international police investigators trying to indict Croatians on corruption charges and war crimes."[124]

In the new millennium SFOR continued to be a reluctant crime fighter. But there were changes, too, for various reasons. One was the de-Americanisation of SFOR. By autumn 2001, a mere 3,200 SFOR troops were American, out of a total of 19,000.[125] European militaries had less stringent force protection requirements than the US military. Also, security conditions in Bosnia were improving fast, making crime-fighting less risky.

Most importantly, the fight against organised crime gained salience in international security, with official discourse becoming martial. In 2002, governments, most of them of EU member states, argued that "if we do not defeat organised crime, it will defeat us."[126] Such discourse went hand in hand with more militarised counter-crime measures. In Bosnia, international actors, frustrated with the slow progress in peacebuilding, increasingly perceived organised crime and corruption as the main problems. By the beginning of the new millennium, organised crime was still pervasive in some areas. For instance, the "Croat borderlands in BiH around Stolac, Siroki Brijeg, and Herceg Novi have become a haven for transnational trafficking in drugs, cigarettes, and oil. Sometimes, Colombian cocaine arriving in Croatian ports is bartered for weapons."[127] Now, pressure on criminals and nationalist parties involved in corruption and criminal collusion increased. High Representative Paddy Ashdown argued that the international community should have given priority to the rule of law rather than to superficial democratic progress.[128] He and other officials within and outside of Bosnia now gave higher priority to crime-fighting.[129]

Growing concern about crime led SFOR to alter its stance. In 1999, SFOR staged Westar, a series of operations directed over several months against a shady network of illegal Bosnian Croat intelligence agencies, nationalist political parties and criminal entrepreneurs based in Stolac, Mostar and elsewhere.[130] Moving against those financing (through front companies and other tricks) and representing 'Herceg-Bosna' was intended to disrupt organised crime, separatism, violent resistance to minority resettlement and other illegal activities obstructing the implementation of Dayton. Especially the dismantling of illegal intelligence services, which were spying on international agencies and their Bosnian staff, was crucial.

Westar and other operations were hampered by SFOR's problems to analyze and use for the purpose of prosecution any incriminating evidence gathered during operations.[131] SFOR thus increasingly drew on the MSU. As mentioned above, MSU crime-fighting was hampered by legal restrictions. But the MSU learned to work around these restrictions. Some information-gathering operations were covert, with MSU personnel wearing plain cloths (the only other element allowed to do this were US Special Forces). The MSU also protected witnesses and provided armed escorts for prisoners.[132] Furthermore, the MSU began to train Bosnian police in raiding crime sites. Thus, in April 2002 the Bosnian police staged a night-time helicopter raid on a brothel where foreign victims of human trafficking were kept.[133]

The effects of international action against crime remain controversial. The OHR sacked numerous Bosnian politicians accused of corruption or of stalling reform.[134] The OHR also sacked police officers based on recommendation from the IPTF. While the vetting process helped to filter out human rights abusers, the process lacked transparency and was rather haphazard.[135] Several years after the termination of the IPTF mission, observers were still criticising the IPFT and UNMBIH for having declared victory prematurely.[136]

The problem that no single institution felt responsible or was strong enough to fight serious crime persisted. There was growing appreciation that improving coordination among international actors and between international and domestic actors was a precondition for fighting organised crime.[137] But the right steps depended too much on individuals. According to an international intelligence official, in 2004 SFOR was keen to arrest Ante Jelavić, a prominent Bosnian-Croat politician presumed to be involved in illegal activities. SFOR commanders were reluctant to use the MSU for prior surveillance, but eventually the official convinced them.[138] Following an MSU surveillance operation, Bosnian police arrested Jelavić in Mostar.[139] Carabinieri officials were present for two reasons: to ensure that the arrest would be carried out correctly and to allow the Bosnian officers involved to present the arrest as having been forced upon them by the international community.[140]

Yet crime-fighting would lag behind when nobody was pushing the issue. One military intelligence official recounts that his predecessor had begun to use SFOR assets for supporting counter-smuggling operations. After taking over in 2004, the official continued these operations by ordering the deployment of drones and helicopters to take pictures in border zones. Yet he would only spend around twenty minutes a day working on this issue, and after three months gave an order to cease such activities, no longer believing in their beneficial effect.[141]

One noteworthy development was a reported decline in human trafficking in Bosnia. Controversy over how and why the trafficking industry changed persists.[142] The IPTF and United States argued that raids on brothels, organised as part of the Special Trafficking Operations Programme, ended the rampant exploitation of women. However, coercive interventions have not addressed the socio-economic root causes of trafficking, have pushed the industry underground and have often failed to protect human rights.[143] NATO learned from earlier mistakes. In 2004 the alliance adopted a zero-tolerance policy banning peacekeepers from buying sex from trafficked persons and, although less explicitly, 'voluntary' prostitutes.[144] It must be noted, however, that the reported decline in human trafficking in Bosnia coincided with a downsizing of SFOR, obscuring clear-cut causality. Moreover, NATO was not in a position to punish soldiers for wrong-doing. Prosecution was a national prerogative and the way national commanders handled allegations of sexual exploitation varied depending on, among other factors, commanders' and countries' views on prostitution.

Security Operations in Other Areas

Several other SFOR activities straddled the boundaries between military and policing tasks. Collecting weapons after war reduces the risk of renewed fighting. IFOR and SFOR paid much attention to controlling heavy weapons. SALW was more difficult because so many people possessed such weapons and because they could be hidden in a backyard or kitchen cabinet. Yet besides endangering a safe and secure environment, thus being a military issue, weapons proliferation is a criminal issue as well. Anti-weapons operations thus inadvertently pushed the military into a policing role. In the most notorious case, in late 2002 SFOR raided a state-owned weapons factory in the northeastern town of Bijeljina. This facility, in conjunction with companies in Serbia, busted UN sanctions against Iraq by supplying weapon parts to the army of Saddam Hussein.[145]

Another example of conceptual blurring is the US-sponsored 'war on terror'. After 9/11, Bosnia became one of the sites where the US tried to counter Islamic militancy. The US focus was on the Mudjahiddin who had supported the Bosniaks during the war, with some staying in Bosnia after the war, often marrying Bosniak women and acquiring Bosnian citizenship. US intelligence activities now turned against potential Wahabi terrorist cells; some suspect Islamists based in Bosnia were even sent to Guantanamo.[146] US SFOR troops now focused on the Muslim population in Bosnia, with ground and aerial patrols searching daily for terrorist training camps and other perceived threats.[147]

While US Special Forces played the main role, the priorities of other actors shifted as well. The MSU began to observe and analyze Islamic groups that might pose a threat to US diplomatic facilities and to SFOR, and also provided area security during counter-terror operations.[148] The 'war on terror' boosted the need for constabulary forces not only for operational, but also for strategic reasons: It diverted US attention away from the Balkans and increased pressure to withdraw troops from Bosnia and Kosovo, thus begging the question of which forces would replace regular forces. Increasing the size and powers of constabulary forces provided part of the answer.

The EU Takes Over

In January 2003 the European Union Police Mission (EUPM) replaced the IPTF. On the military side, in late 2004 EUFOR Althea replaced SFOR. NATO retained important functions, especially with regard to defence reform and operations against suspected war criminals. Yet the main international actor in the fight against serious crime now was the EU. Bosnia presented a crucial test for the EU. The organisation was under tremendous pressure to prove its ability to manage crises and build peace in a country where it had miserably failed before (especially Bosniaks had more faith in Washington). Moreover, EUFOR Althea was the largest military operation of the nascent European Security and Defence Policy (ESDP). Further, the EU hoped that by having military and police missions under the umbrella of one organisation, coordination would be easier than before, when NATO and the UN were uncomfortably working alongside one another. Yet events would soon prove such hope was premature.

With 7,500 personnel EUFOR was a much smaller mission than SFOR. Many EUFOR soldiers, especially those from EU member states (EUFOR also included troops from non-EU member states), simply changed hats and badges after the termination of SFOR, thus ensuring a degree of continuity. EUFOR benefited from the facts that most displaced persons had returned; that the domestic military and, to some degree, intelligence services were under international control; and that the risk of violence against international personnel or civilians was much lower than before.

EUFOR was tasked with monitoring the storing and movement of weapons and ammunition as well as supporting defence reform.[149] EUFOR's capabilities were also tested by suspected war criminals. Radovan Karadžić, Radko Mladić and others indicted by the ICTY continued to elude arrest, allegedly benefiting from a network of supporters involved in organised crime.

It soon became evident that the mission faced a dilemma similar to the one SFOR had faced: Both military activism and a lack of activism in the fight against serious crime was problematic. However, there was an important difference: International actors now acknowledged that the fight against serious crime, especially organised crime, was crucial for post-conflict stabilisation and peacebuilding. In addition, the military had gathered experience in fighting crime and in collaborating with law enforcement agencies over the previous years and this experience came in handy now. These changes help to understand why the fight against organised crime became a central EUFOR task during the first term. All but in name, EUFOR became part of Bosnia's convoluted law enforcement architecture.[150]

EUFOR assumed responsibility for ensuring a safe and secure environment in December 2004. At that time much progress had been made. International actors had created unified Bosnian armed forces and integrated the country's different intelligence services.[151] This was important because of links between intelligence elements, organised crime and indicted war criminals. Bosnian police forces performed better, too.

However, law enforcement continued to suffer from ethnic division, corruption, political appointments of police officers and a lack of equipment and intelligence-gathering capabilities.[152] It also suffered from the fragmented structure of the Bosnian polity. By 2002 it could still take police from one of the two Entities (the Federation and the RS) eight hours to inform their counterparts of criminal movements across the de-facto inter-ethnic boundary line.[153] Police cooperation among the Federation's cantons was (and continues to be) deficient as well. Bosnian police forces lacked many of the instruments needed to fight serious crime, such as phone-tapping; witness protection; asset forfeiture; forensic services (including a national DNA database); electronic national data bases; and effective laws, courts and prisons.

EUPM was unable to fill the law enforcement void. It did not have an executive crime-fighting mandate and was confined to supervising domestic police reform and equipping and advising Bosnian police. In its first term the EUPM's mandate did not even cover organised crime – this important task was added only later.[154] The EUPM also had no power over prosecutors and judges.[155] Compounding the difficulty of the mission to fulfill its task to promote the rule of law was the fact that the handover from the IPTF was all but smooth. IPTF officials reportedly failed to hand over hundreds of files on organised crime, especially human trafficking, to the EUPM; the files were either archived in New York or destroyed. Information about around 1,500 potential victims of trafficking and hundreds of potential traffickers was thus lost, and the EUMP and domestic law enforcement agencies had to start from scratch.[156] As if this was not enough, the EU itself made life difficult for EUPM officials. Because Brussels did not provide implementation guidelines or assessment protocols,[157] EUPM officials had to improvise at the police stations across Bosnia where they were co-located.

Also, the coordination of counter-crime activities was a major problem. Coordination was flawed "on the ground in the region, between EU capitals, between EU institutions and EU capitals, and within the EU institutions in Brussels".[158] It quickly became apparent that intra-institutional cooperation, i.e., cooperation among the various EU actors in Bosnia, was as much a problem as inter-institutional cooperation, i.e., cooperation between the EU and other international organisations.[159] As EUFOR, during its first term, became directly involved in counter-crime operations, the EUPM accused EUFOR of stepping onto civilian turf.

EUFOR and Law Enforcement From 2004 to 2005[160]

EUFOR's first commander was British General David Leakey. He had been tasked by Javier Solana, the High Representative for EU Common Foreign and Security Policy (CFSP), to ensure that EUFOR would be 'new and distinct' and that it would 'make a difference'.[161] EUFOR's key novel military task was to support the EU's Mission Implementation Plan for Bosnia – even though none of the items clearly fell within the classical remit of military forces. The 'key supporting task' was to support the fight against organised crime. The key difference between SFOR and EUFOR was EUFOR's enhanced military support of civilian institutions. Leakey argued that supporting the MIP and supporting crime-fighting "were two sides of the same coin" and would also help EUFOR fulfil another key supporting task, the arrest of ICTY-indicted war criminals.[162]

Leakey and other EU decision-makers saw organised crime as depriving the state of badly needed tax revenues, undermining the faith of citizens in institutions and funding war criminals. Military involvement in crime-fighting was seen as necessary due to the weakness of domestic institutions. Moreover, military planners – correctly – argued that EUPM was having a difficult start-up phase, which meant that EUPM was unable to facilitate the coordination of counter-crime activities among the various agencies involved. These actors included EUPM, the head of the rule of law unit at OHR, the two Entity police forces and state-level law enforcement institutions.[163] The most important state-level law enforcement institutions were SIPA (the State Information and Protection Agency, later renamed State Investigation and Protection Agency), the BiH Border Police, the Bosnian intelligence agency (OSA-OBA BiH), the State Court, and customs, agricultural and taxation authorities. EUFOR decided that it had to fill the gap. It did so by identifying specific types of crime, and by working with those police officers it regarded as trustworthy, competent and motivated.[164] Leakey emphasised that EUFOR would have an indirect role, distinguishing

> between what was an appropriate military activity for EUFOR soldiers and what was a police task. I laid down one clear principle to guide EUFOR: soldiers would create the conditions in which the BiH law enforcement agencies not only 'could' but 'would have to' do their duty. In other words, EUFOR would help discover a crime or illegality (e.g. fuel smuggling or illegal timber cutting), but would 'freeze the scene' and hand it over to the BiH authorities to deal with the legal and law enforcement technicalities. This avoided EUFOR soldiers being involved in the specialised police work of handling evidence or appearing as witnesses in subsequent legal proceedings.[165]

Practice soon revealed, however, that clear-cut distinctions between military and policing work were hard to maintain. Moreover, Leakey's strategy was problematic because it was based on the assumption of smooth military-police cooperation. Leakey shared much with High Representative Paddy Ashdown, who was also the EU Special Representative to Bosnia. Both were British; Ashdown had a military background; and both perceived the rule of law as lagging behind. Leakey and Ashdown formally met once a week and talked on the phone every day.[166] Relations were tense, however, between Leakey and the head of the EUPM. Moreover, Leakey's assumption that Bosnian law enforcement agencies would be able to share the burden overestimated the political will and capacities of Bosnian institutions (as well as EUPM) to effectively counter crime. All this meant that EUFOR would encroach on policing more than Leakey had probably anticipated.

When EUFOR replaced SFOR, one of the most visible criminal activities in Bosnia was illegal logging. Bosnia is not rich in natural resources. Timber, although of relatively low quality, is one of the country's valuable assets. Bosnia's forests were cut down at an alarming pace which led to environmental destruction and deprived the state of tax revenues.

EUFOR argued as well that organised crime groups were involved in illegal logging and that organised crime was funding networks that supported suspected war criminals. According to the official EUFOR journal: "It is the same organized crime gangs that run drugs, prostitution and people smuggling that carry out illegal logging. These criminal organizations are the same organizations that protect and support PIFWCs and are obstructing BiH's way to a more prosperous future as a member of the European Union."[167]

Leakey, trying to expand military activities into the civilian realm, faced opposition from various sides. Some EU member states, such as Germany and the Nordic countries, were reluctant to blur the lines between military and policing work. Moreover, many EUPM officials had reservations about EUFOR's construction of a continuum of different criminal activities and war crimes, not least because EUFOR failed to back up its allegations with hard evidence.[168] Yet uncertainty was not an issue for EUFOR. The mission, under Leakey's leadership, saw operations against 'organised crime' as the area where EUFOR could quickly make a difference. Leakey justified EUFOR activism in functional terms, referring to EUFOR assets that included

> considerable surveillance capabilities (day and night, ground-based and overhead); the capacity of the headquarters at all levels to coordinate and plan operations, and to conduct 'after action reviews'; the agility of the force to deploy to and concentrate in any part of BiH at any time; the capacity to undertake protracted operations without such limitations as overtime payments for long working hours; the flexibility of the military's communications; the availability of a large number of soldiers (6,500) to cover big geographical areas; [and] the huge intelligence database and intelligence gathering capability […].169

From late 2004 onward, and until fall 2005 when operations were scaled back, EUFOR set up roadblocks across Bosnia. These were manned by soldiers, yet Bosnian police were present as well. EUFOR soldiers would search vehicles, including trucks carrying timber. In several instances EUFOR detained suspected smugglers.[170] Moreover, EUFOR surveilled and patrolled rural areas and forests. Those cutting down trees illegally, and drivers and passengers transporting timber from illegal logging operations, would be held by EUFOR soldiers and handed over to Bosnian police who would make the arrest.

In a series of operations (named, among other things, Snowstorm, Longhorn, Spring Clean 1-6, Robust Pose, House Care, Woodpecker, Lucky

Harvest and Deep River) soldiers erected checkpoints and staged patrols. The aim was to seize illicit timber, weapons, drugs and smuggled fuel, and to detain smugglers and traffickers.[171] Some results of tactical military-police cooperation were impressive. EUFOR soldiers found numerous weapons including anti-tank mines, machine guns, mortars and rocket-propelled grenades, as well as significant amounts of ammunition. They were also present when Bosnian police seized substantial amounts of drugs. In one instance in April 2005, 27 kg of heroin were seized at a border crossing near Bijeljina.[172] But more often seizures of goods were insignificant. EUFOR constabularies, the Integrated Police Unit (IPU, see below), conscientiously listed seized items that included "12.71 cubic metres of wood without proper documentation", a narcotising spray, ten grams of marihuana, a toy gun and small amounts of smuggled cigarettes.[173] EUFOR handed over numerous people to the Bosnian police, some of them suspected of major offences. Others, however, were found to carry knives, to illegally have crossed a border, or to have altered their truck tachographs.[174] EUFOR hoped to receive information on crime, among other means, by setting up a hotline for people wishing to report suspicious activities.[175]

EUFOR further engaged in crime-fighting by controlling Bosnia's rugged, over 1,500km long frontiers. The country counted 400-500 border crossing points.[176] Most of them were weakly controlled, or not controlled at all, since the Border Police lacked the personnel to organise foot patrols. Such points were often used for illegal transactions. Simply closing the points to all traffic (whether to individuals or to 4-wheel-drive vehicles) was not possible because local communities depended on trans-border commerce. By patrolling border zones and stationing soldiers at crossing points, EUFOR hoped to check smuggling and trafficking. To the extent possible, it tried to cooperate with the Border Police.[177]

The impact of EUFOR activities on organised crime is ambiguous. Counter-crime operations gave soldiers something to do – boredom was one of the main problems as security in the country improved.[178] EUFOR also provided reassurance to citizens fearing a renewed security gap following the departure of SFOR; EUFOR sent a signal of resolve that criminals would not be able to operate with impunity.[179] General Leakey and EUFOR (as a whole) never failed to underline that law enforcement was a policing task. Yet international actors felt that Bosnian institutions were too weak and lacked the motivation to enforce the law.[180] On the other hand, they benefited from EUFOR in that they received logistical, material and personnel support. EUFOR drew up diagrams depicting the presumed structure of criminal networks, particular crime problems in different parts of the country and how the various security sector actors cooperated. EUFOR would show some of these diagrams to international prosecutors.[181] Also, it is likely that EUFOR tipped off police on numerous occasions. The criminal justice sector benefited as well. A State Court prosecutor underlines the value of EUFOR's contributions in the fight against organised crime. "We received lots of intelligence bits, things like who does what where when, from EUFOR that never went into the records. It was very important to us."[182]

What was positive, too, was that EUFOR largely avoided exacerbating crime, especially human trafficking. Stricter military regulations made it difficult for soldiers to frequent houses of prostitution, and awareness campaigns became part of pre-deployment training. While there may have been incidents that violated standards promulgated for ESDP missions, there were fewer violations than before. In one case, EUFOR soldiers allegedly brought prostitutes onto a military compound in Herzegovina.[183] Overall, EUFOR had learned from the mistakes of NATO.[184]

But there were still many problems. Military involvement in crime-fighting on the operational level, besides undermining internationally-sponsored SSR norms, underlined the continuing weakness of Bosnian law enforcement agencies. The prosecutor cited above, besides stressing the value of information and intelligence gathered by EUFOR, also pointed out the limits of military crime fighting. In one case, EUFOR seized 100,000 US-Dollars from a suspect. Yet since EUFOR had not followed proper procedures (among other mistakes, it held onto the money for too long), the evidence was not admissible in court.[185] This incident illustrates the lack of soldiers' policing skills. A military intelligence official with many years of experience working with the OHR underlines that the record of NATO and EU military forces in securing the chain of evidence in Bosnia is poor. According to the official, this problem results very much from the often legally controversial, or outright illegal, ways in which the military, including constabulary forces, gather intelligence.[186]

Militarising border control was not a smooth process either, as described by one EUPM official.[187] On several occasions, EUFOR patrols along the border made mistakes in apprehending smugglers and seizing their assets, as they were not informed about proper procedures and relevant laws. The official said that EUFOR lacked knowledge on border control, also because six-month rotation periods were too short for soldiers to understand the complicated procedures. On the symbolic level, EUPM officials argued that a visitor coming to Bosnia should not see, as the first international representative, a foreign soldier. EUFOR activities also suffered from the displacement effect: EUFOR succeeded in disrupting illegal logging temporarily, at the sites where it intervened. Yet quickly, trees were cut down elsewhere and transport routes changed.

By summer 2005, it was apparent that EUFOR had achieved tactical, not strategic victories against organised crime. This lent credibility to EUPM's calls to scale down military activism. Up to then, relations between EUFOR and EUPM had been tense. This was not least due to animosities between EUFOR Commander Leakey and the (Irish) EUPM Head of Mission. While EUFOR accused EUPM of neglecting organised crime, EUPM accused EUFOR of incompetently encroaching on policing turf. This episode underlines that adversarial relationships between individuals can exacerbate institutional turf battles.

Law Enforcement from 2005 to 2008

In fall 2005 EUFOR scaled down involvement in counter-crime operations. The time was ripe for civilian primacy over policing. EUPM by now had overcome some of its initial deficiencies. Moreover, as new heads of missions took over, relations between EUFOR and EUPM improved. In September 2005 EU representatives in Bosnia formulated the co-called Seven Principles that subsequently governed relations between EUFOR and EUPM.[188] In May 2006 the EU formulated Common Operational Guidelines, based on these principles.[189] The principles and guidelines prescribed that Bosnian law enforcement institutions could draw on the operational capabilities of EUFOR, but that EUPM would coordinate such support (the EU Special Representative was to coordinate all activities on the political level). Thus, EUPM effectively placed itself between Bosnian institutions and EUFOR, at last becoming the prime international law enforcement actor. Subsequent EU documents emphasised that requests for EUFOR support would be limited to technical capabilities.[190] Yet even though the EU tried to curtail EUFOR involvement in law enforcement, the role of EUFOR de facto went beyond the mere technical.

The greater assertiveness of EUPM was bolstered by a change in mandates: now, the mission was tasked to support the fight against organised crime. Differences between EUFOR and EUPM were smoothed by an increasing number of constabulary forces joining EUPM. The Carabinieri had around 15 officers within EUPM and the French Gendarmerie was represented as well.[191] Thus, while the military was being policised, the police was being militarised. Coordination between EUPM and EUFOR was ensured, among other things, by fortnightly meetings.[192]

EUPM was not given an executive mandate; the mission was still limited to monitoring and advising Bosnian institutions. Much hope was placed into these institutions. A Targeting Board composed of domestic and international security actors would define priorities. Bosnian actors subsequently would contact EUPM, and EUPM would, if needed, ask EUFOR to provide support, especially intelligence. EUFOR, depending on the classification level, would then allow EUPM to share EUFOR intelligence with Bosnian institutions.[193]

Due to EU and US support, the personnel, material and technological capacities of SIPA and the Border Police improved. SIPA could count on relatively effective SWAT teams used for high-risk operations. SIPA even conducted operations against suspected war criminals, although 'internationals' still dominated intelligence gathering and operational planning (see below). However, problems lingered on, making it difficult for the military to share intelligence. Many Bosnian police officers were selected on the basis of their political affiliation, instead of merit. Effective and legitimate police work was also undermined by the fact that police at times would not target powerful criminals due to fear, corruption, or war-time bonds between police and criminals.[194] Understaffing was a problem as well.[195] According to a SIPA official interviewed in summer 2008, the institution was operating on 60 percent of the planned staff level. In addition, SIPA depended on international intelligence support (e.g., in the fields of computer and communication forensics) and international involvement in investigations.[196] Material support was needed, too. Here, CIVPOL officers complained about improper behaviour by their local counterparts. One EUPM official claimed that jet stream speedboats donated to the Border Police in 2003 were not properly maintained and thus became dysfunctional, and that there was no stocktaking, which led to the disappearance of equipment.

The use of IT was fraught with problems, too. IT infrastructure delivered to improve the exchange of information among the various elements of the Border Police was not used. Thus, by summer 2008 there still was no joint criminal justice database. The US, as part of its International Criminal Investigative Training Assistance Program (ICITAP), had delivered servers, but they were not set up. Instead, the Bosnian Border Police used several parallel, inefficient systems, such as Microsoft Excel tables. An EUPM officer explains the lack of information sharing and a reluctance of Bosnian officials to feed data into the system, as well as corruption and a lack of primary data.[197] Not just the Border Police used inefficient methods. In the Federation, Cantonal Ministries of Security were running their own separate databases.[198]

The lack of centralised information systems meant that police, especially when working with their counterparts from the other Entity, relied on informal cooperation, often using their personal mobile phones to inform their colleagues about the whereabouts of suspects.[199] Criminals did not fail to exploit such weakness. Bank robbers, for instance, allegedly crossed weakly policed parts of the inter-ethnic boundary line after committing their crimes.[200]

One of the biggest worries has been the Bosnian criminal justice system. This system, which was a legacy both of Communism and the war, has haunted crime-fighters ever since the end of the war; it did not give those with power and influence much to fear from prosecutors and judges.[201] By mid-2000 many problems had still not been rectified. Prosecutors still did not know, for example, how to take DNA samples at crime scenes (according to Bosnian law this is the responsibility of prosecutors). Moreover, relations between the police and prosecutors, who both needed to collect evidence, were conflictual due to unclear divisions of labour.[202] The role of judges was questionable, too. According to one international prosecutor, there has been a reversal rate of over 90 percent for organised crime cases following a first ruling, due to a mix of corruption, incompetence and fear.[203]

While many of these problems were home-made, international actors have shared the responsibility to rectify them. Internationally-sponsored training programmes have focused on the police and less so on the judiciary. Both domestic and international prosecutors have faced an overwhelming workload, yet have been given scant resources. Prosecuting large cases (which could involve up to 10,000 pieces of evidence and 100 witnesses) has thus been challenging.[204] In 2007, merely four international prosecutors, six national prosecutors, and seven clerks were working on 500-600 cases.[205] Moreover, training has not been provided over long periods of time, undermining the effective use of sophisticated equipment as well as techniques such as fingerprint analysis. With regard to the legal framework, international actors have exported a confusing mix of common and civil law practices to Bosnia.[206] Also, EUPM has focused too much on strategy, and too little on implementation.[207] Witness protection has been a problem, too. According to one prosecutor, the Court was unable to find witnesses who were not terrified to testify.[208]

Many policing problems were legacy issues of the war and the Dayton agreement. The latter has created "the world's most decentralised state"[209] and has been "interpreted both as a blueprint for partition and for the consolidation of a unitary state"[210]. In 2007, a heated debate erupted over international pressure on Bosnia to reform its police. The OHR, EUPM and other institutions pushed for an integration of the country's numerous police forces but met fierce resistance from the RS. RS Prime Minister Milorad Dodik, who had morphed from a politician supported by the West to a perceived spoiler of stabilisation efforts, argued that efforts to centralise policing violated the spirit and letter of Dayton. Especially RS politicians did not want strong state-level institutions and this undermined the effectiveness of SIPA and the Border Police. The lack of consensus over the future of Bosnia has been an obstacle to ordinary police work, and even more so to intelligence-led operations. Although by mid-2008 databases were installed, RS officials in particular were often unwilling to share intelligence.[211]

Those opposed to a more centralised model of policing argued that police cooperation on an operational level was better than reformers would have it.[212] This is true. But there was a risk that the police, if not integrated and ethnically mixed, would identify more with members of 'their' ethnic group. To some extent, the adage that a cop is a cop holds true in Bosnia. But there is still a risk of biased policing. One journalist underlines the continuing politicisation even of SIPA, touted as the most visible success of international police reform: If SIPA does a raid in Banja Luka, Serbian SIPA officers do not want to participate. If there is a raid in Mostar, the Croats do not want to participate.[213] The risk of police disunity is particularly high at times of political crisis.

Proponents of reform, in response to the objection that many countries do not have unified, centralised police forces, said that Bosnia was too small and too poor to afford the post-Dayton policing system.[214] With 15 different criminal law enforcement agencies existing in 2009, the system was complex indeed. In addition to SIPA and the Border Police, the two Entities each had their own police force, Brčko had its own force, and so did each of the 10 cantons in the Federation. With over 17,000 police officers for a population of 4,2 million people, Bosnia had one of the highest ratios of per capita police officers in the world. There were also 15 Interior Ministries, as well as 15 police laws and 11 weapons laws.[215]

EUFOR and Law Enforcement from 2005 to 2008

The problems described above meant that EUFOR would continue to play an important role in law enforcement. International interlocutors emphasised that direct military intervention in policing was a thing of the past; they stressed that after EUFOR's first term, law enforcement was in the hands of the police, especially the Bosnian police. However, a close-up look at the operational level reveals that EUFOR involvement in law enforcement was more than residual, contrary to the mantra of security practitioners.

One of the prime areas of activity was the search for suspected war criminals who had been indicted by the ICTY. Over the years, the list of fugitives became shorter and shorter, containing only two names by the summer of 2009 (Ratko Mladić and Goran Hadžić).[216] NATO was the institution responsible for PIFWC operations, but de facto it shared this responsibility with the EU. On the operational level, regular EUFOR troops, such as those from the UK, supported PIFWC operations.[217]

EUFOR relied on Military Police investigators for advising Multinational Task Force (MTF) Commanders and on G-2 (military intelligence) for handling policing matters and liaising with Bosnian law enforcement agencies.[218] Yet the most important actors were EUFOR's IPU.[219] Most of the IPU officers, as had been the case with NATO's MSU, were Carabinieri; Italy had been the framework nation for the MSU and now was the lead nation supporting the IPU. The IPU also included constabulary forces from the Netherlands, Turkey and other countries. IPU could substitute for domestic security forces and deploy formed, homogenous units, thus avoiding the problems with heterogeneity that had plagued the IPTF and other missions. These units engaged in police tasks, especially CRC and surveillance operations. The IPU also had at its disposal specialised elements assembled on a case-by-case basis, such as forensics experts, anti-terror specialists and investigators with special skills.[220]

The increasing use of constabulary forces in Bosnia reflected a learning process on the part of NATO and the EU, as well as on the part of entrepreneurial commanders such as General Leakey. On the operational level, the presence of the right individuals at the right time and place mattered a lot as well. A British intelligence official, seeing that EUPM in the beginning did too little, managed to bring the main crime-fighting institutions together. The State Prosecutor would say what he needed and EUFOR, especially the IPU, would then discuss the operational details. The IPU, according to the official, was enthusiastic from the beginning.[221]

One of the main advantages of the IPU was that it was the only part of EUFOR operating across Bosnia. The IPU staged numerous operations.[222] One of their tasks was to support NATO in defence reform. Moreover, as shown below, CRC and the fight against organised crime were central preoccupations of the IPU. Yet the activity that put the IPU into the limelight was its attempts to arrest PIWCS. Operationally, EUFOR's IPU, which had executive powers, became the dominant actor in this area. Due to fears of corruption and collusion, Bosnian security forces were not allowed to participate in the planning of major operations; they would be called in at a late stage, yet often without being informed about operational details.

Relations between the ICTY and EUFOR were tense; EUFOR contingents often failed to share information and intelligence with the ICTY, sending information to their respective national capitals instead.[223] The IPU was an exception, however. They staged numerous raids on the homes of suspected war criminals and their supporters. The IPU was therefore a major source of support for ICTY prosecutors in The Hague. According to a Bosnian journalist specialising on war crimes, the Carabinieri had become the ICTY's closest partners in the country.[224] In May 2007, for instance, the IPU helped the Bosnian police to arrest Zdravko Tolimir, who was then flown to The Hague.[225] In another case, in January 2006 international forces, most probably IPU officers, shot dead the wife and wounded the son of Dragomir Abazović, a Bosnian Serb wanted for war crimes committed against Muslims in the Rogatica area. As he tried to flee, his wife and son reportedly opened fire on the troops.[226] Abazović was not on the list of suspects wanted by the ICTY, but had been indicted by a court in Sarajevo (and, after his arrest, was later released from custody on a legal technicality). The incident showed that IPU operations could turn violent and draw public criticism.[227] It also showed that the IPU targeted not only PIFWCs wanted by prosecutors in The Hague, but pursued lower-level war crimes suspects as well. The IPU at times also arrested individuals suspected of corruption and trafficking, with Bosnian security forces limited to an assisting role.[228]

EUFOR's crucial role in law enforcement becomes clear when looking at intelligence operations. Especially the Carabinieri had both the know-how and the technical assets to stage surveillance operations. According to a EUPM official, tapping telephones would not be possible without the IPU.[229] EUFOR officials never failed to reiterate the mantra that the mission was merely supporting domestic law enforcement institutions through EUMP. Indeed, the IPU were not allowed to run investigations independently. Still, IPU involvement was direct. For instance, IPU officers listened in on phone conversations.[230] Many operations resulted from autonomous intelligence gathering by the IPU, such as raids on possible sites of arms trafficking in the outskirts of Sarajevo in February 2005.[231] EUPM officials felt that the IPU were keen to do as much law enforcement as possible,[232] an impression corroborated by the long list of IPU operations.

The IPU have also built domestic capacity. The institution benefiting most from the IPU was SIPA. The IPU supported SIPA logistically and taught SIPA surveillance techniques, such as how to plant listening devises. In 2006 and 2007, SIPA asked for IPU help in operations against organised crime, each of which lasted for three months.[233] In addition to helping SIPA with surveillance, the IPU strengthened SWAT teams of SIPA. These strengthened teams ran under the name of Special Support Units (SSUs) and were set up in mid-2005. There were Alpha, Beta and Gamma teams (the Alpha team was used for high-risk operations). These elite forces (whose salary exceeded the salary of regular SIPA officers by 50 percent) were to be used against hostage takers, kidnappers, terrorists, suspected war criminals and other dangerous individuals. In autumn 2007, for instance, the IPU trained SIPA SWAT teams on how to free hostages.[234] The IPU provided the SSU with intelligence as well.

According to an EUPM officer, the SSUs were well-manned, trained and equipped, representing an example of successful international support.[235] The SSU produced impressive output. Only in the first half of 2008, SIPA's SWAT teams arrested 80 persons suspected of having committed war crimes and organised crime activities.[236] Close relations between the 'paramilitary' IPU and 'paramilitary' Bosnian police forces underline the paramilitarisation of security practices in Bosnia. Both on the international and domestic side, the structure and outlook of security actors increasingly defied clear-cut categorisation between internal and external security, and policing and military work.[237]

A crucial activity of constabulary forces is CRC. CRC is now a central military preoccupation in peace operations (see also the Kosovo case study in this book). In Bosnia, the IPU stood ready to engage in this task, underlining that EUFOR had learned from the failure of IFOR and SFOR to deal with angry crowds. In addition, the IPU provided CRC training to Bosnian police forces.

The IPU were thus a crucial EUFOR asset. Yet EUFOR as a whole shifted to intelligence-led operations in the fight against serious crime, using sophisticated surveillance methods and equipment. For instance, reports about cannabis cultivation in Herzegovina led EUFOR to take pictures from the air.[238]

The fight against serious crime in Bosnia has defied clear-cut categorisation as the lines between military and policing work, intelligence and information and coercive and humanitarian operations have been blurred. This becomes obvious when looking at Liaison and Observation Teams (LOT) houses. The LOT house concept, developed by SFOR in 2003,[239] was expanded by EUFOR. Due to the much improved security situation, EUFOR deployed soldiers to cities, towns and villages where they would live in rented houses.[240] Keeping a low profile, e.g., by being lightly armed, LOT house personnel's task was to reassure the population that EUFOR (whose strength, in February 2007, was reduced to 2,500) had not left the country to its own devices.

Moreover, LOT houses worked on so-called quick-impact projects. Officially, LOT personnel did not conduct CIMIC operations. But they would buy bed sheets for university dormitories, give tinned food to boy scouts, and equip schools with fire extinguishers.[241] Some tasks could not be more remote from what a soldier is trained for. In one LOT house, soldiers spent much time helping people fill out pension claim forms. Bosnians who had worked in Western Europe and who were confused by the complicated forms or lacked language skills would come to the LOT house. In some cases, EUFOR soldiers would liaise with insurance companies in their home country to clarify matters.

Yet the main task of LOT house personnel was to support EUFOR Headquarters by collecting information that would help detect any potential security problem at an early stage. LOT house soldiers became the "eye and ear of the EUFOR Commander"[242] and the "friendly face of EUFOR"[243] To interact closely with citizens, they needed soft skills such as knowledge about local politics, history, culture and language.[244] The LOT houses thus epitomised the light military footprint strategy of EUFOR. LOT house personnel met mayors, police chiefs, priests, imams, directors of schools, and, during their frequent patrols (or, to use the term preferred by LOT house personnel, "walks"), ordinary citizens. To find out about local politics, security risks and security perceptions,[245] soldiers had to become diplomats, administrators and humanitarian workers. One LOT house officer said: "We are not really doing military work here. Instead, we are doing market research on mayors and police chiefs. Actually, citizens here would need civilians knowledgeable, for instance, about EU regulations regarding the quality of products. But such experts probably would not want to live in the simple house that we have here."[246] The commander of another LOT house says that in his home country he would train in tank warfare, but that in Bosnia he essentially had a civilian job.[247]

Most soldiers managed to cope not so much because of their pre-deployment training, which often was rudimentary. More importantly, soldiers used their common sense to adapt to an essentially non-military role and also relied heavily on interpreters who simultaneously served as guides and local area specialists.[248] EUFOR headquarters, as well as national contingent commanders, greatly benefited from the reports sent by LOT house personnel. EUFOR emphasised that the LOT houses did not gather intelligence and were not involved in the fight against serious crime. But indirectly, they were involved. Although LOT houses did not resort to covert means, the difference between information and intelligence gathering was academic on the ground. For example, LOT house personnel in Pale, in early 2006, gathered information on illegal logging.[249]

Many LOT house soldiers had reservations about their role. Besides the hardship of being confined to a small space in a remote area for six months, the seven soldiers manning a LOT house in an Eastern Bosnian town felt frustrated that they were involved in humanitarian tasks while being unable to tackle security problems. Fighting serious crime, especially organised crime, was not within the remit of LOT house personnel. Their knowledge about dangerous groups and individuals led to feelings of powerlessness. According to one LOT house officer, local strongmen and criminals were heavily armed. To effectively challenge those committing acts of violence and crime, the officer would need an entire platoon instead of just the few lightly armed soldiers currently under his command. The officer said that the vulnerability of the LOT houses created a hostage-like situation.[250]

The IPU, which did have the capabilities and the mandate to act against serious crime, were resented by LOT house personnel. The IPU were the only element of EUFOR that had a mandate to operate theatre-wide across Bosnia. They operated by raiding houses of suspected war criminals or to collect weapons. The secrecy level of these operations was such that LOT house personnel were not informed beforehand. The LOT house officer referred to in the paragraph above said that heavily armed Carabinieri would stage an unexpected and sudden operation in their Area of Responsibility, and then leave shortly afterwards. His LOT team would then have to explain the rationale for the operation to the local population. He would only learn about the operation upon the arrival of the IPU or the next day. Therefore, he wished that the IPU would stay away from his area.[251] As shown in the next chapter, troops also resented similar constabulary activities in Kosovo.

A perennial problem of peace operations is the lack of information and intelligence sharing among the various stakeholders. Officially, the EUFOR Commander was to be informed about activities that impinged on security in Bosnia. Yet in many cases, information and intelligence first went to the capitals of troop-contributing nations (especially those with the means to collect intelligence), and often never came back. One Bosnian journalist said that he regularly met with EUFOR contingents from two countries to exchange what essentially was a mix of information and intelligence. It often happened that EUFOR personnel from other countries, who had obviously not been informed by the two contingents, would ask him the same questions.[252]

One of the prime sites of EUFOR activities was at the border. EUFOR supported border policing in various ways. Most directly, it dispatched patrols. Due to personnel and material shortages affecting the Border Police, most of Bosnia's border-crossing points were still weakly policed. Thus, EUFOR border controls continued in 2006.[253] Pressure to keep a low profile meant that EUFOR support became less visible after its first term. EUFOR then focused on the green border by reinforcing, or substituting for, Border Police patrols. EUFOR also used its superior technological assets for taking aerial imagery of border zones. Such imagery provided valuable information and intelligence both to EUPM and Bosnian police. Often, the IPU provided tip-offs about illegal activities.[254] EUFOR monitored various illegal activities, including the smuggling of cattle and cigarettes.[255]

A prime mechanism through which EUFOR straddled the boundary between civilian and military work was through the training and equipping of Bosnian law enforcement agencies. EUFOR supported the Bosnian Border Police by providing hardware such as night-vision goggles, maps, and data such as aerial imagery. EUFOR also taught the Border Police how to use GPS technology and how to read grids on military maps. Border policing reveals EUFOR's difficulty to keep a low profile and at the same time effectively support border control, under the condition of diminishing personnel and material resources.

By summer 2008, international and Bosnian officials, when asked about the role of EUFOR in border policing, automatically answered that this was a job for the Border Police. However, they acknowledged that due to understaffing and logistical shortcomings, the Border Police depended on military support. A senior EUPM planner was ready to ask for EUFOR helicopter support. The official emphasised that the actual surveillance and also apprehension of suspects would be done by Bosnians (and would require a good knowledge of areas mined during the war), as it would violate European standards if military forces assumed policing functions.[256] The Bosnian Border Police welcomed the prospect of EUFOR once again assuming a greater role in border control.[257]

EUFOR activities in the murky military-police grey zone reveal that EUFOR was not only a military mission. Supporting the fight against serious crime had become a prime EUFOR activity. By 2008, EUFOR had shrunk to 2,500 personnel, many in support functions. The threat of war had receded, although the political crisis in 2007 sparked by the controversy over police reform led the EUFOR Commander to state that EUFOR would intervene in case of another war (a statement that exacerbated, instead of calmed, perceived insecurity).[258] The main EUFOR element to counter any serious security threat was a multinational manoeuvre battalion. More importantly, in case of trouble EUFOR would deploy over-the-horizon forces. Yet the most crucial elements of EUFOR were now the LOT houses and the IPU, with the latter indicating the shift from war fighting to crime fighting in peace operations.[259]

The Tricky Question of Effectiveness[260]

What are the effects of military support of the fight against serious crime? Any attempt to answer this question is challenging for several reasons. First, there is a scarcity of data on serious crime, especially organised crime. Both criminals and security forces using intelligence try to stay out of the limelight. The poor capacities of the Bosnian government and the fragmentation of the 'international community' further impede the collection of data. More generally, there is no agreement as to the exact nature of serious crime, especially organised crime, and how to measure it.[261]

Second, attempts to establish causal links between military support against serious crime, on the one hand, and changes in the criminal landscape, on the other, are risky. The military is not the only, nor the main, actor fighting serious crime in Bosnia. Police are more important. Separating the causal effects of military activities from those of police activities is impossible. Also, there are many other actors, international and domestic, who have implemented a host of programmes, coercive and non-coercive, that have also had an impact on crime. The lack of success is equally difficult to explain. For instance, if NATO and EU soldiers had been better at collecting and sharing intelligence with international and domestic prosecutors in Bosnia, prosecution outcomes may have been more impressive than they are. However, the overall effect may still have been minimal, given the desolate state of the Bosnian criminal justice system. Moreover, the Bosnian parliament has often failed to enact the laws that are needed to fight serious crime.[262] The military cannot alleviate these shortcomings.

Attempts to assess effectiveness warrant a third note of caution. Contingent factors have changed the face of serious crime in Bosnia. One such factor is demography. In contrast to the demographics in the early 1990s, by 2009 the Bosnian populace was old on average.[263] This information helps to account for low rates in conventional crime such as murder and robbery in Bosnia (these crimes are usually committed by young men living in cities). These rates, in turn, are important indicators of the non-pervasive nature of violent organised crime.[264] Other factors matter as well. Waging the same kind of warfare against civilians as before would no longer be possible, due to a lack of heavy weapons and ammunition. Moreover, compared to the previous ethnic patchwork, the different parts of Bosnia are more homogenous now, as a consequence of 'ethnic cleansing' and people selling their houses. There are thus fewer incentives to engage in inter-ethnic crime.

Some contingent factors relate to military activities that – inadvertently – have changed the scope of serious crime in Bosnia. As shown below, there are indications that human trafficking in Bosnia has declined over recent years. This decline has many causes. One of them is that NATO, the EU and troop-contributing nations have promulgated zero-tolerance policies against peacekeepers' involvement in human trafficking. However, the withdrawal of troops (from IFOR's 60,000 to EUFOR's 2,500) has been a more important factor: As international clients disappeared, business opportunities for human traffickers shrunk.

Another related issue is how to operationalise effectiveness. Several indicators are on offer. The most convenient ones for security sector actors are output and outcome indicators. Output indicators would be, for example, the number of times the military has trained Bosnian police forces, the amount of material donated, or the number of joint military-police patrols. Outcome indicators would focus on the usage of knowledge and equipment provided by the military to the police. At peak times, such as during EUFOR's first term, output and outcome were impressive.

However, the crux is impact. Impact indicators would include the number of serious criminals convicted as a consequence of military activities, the number of returnees saved by the military from rioting mobs and the number of war criminals arrested. Even more tricky to assess are broader impact indicators, such as a reduction in organised crime as a consequence of direct military involvement in law enforcement, or enhanced policing capacities as a consequence of military support. Such indicators, due to the methodological problems mentioned above (such as the lack of data and causal complexity), are difficult to observe.

Still: Available data shows that serious crime in Bosnia has changed over years. Moreover, one can plausibly argue that while the military has made a positive contribution to crime-fighting, the impact of military crime-fighting should not be overestimated. There has been a decline in the more violent forms of serious crime. While IFOR and the first rotations of SFOR turned a blind eye to war criminals, SFOR stepped up operations and EUFOR accelerated this trend.

CRC became a less pressing issue over time. There have been some violent demonstrations, for example in Banja Luka following the proclamation of an independent Kosovo in February 2008. There have also been isolated attacks against minorities and refugees. But compared to the years after Dayton, inter-ethic crime has become less of a problem – also because, as mentioned above, many of those finding themselves as minorities have sold their properties, or because mainly old people inhabited areas from which they had been expelled during the war. IFOR and SFOR had many problems with CRC. In the first decade of the new millennium, CRC was given higher priority. Assessing EUFOR's performance in this area is difficult since the mission had not faced a serious test by early 2009. But it is important to note that EUFOR provided much CRC training to Bosnian law enforcement agencies.

The most dynamic changes pertain to organised crime. As shown above, Bosnia in the aftermath of Dayton was a haven of smuggling and trafficking. Organised crime activities often went hand in hand with violence committed against criminal competitors, members of security forces that could not be bribed or intimidated and victims such as women trafficked into sexual exploitation. In the new millennium, the face of organised crime changed. Human smuggling declined concomitantly with more stringent migration controls. By 2008, Bosnia continued to serve as a transit country, especially for people from China, India and Turkey smuggled to Western Europe,[265] as well as for ethnic Albanians going west.[266] But the numbers of people smuggled were probably in the hundreds, no longer in the thousands as in the 1990s.

A similar trend can be observed with regard to human trafficking. In the 1990s, possibly thousands of women, mostly from Eastern Europe, worked in Bosnian brothels. A combination of the withdrawal of 'internationals', zero tolerance policies, more stringent border controls and raids on brothels forced some traffickers out of business and others to change their modus operandi. The decline of trafficking is indicated by a decreasing number of identified victims.[267] Law enforcement pressure has, to some extent, pushed the industry underground as well. To reduce risk traffickers use private apartments instead of brothels, mobile phones instead of landlines and domestic victims instead of women from abroad. They also pay victims to reduce their incentives to contact the police.[268]

Drugs are one of the most lucrative sources of revenue for organised crime groups. Over recent years, only relatively small amounts of drugs were confiscated in Bosnia.[269] This may indicate that police work is not sufficiently intelligence-led and that traffickers outsmart security forces. Yet it may also indicate that the famous Balkan drug smuggling routes partly bypass Bosnia, or that Bosnia is not an important storage site.[270] Also, due to factors such as the lifting of sanctions, more effective control of intermediate merchants, a harmonisation of taxes, and better border controls, the smuggling and trafficking of cigarettes, fuel, textiles, and other goods have decreased over recent years.

It must also be noted that many of the factors allegedly facilitating organised crime are inconclusive. For example, it is often said that Bosnia's rugged terrain makes smuggling and trafficking easy. However, mountains, rivers and winding roads are not only an asset, but can also be an impediment. When criminals have to transport people or goods on small, winding roads, checkpoints on those roads pose a greater risk than checkpoints along major highways, where only a small percentage of cars can be searched. Moreover, the large number of international and domestic security forces operating in Bosnia (Bosnia has one of the world's highest per capita numbers of police officers) poses risks to criminals. Why should criminal networks traffic through Bosnia if they can use the highway linking Sofia, Belgrade and Western Europe instead, or if they can go through Kosovo and Southern Serbia to the coast of Montenegro?

All this does not mean that there is no organised crime in Bosnia. But, according to an EU official in Bosnia, there is "small-town organised crime".[271] A UN report published in spring 2008 largely confirms this view.[272] Despite the public perception of Bosnia being a haven of organised crime, the situation in the country is very different from the one in Kosovo (see next chapter) or many Western European countries. Bosnia has seen a decline in the more violent forms of organised crime, especially the trafficking of people, drugs and weapons. By early 2009, these crimes were still being committed, yet on a much reduced scale. Relatively new criminal activities have entered the fore, such as the trafficking of stolen vehicles.[273] And loggers continue to illegally clear forests. Yet these activities, despite the economic and ecological damage they cause, have not posed major threats to the stability of Bosnia.

More worrying is the shift to business crimes such as tax evasion, privatisation fraud and money laundering. Those formerly engaged in more violent crimes now try to appear as legitimate entrepreneurs. Ivan Stanchev writes about crime in the Balkans: "If there are positive developments, they result not from intentional policies to contain crime but rather from processes of converging black economic activities into shadow and 'white' entrepreneurship."[274] According to an international prosecutor, there is now a corporate approach to crime.[275] International actors have mainly been concerned about the smuggling and trafficking of people and goods – despite the pernicious economic and social effects of white-collar crime.[276]

What then has been the record of militarised crime-fighting in post-Dayton Bosnia? While SFOR largely neglected organised crime, EUFOR became deeply involved in crime-fighting in its first term. Success was not strategic. There has been much military output (counted in the number of checkpoints, patrols, and surveillance operations), outcome (counted, for instance, in military-supported and induced police operations) and tactical impact (such as the displacement of trafficking routes and illegal logging sites the arrest of smugglers and traffickers). Yet strategic impact – a reduction in crime – is harder to discern. Whenever EUFOR stopped an illegal activity in one place, the hydra would pop up somewhere else – the well known displacement effect that can haunt law enforcement anywhere.[277] According to a (restricted) 2006 EU report, counter-logging operations, "usually EUFOR-initiated, have yielded little criminal intelligence and no significant results." To reduce illegal logging, it is more promising to license saw mills, certify timber, increase the number of inspectors and tax officials, and reduce the demand for cheap timber from EU member states, rather than to stage military-style interruption operations.[278] There are sound arguments against military involvement in counter-drug operations as well. Taking aerial images, as EUFOR did, is a relatively benign activity, but it puts the military on a slippery slope. There have been few indications of large-scale cannabis cultivation anywhere in Bosnia.[279] In any case, the US 'war on drugs', at home and abroad, provides ample lessons for the ineffectiveness and collateral damage of coercive drug policies.[280]

Some counter-crime operations have smacked of military activism, instead of a functional – and legitimate – response to obvious security problems. According to one British military officer, EUFOR had to do something after taking over from SFOR. It did not matter much what it did, but EUFOR had to make a difference. The mission thus became involved in law enforcement.[281] An EU official says that EUFOR should not have become involved in counter-logging and other operations. But EUFOR had the personnel and material capacity; also, military tasks such as controlling cease-fires had receded to the background.[282] For EUFOR, counter-crime initiatives carried advantages that were largely secondary to the primary objective of reducing the burden of crime on society. One EUFOR commander said that "more important than the tactical results was the learning process how to develop the cooperation with the Local

Authorities."[283] General Leakey emphasised that by enabling Bosnian authorities to "touch the untouchables", EUFOR helped the public, police and the media to defend themselves against criminals.[284]

Crime-fighting is too important to serve as testing ground for CIMIC. A more systematic targeting of individuals, groups and criminal markets, as well as the use of less coercive methods (whether in the fields of demand reduction, harm reduction, or financial regulation) is more likely to reduce smuggling and trafficking than 'doing something'. Since non-coercive methods are beyond the remit of the military, and since even in the coercive realm military contributions to law enforcement have lacked effectiveness, the positive impact of NATO and EU counter-crime operations should not be overestimated. Taking action against weapons smuggling, for instance, is more obviously a military duty than is the case with illegal logging or drug trafficking. Indeed, both NATO and EU forces have tried to reduce the supply of weapons in and to Bosnia. By late 2008, there were few indications of Bosnia being an important weapons smuggling hub, in contrast to the 1990s. Yet this possible decline not only reflects more stringent (military) control mechanisms, but also the fact that many weapons have been sold or destroyed and markets, especially the one for cheap weapons such as the AK 47, are saturated. The ability of military forces to reduce white-collar crime – the form of crime that has complemented and partially substituted more traditional types of organised crime in the Balkans – is even more limited.

These caveats notwithstanding, the effects of military contributions should not be underestimated either. As shown above, prosecutors working on organised crime cases have received valuable hints from EUFOR. Assessing the extent to which information, intelligence and evidence gathered by EUFOR have led to the successful prosecution of offenders is difficult. Even prosecutors and judges often do not know how evidence was collected and who collected it; external observers are even harder pressed to get the full picture. Despite this caveat, the military did support prosecutors. The fact that conviction rates for organised crime in Bosnia are unsatisfactory is more a reflection of police and criminal justice failures than the inability of the military to do police work.

Moreover, effectiveness is also about symbols. The failure of IFOR and SFOR to take on spoilers has undermined the trust of many Bosnian citizens in international forces.[285] Images of soldiers standing by while human rights were violated, property was destroyed and laws were broken have had a negative effect on the credibility of the international state- and nation-building project in Bosnia as a whole. Military activism, on the other hand, even though not necessarily effective in strategic terms, has sent a signal to citizens that crimes would not be committed with impunity.

Conclusion

Has military involvement in law enforcement in post-Dayton Bosnia come close to the ideal-type strategy as outlined in the conclusion? The empirical analysis reveals a mixed picture (see also the summary of the main findings in the conclusion). The question is therefore whether the lessons from Bosnia have been transferred to other post-war countries. The prime test case is Kosovo. As in Bosnia, serious crime has posed a major challenge to international stabilisation and peacebuilding attempts in Kosovo. The next chapter shows how, in light of the Bosnian experience, NATO has coped in this other international protectorate.

Notes

1 Bose 2002: 33; Zaalberg 2006: 490, endnote 2.

2 Dziedzic and Bair 1996.

3 Kaldor 2005: Chapter 3;. See also Münkler 2005 : Chapter 4.

4 Kaldor 2005: 53.

5 Andreas 2008.

6 Rumiz 2000: Chapter 6; Bose 2002: 36-37.

7 Andreas 2004: 44. See also Donais 2003: 365.

8 Bose 2002: 7.

9 See Zaalberg 2006: 253.

10 Malcolm 2002: 270.

11 On the structural problems in the Dayton agreement, see Sharp 1997/1998: 113-123.

12 Quoted in: Center for Democracy in Vienna 1998: 145.

13 Perdan 2006: 188.

14 Sharp 1997/1998: 125-126.

15 Zaalberg 2006: 245. One of the most prominent persons acknowledging the problematic segregation of military and civilian aspects of Dayton was Richard Holbrooke (Holbrooke 1998).

16 On the following, see Dziedzic and Bair 1998; Perito 2004: 120; Bose 2002: 33; Zaalberg 2006: 494, endnotes 52 and 53; Sele 1999; Sharp 1997/1998: 119.

17 Quoted in: Perito 2004: 121. See also pp. 127-128, and: SACEUR (US General) George A. Joulwan: Department of Defense Press Briefing: US Department of Defense, Operation Joint Endeavor Fact Sheet No. 004-B (7 December 1995); IFOR nije poduzeo ništa (IFOR did not do anything), in: Dnevni Avaz, 30 August 1996.

18 Quoted in: Zaalberg 2006: 256.

19 Zaalberg 2006: 258. It must be noted that non-US forces, such as British and Dutch soldiers, were tougher on the Bosnian police than was the case with US forces (Zaalberg 2006: 260-262).

20 For one example, see Almasa Hadžić: Srpski specijalci upali u Mahalu (Serbian special police entered Mahala), in: Dnevni Avaz, 30 August 1996.

21 Quoted in: Zaalberg 2006: 265.

22 Quoted in: Murphy 2004: 359.

23 Zaalberg 2006: 262.

24 See Palmer and Posa 1999; Sharp 1997/1998: 121; Ritscher 2005: 119.

25 Sharp 1997/1998: 120 and 122.

26 See Murphy (2004) for an insider account of how the notion of neutrality hampered effective international responses to the Bosnian war during wartime.

27 This view was not unrealistic: As late as 1998, SFOR convoys could come under fire. Interview with former SFOR official, Sarajevo, November 2007.

28 Zaalberg 2006: 254; Perito 2004: 115.

29 Holbrooke 1998: 252.

30 On the travails of the IPTF, see Dziedzic and Bair 1998; Sharp 1997/1998: 118; Perito 2008: 57-59; Stark 2004: 12-13.

31 Dziedzic and Bair 1998.

32 Colum Lynch, UN Police in Bosnia: Who's Watching?, in: Washington Post, 30 May 2001. As late as 2007/2008, Bosnian officials enjoyed telling jokes about the IPTF.

33 See Clark 2001: 55-56. On Washington's curtailing the role of the UN in post-Dayton Bosnia, see Daalder 2000: 153-154.

34 Quoted in: Zaalberg 2006: 249. See also Holbrooke 1998: 324; Šabić 2005: Part III. The fact that Bildt and Smith did not get on set a bad precedent for civil-military relations at an early stage.

35 See Rose 1998.

36 See Fukuyama 2006: 237 (also for further references). This view implies that holding elections later would have reduced the power of ethnic politics. However, as late as 2009, viable alternatives to ethnic politics seem ephemeral. The impact of the timing of the elections on whom the victors would be may therefore be less important than critics of the decision to hold elections in 1996 assume. A more important disadvantage of holding early elections arguably was that the elections put war-time leaders in charge of the transition period (many of them were later removed through the use of the Bonn powers), with negative consequences for the implementation of the Dayton agreement. I thank an anonymous reviewer for commenting on this point.

37 Interview with former IFOR/SFOR officer, Sarajevo, October 2007.

38 U.S. Army Peacekeeping and Stability Operations Institute 2000: 17.

39 See Zaalberg 2006: 263-265.

40 Quoted in: Perito 2004: 129.

41 Quoted in: Zaalberg 2006: 264.

42 Caplan 2004: 56-57; Chandler 2005: 340-345.

43 U.S. Army Peacekeeping and Stability Operations Institute 2000: 4.

44 See Caddick-Adams 1998; Sharp 1997/1998: 128; Zaalberg 2006: 275-284. It must be noted that CIMIC projects were problematic for various reasons, including the risk to involve war criminals (Siegel 2001: 108).

45 U.S. Army Peacekeeping and Stability Operations Institute 2000: 10, footnote 17.

46 Stark 2004: 14; Crane 2005.

47 Perito 2004: 158.

48 Interview with Italian Embassy official, Sarajevo, November 2007.

49 See Perito 2004: 131-140.

50 Zaalberg 2006: 265.

51 Zaalberg 2006: 266.

52 Murphy 2004: 367. According to critics (and as alleged by Karadžić during his trial in The Hague following his arrest in 2008), Western powers had promised Bosnian wartime leaders that they would not be prosecuted if they did not obstruct the peace (see also the movie "The Hunting Party" starring Richard Gere, in which international troops try to prevent three lone journalists from catching an indicted war criminal, who is a thinly altered image of Karadžić). Richard Holbrooke has denied that any deals had been struck. See Holbrooke Denies US Deal with Karadžić, in: France 24, 31 July 2008, available at http://www.france24.com/en/20080731-holbrooke-denies-us-deal-with-karadzic-karadzic-usa (download 14 January 2009). See also CIA Protected Karadžić, in: B92, 10 August 2008, available at http://www.b92.net/eng/news/crimes-article.php?yyyy=2008&mm=08&dd=10&nav_id=52591 (download 14 January 2009); Marlise Simons, Study Backs Bosnian Serb's Claim of Immunity, in: The New York Times, 21 March 2009.

53 Sharp 1997/1998: 134.

54 Sudetic 2000; Zaalberg 2006: 268; International Crisis Group 2000; International Crisis Group 2001: 12.

55 London thwarted Karadžić's arrest, in: B92, 9 August 2008.

56 Sharp 1997/1998: 123; Zaalberg 2006: 265.

57 In Bosnia, Britain drew upon its experiences in Northern Ireland, a 'corporal's war', with regard to training, doctrine, and capabilities. According to a British military officer, British forces can fairly easily slip into the role of arresting a suspect and handing the suspect over to the police, to conduct intelligence-led operations and to strike a close relationship with the local population. They can do so because officers and non-commissioned officers are trained to patrol streets and take decisions quickly without first getting permission from higher up in the chain of command. For the officer, this was the future of modern armed forces. (Interviews, Sarajevo, November 2007 and July 2008; see also Zaalberg 2006: 261 and 267.) For a more critical view, see Hills 2001: 86-90.

58 Interview with Military Attaché from EU member state, November 2007, Sarajevo; Susanne Koelbl, "Gegen das Böse kämpfen", in: Der Spiegel 31/2001, 24 September 2001: 42; Zaalberg 2006: 268.

59 See Aufmarsch einer starken Truppe in Pale, in: Süddeutsche Zeitung, 3 April 1998.

60 Zaalberg 2006: 268.

61 Murphy 2004: 368.

62 International Crisis Group 2002: 56.

63 Zaalberg 2006: 269.

64 See Srpski specijalci pod kontrolom (Serbian special police under control), in: Oslobođenje, 11 August 1997.

65 Perito 2004: 150 and 157.

66 Perito 2004: 176.

67 See, for example, Emir Spaho: Karadžić je bio na palama, ali nije uhapšen (Karadžić was in Pale, but he was not arrested), in: Ljiljan, 14 April 1998.

68 See International Crisis Group 2000: 70.

69 International Crisis Group 1999: 6 and 52.

70 Sloan 2003: 91; Currie 2007: 365.

71 For a criticism of the Court's handling of a well-known case, see Scharf 1998.

72 On this incident, see the OHR website, available at http://www.ohr.int/other-doc/contact-g/default.asp?content_id=3604 (download 1 December 2008), as well as Dziedzic and Bair 1998; International Crisis Group 1997; International Crisis Group 2000b: 19-20.

73 For accounts of this incident, see Perito 2004: 9-24; Zaalberg 2006: 272.

74 Zaalberg 2006: 272.

75 Perito 2004: 17.

76 Perito 2004: 20.

77 Perito 2004: 29.

78 Zaalberg 2006: 273.

79 Perito 2004: 147.

80 Belloni 2005: 442.

81 Interview with German military officer, Sarajevo, July 2008.

82 Perito 2004: 30.

83 Perito 2004: 137. See also Elizabeth Neuffer, NATO Plans 'Paramilitary' Force in Bosnia, in: The Boston Globe, 23 February 1998.

84 In 2003, the MNDs became Multinational Task Forces (MNTFs). This new organizational structure increased the influence of troop contributors other than the US, France and the UK.

85 Perito 2004: 161.

86 Zaalberg 2006: 270; Perito 2004: 154.

87 Perito 2004: 150-156.

88 Stark 2004: 7.

89 Interview, Kosovo, autumn 2008.

90 Perito 2004: 150-151.

91 Interview, Kosovo, autumn 2008.

92 See 11th Report of the High Representative for Implementation of the Peace Agreement to the Secretary-General of the United Nations, 14 October 1998, available at http://www.ohr.int/other-doc/hr-reports/default.asp?content_id=3674 (download 24 November 2008).

93 Perito 2004: 163-164. See also Zaalberg 2004: 270.

94 Zaalberg 2006: 270.

95 Perito 2004: 167-168.

96 U.S. Army Peacekeeping and Stability Operations Institute 2000: 10-11.

97 Zaalberg 2006: 274 and 498, endnote 123.

98 International Crisis Group 2000b: 61.

99 Descriptions of the events can be found in Mappes-Niediek 2003: 173-174; International Crisis Group 2001: 4-5; Perito 2004: 174-175; Rivolta a Mostar, undici Carabinieri feriti, Croati di Bosnia assaltano la banca commissariata dall'UE, in: La Stampa, 7 April 2001.

100 See International Crisis Group 2000b.

101 International Crisis Group 2001: 4. On the problems of intelligence sharing in Bosnia, see Peavie 2001; U.S. Army Peacekeeping and Stability Operations Institute 2000: 29.

102 Quoted in: NATO in the Middle, in: The Economist, 14 April 2001.

103 International Crisis Group 2001: 5.

104 Perito 2004: 179.

105 Bose 2002: 155-157; Robert Wright: Tensions in Bosnia Pose Test for the West, in: Financial Times (London), 23 May 2001.

106 Perito 2004: 180.

107 International Crisis Group 2002: 7.

108 Quoted in: International Crisis Group 2002: 57.

109 Heimerl 2005; Bose 2002: 34. Many people returned only briefly to sell their houses.

110 See Robert Fisk, How Sarajevo has become the springboard into Europe, in: The Independent, 5 February 2001; Andreas 2004: 46; Andreas 2008: 126-127.

111 U.S. Army Peacekeeping and Stability Operations Institute 2000: 22.

112 Perito 2004: 171.

113 Perito 2004: 169-170; International Crisis Group 2001b: 4; Andreas 2004: 46; Andreas 2008: 132-136.

114 Interview with OHCHR official based in Bosnia in the 1990s, Geneva, September 2006; International Crisis Group 2002: 30, footnote 209.

115 See Human Rights Watch 2002; Mendelson 2005; International Crisis Group 2002: 28-32; International Crisis Group 1999: 49; Vandenberg 2007; Fako 2007; Andreas 2008: 128-132.

116 See Human Rights Watch 2002: 54-55 and 62-68.

117 Limanowska 2002: 65.

118 On US-sponsored prostitution in Korea, see Moon 1997.

119 International Crisis Group 2002: 21.

120 See Human Rights Watch 2002.

121 Interview with OHCHR official based in Bosnia in the 1990s, Geneva, September 2006.

122 International missions and agencies largely failed to punish individuals who used the services of trafficked persons, but instead simply withdrew such individuals from Bosnia. To be sure, it was only in the late 1990s that human trafficking was portrayed as a serious crime around the world. The UN did not define human trafficking until 2000, when a protocol was signed in Palermo, Italy. In the years after Dayton, NATO personnel lacked understanding of human trafficking. Nevertheless, acknowledging the severe impact of human trafficking on human rights and post-conflict stabilization did not require in-depth legal, cultural, or economic knowledge; the absence of such knowledge does not exonerate the individuals and institutions that failed to address a highly visible problem.

123 Vandenberg 2007: 87.

124 Zaalberg 2006: 274.

125 Bose 2002: 273, footnote 27.

126 London Statement 2002.

127 Pugh and Cooper 2004: 175. See also Donais 2003.

128 Paddy Ashdown, What I Learned in Bosnia, in: New York Times, 28 October 2002; Ashdown: Uspjeh nacionalnih stranaka je rezultat razočaranja, in: HINA news agency, 10 October 2002; JISB Interview 2007: 108; Ashdown 2007: 71-78 and 222-224. This

view was echoed by Wolfgang Petritsch, another High Representative, at a discussion on peacebuilding at a Geneva-based institute, May 2006.

129 For criticism of the export of the 'rule of law' to Bosnia, the use of executive powers by international actors in Bosnia, and the lack of local ownership in crime-fighting, see Chandler 2005; Knaus and Martin 2003; Fagan 2005; Merlingen and Ostrauskaite 2005: 230; European Stability Initiative 2007b; Schroeder and Friesendorf 2009; Hozic 2007; and the contributions to a Special Supplement of the Journal of Intervention and State Building, December 2007. For an insightful critique of crime-fighting in Southeast Europe more generally, see Woodward 2004. For a deconstruction of Western views of the Balkans, see Todorova 1997.

130 See Ritscher 2005: 121; International Crisis Group 2000b: 30; International Crisis Group 1999: 46; U.S. Army Peacekeeping and Stability Operations Institute 2000: 32, footnote 33.

131 International Crisis Group 2001: 8, footnote 21.

132 Perito 2004: 171.

133 Perito 2004: 180. See also Specijalci protiv kriminala (special police against crime), in: Oslobođenje, 3 August 2002.

134 Critics have argued that the international obsession with corruption has had a paradoxical effect: Allegations of corruption have sowed a feeling of insecurity, which has led people to vote for 'their' nationalist party, even if party members were corrupt (see Chandler 2002: 111-112).

135 Of around 18,000 police officers assessed between 1996 and 2002, the UN declared 793 unfit for office (European Stability Initiative 2007; for a different figure, see Merlingen and Ostrauskaite 2005b: 304).

136 Interviews, Sarajevo, 2007-2008.

137 On the deficient coordination of international rule of law activities in Bosnia, see Schroeder and Friesendorf 2009; International Crisis Group 2001c; International Crisis Group 2002b: 4-12.

138 Interview, Sarajevo, July 2008.

139 See Anes Alić, Influential Bosnian Croat Trio Arrested, in: Transitions Online, 27 January 2004, available at http://www.ceeol.com/aspx/issuedetails.aspx?issueid=996d82e5-50c5-11d8-91f3-0000b4a60532&articleId=656ba406-51a0-11d8-91f3-0000b4a60532 (download 24 November 2008).

140 Interview with international intelligence official, Sarajevo, July 2008.

141 Interview, Kosovo, autumn 2008.

142 Arsovska 2008.

143 Interviews with police and NGOs in Bulgaria, Macedonia, Kosovo and Bosnia, 2006-2008; Friesendorf 2006; Friesendorf 2007b; Berman and Friesendorf 2008; Limanowska and Rosga 2004; Limanowska 2005; Fako 2007: 9-10.

144 See Allred 2006.

145 Anastasijevic 2006: 19; Dragan Stojkovic and Dragan Stanimirovic: Balkan Arms to Iraq, in: Time Magazine, 30 October 2002, available at http://www.time.com/time/world/article/0,8599,385886,00.html (download 14 April 2009); International Crisis Group 2002c; Vetschera and Damian 2006: 32-33.

146 Mappes-Niediek 2003. 177. One of the flaws of 'counter-terrorism' in Bosnia was that from the perspective of Bosnian citizens, terror against returnees was a much greater problem than foreign terrorism. Yet international actors did not give priority to the

former, not considering it a form of terrorism (on the pathologies of the 'war on terror' in Bosnia, see Innes 2005).

147 Stark 2004: 11.

148 Perito 2004: 177.

149 These tasks were crucial to prevent one type of serious crime: a renewed outbreak of fighting that would manifest itself as inter-ethnic crime. Typical military functions in peace operations, such as separating former combatants (in the immediate post-war phase) and monitoring weapons and ammunition (a long-term task) are part and parcel of fighting serious crime.

150 Ahić 2007: 11.

151 See Perdan 2008.

152 See International Crisis Group 2002.

153 International Crisis Group 2002: 11, footnote 56.

154 Penksa 2006.

155 Interview with EUPM official, Sarajevo, July 2008.

156 Mendelson 2005: 63-64.

157 Penksa 2006: 10.

158 Montanaro-Jankovski 2005: 23. See also Osland 2004.

159 I owe this point to Ursula C. Schroeder.

160 This section partially draws on Friesendorf and Penksa 2008. I am grateful to Susan E. Penksa for sharing her insights on EU policymaking toward Bosnia with me.

161 Leakey 2006: 59.

162 Leakey 2006: 62. See also Michael Evans, EU Force to Take on Pimps, Drug Barons and Smugglers, in: The Times (London), 29 November 2004; Antonio Prlenda, Vojskom na mafiju (army to combat mafia), in: Oslobođenje, 24 November 2004.

163 Policija nije dovoljno jedinstvena da bi se suprotstavila kriminalu (local police forces are not united enough to prevent crime), in: Dnevni Avaz, 25 May 2005.

164 Interview with British military officer, Sarajevo, July 2008.

165 Leakey 2006: 63-64.

166 Talk of General Leakey at a Geneva-based institute, 2006.

167 Baillie 2005. See also Nije Naveden: EUFOR čuva bukve (EUFOR guarding trees), in: Oslobođenje, 11 May 2005.

168 Interview with EUPM official, Sarajevo, July 2008.

169 Leakey 2006: 63.

170 See the 2005 issues of EUFOR Forum, the mission's official journal.

171 Percival 2005; December 2005 edition of EUFOR Forum; for an example of efforts to collect stolen weapons, see Snježana Karić: Gdje nestaje oružje iz kasarni BiH (Where the weapons from the BiH barracks have gone), in: Nezavisne Novine, 8 January 2006.

172 EUFOR and Bosnian Police Carrying Out Joint Anti-Crime Operations, in: HINA news agency and BBC Monitoring, 19 April 2005.

173 For lists of these and other items see Vacca (2005), as well as the descriptions of specific IPU operations, available at http://www.euforbih.org/eufor/index.php?option=com_content&task=view&id=16&Itemid=32 (download 17 December 2008).

174 Ibid.

175 Nije Naveden: Telefonska linija za dojave o kriminalu (phone line to combat crime), in: Oslobođenje, 19 January 2005.

176 In fall 2007, there were four international airports, 54 international crossing points, 33 local crossing points and 350-400 weakly controlled crossing points. Interview with EUPM official, Sarajevo, November 2007.

177 See Nije Naveden: Pomoć DGS u suzbijanju krijumčarenja (helping the Bosnian Border Police to prevent smuggling), in: Oslobođenje, 2 June 2006.

178 Interview with British military officer, Sarajevo, November 2007.

179 Interview with Bosnian security expert, Sarajevo, October 2007.

180 These institutions disputed their alleged weakness and lack of motivation. Interview with SIPA official, Sarajevo, June 2008.

181 Interview with a prosecutor, Sarajevo, October 2007; interview with a British military officer, Sarajevo, July 2008.

182 Interview, Sarajevo, June 2008. According to the official EUFOR journal, "as well as concrete results like drug seizures and arrests, 'Spring Clean 3' also [...] provided huge amount of information and intelligence to MNTF(N) and local authorities" (Miettinen 2005).

183 Interview with EU Council official, January 2007.

184 To be true, the EU benefited from the fact that by the time it replaced NATO, human trafficking was a much better-known problem. If SFOR had been an EU mission, its soldiers would have engaged in trafficking, as NATO soldiers had done. Only in 2002-2003 did governments and military leaders begin to heed calls to stop fueling trafficking

185 Interview with international prosecutor, Sarajevo, October 2007; email communication with the same prosecutor, spring 2008.

186 Interview, Sarajevo, July 2008. For an example of allegations about rule-violating behavior, see Alexander Richter and Joachim Dethlefs: Soldaten als Reporter auf Geheimmission, in: Tagesschau, 17 February 2006, at www.tagesschau.de/inland/meldung133236.html (download 16 April 2009).

187 Interview, Sarajevo, November 2007.

188 European Union 2005. See also Penksa 2006: 20. According to a senior EU police officer, he and other officials formulated the principles in one single night. Interview, Southeast Europe, November 2008.

189 European Union 2006.

190 Such (restricted) documents include the six-monthly EUMP review sent by the EU Council Secretariat to the Political and Security Committee and to non-EU countries contributing to the EUPM.

191 Interview with Italian and French Embassy officials, Sarajevo, November 2007.

192 Interview with EUPM official, Sarajevo, November 2007.

193 Interview with EUPM official, Sarajevo, November 2007.

194 Interviews with EUPM officials, Sarajevo, November 2007. See also De Graaf 2005: 172.

195 Interviews with EUPM officials, Sarajevo, 2007 and 2008.

196 Interview, June 2008. While SIPA appreciated international support, representatives complained that the institution was excluded from PIFWC operations (interview with SIPA official, June 2008). This exclusion reflects a lack of trust and the desire to limit the number of actors involved in highly sensitive domains.

197 Interview with EUPM official, Sarajevo, summer 2008. See also Wisler 2007: 265.

198 Interview with official in BiH Ministry of Security, Sarajevo, November 2007.

199 Interview with Bosnian security officials, Banja Luka, November 2007.

200 Interview with Bosnian police official, Banja Luka, November 2007.

201 See International Crisis Group 1999b (e.g., page 19).

202 Interviews with Bosnian security officials, Banja Luka, November 2007.

203 Interview, Sarajevo, October 2007. See also International Crisis Group 2007: 11-14.

204 Interview with international prosecutor, Sarajevo, June 2008.

205 Interview with international prosecutor, Sarajevo, October 2007.

206 Interview with EUPM official, Sarajevo, November 2007.

207 In early 2009, the International Crisis Group (2009: 25) harshly criticized the EUPM's crime-fighting record.

208 Interview, Sarajevo, October 2007.

209 Bose 2002: 75.

210 Glenny 1999: 651.

211 Interview with EUPM official, Sarajevo, July 2008.

212 European Stability Initiative 2007b; Parish 2007: 18-21; interview with Bosnian police officer, Banja Luka, November 2007.

213 Interview, Sarajevo, July 2008.

214 Interview with EUPM official, Sarajevo, November 2007.

215 Interview with EUPM official, Sarajevo, July 2008.

216 By contrast, there were approximately 13,000 lower-level suspected war criminals who had not been prosecuted (Interview with Bosnian journalist, Sarajevo, fall 2007).

217 Interview with British military officer, Sarajevo, July 2008.

218 Dimitrios 2006.

219 By summer 2008, the EU considered several options for reforming the EUPM. One was to rename the institution, strengthen its judicial elements and integrate the IPU as the robust element of the new mission. The IPU would thus no longer be under military, but under civilian command (interview with EU official, Sarajevo, July 2008).

220 Interview with EUFOR official, November 2007, Sarajevo. The perceived success of the IPU in Bosnia led, in late 2007, to the IPU becoming the first mission of the newly-created European Gendarmerie Force based in Vicenza, Italy.

221 Interview, Sarajevo, July 2008. In convincing commanders of regular EUFOR elements to support law enforcement, the official benefited from his contacts to the British military, other intelligence officers, the OHR, and the State Court.

222 For a list, see http://www.euforbih.org/eufor/index.php?Itemid=32&id=16&option=com_content&task=view (download 17 December 2008).

223 Interview with a Bosnian investigative journalist, Sarajevo, November 2007.

224 Interview, Sarajevo, November 2007.

225 Interview with EU member state Embassy official, Sarajevo, November 2007.

226 Sena Avdić: Zašto međunarodni vojnici ubijaru Srbe (Why International Soldiers Are Killing Serbs), in: Slobodna Bosna, 12 January 2006; Nicholas Wood, Bosnian Was Killed After Firing Shots, Peacekeepers Say, in: New York Times, 8 January 2006, available at http://www.nytimes.com/2006/01/08/international/europe/08bosnia.html (download 21 November 2008).

227 For a condemnation of EUFOR's failure to cooperate with domestic law enforcement institutions in the arrest, see EUFOR prekoračio mandat (EUFOR breaches its mandate), in: Nezavisne Novine, 24 April 2006.

228 For an example, see Senad Mešetović: Hapšenje mafijaša (Mafia Arrests), in: Oslobođenje, 28 August 2006.

229 Interview with EUPM official, Sarajevo, November 2007.
230 Interview with EUPM official, Sarajevo, November 2007.
231 See EUFOR Forum, December 2005 edition, p. 25.
232 Interviews with EUPM officials, Sarajevo, November 2007.
233 Interview with SIPA official, Sarajevo, June 2008.
234 Interview with EUFOR official, Sarajevo, July 2008.
235 Interview, Sarajevo, November 2007.
236 Interview with SIPA official, Sarajevo, June 2008.
237 EUFOR was not the only agent of change. For instance, SIPA received sniper training from the US military as part of training courses taking place in the US.
238 Interview with EUPM official, Sarajevo, November 2007.
239 Packett et al. 2005.
240 This paragraph is based on direct observation of the work of, and interviews with, LOT house personnel in a town in Eastern Bosnia in winter 2007/2008 and in Herzegovina in summer 2008.
241 Interview with LOT house officer, Herzegovina, summer 2008.
242 Interview with Military Attaché from EU member state, November 2007, Sarajevo.
243 Interview with LOT house officer, Eastern Bosnia, November 2007.
244 Interview with EUFOR officer, Banja Luka, November 2007.
245 The price of market goods was one indicator of security perceptions. In fall 2007, the political crisis triggered by the stalemate over police reform led citizens to stock up on supplies, and prices to rise as a consequence. Especially rising cooking oil prices raised fears among citizens who remembered that the outbreak of the war in 1992 had coincided with high cooking oil prices. To understand what was happening, LOT house soldiers were dispatched to photograph price tags in shops.
246 Interview, Eastern Bosnia, winter 2007/2008.
247 Interview with LOT house officer, Herzegovina, summer 2008.
248 According to a LOT house officer (interview, Herzegovina, summer 2008), "we probably rely too much on interpreters, but we don't have a choice."
249 See EUFOR Forum, March 2006 edition, p. 10.
250 Interview with LOT house officer, Eastern Bosnia, winter 2007/2008.
251 Interview with LOT house officer, Eastern Bosnia, winter 2007/2008.
252 Interview, Sarajevo, summer 2008.
253 Interview with EUPM official, Sarajevo, November 2007.
254 Interview with Bosnian Border Police Official, Sarajevo, July 2008.
255 Interview with Bosnian Border Police Official, Sarajevo, July 2008.
256 Interview, Sarajevo, July 2008.
257 Interview with Bosnian Border Police official, Sarajevo, July 2008.
258 See European Stability Initiative 2007b: 1; Dnevni List, EUFOR je spreman intervenirati u slučaju novog rata (EUFOR ready to intervene in case of another war), in: Oslobođenje, 31 October 2007.
259 On this shift more generally, see Andreas and Price 2001.
260 This section partially draws on Schroeder and Friesendorf 2009. I thank Ursula C. Schroeder for her insights and ideas.
261 Van Duyne et al. 2004; van Dijk 2007.
262 On problems with a law on asset forfeiture, see Rausch 2006: 64.
263 UNODC 2008: Part I.

264 UNODC 2008: 97.
265 Interview with prosecutor, Sarajevo, summer 2008.
266 Interview with Bosnian Border Police official, July 2008.
267 See Friesendorf 2007b.
268 Interviews with prosecutors, the police, and NGOs in various parts of Bosnia, 2006-2008.
269 European Commission and Council of Europe 2007: 19.
270 See European Stability Initiative 2007b: 6.
271 Interviews, Sarajevo, August 2006 and fall 2007.
272 UNODC 2008. See also Penksa 2006: 21; European Commission and Council of Europe 2007.
273 See Friesendorf, Schroeder and Deljkić forthcoming.
274 Stanchev 2005: 32.
275 Interview, Sarajevo, October 2007.
276 Ironically, the free-market, 'liberal peace' spirit exported to Bosnia by governments and institutions such as the World Bank has exacerbated poverty through cuts in welfare spending, thus providing organized crime groups with a pool of labourers. Michael Pugh argues that the shadow economy is a "coping mechanism, one made all the more attractive by the impact of neoliberal restructuring" (Pugh and Cooper 2004: 146; see also Pugh 2002: 475-477; Pugh 2005: 459). Thus, in 2002, according to the World Bank, grey and black market activities made up between 50 and 60 percent of Bosnia's GDP (see Andreas 2008: 119). The implantation of capitalism has also facilitated business crime, such as the fraudulent privatization of state assets.
277 On this effect in a different context, see Friesendorf 2005.
278 Friesendorf and Penksa 2008: 689-690; author email exchange with official from the Forest Stewardship Council, March 2008.
279 See, for example, the discussion of drug problems in Bosnia in UNODC 2008.
280 Friesendorf 2007.
281 Interview, Sarajevo, summer 2008. See also Penksa 2006: 20.
282 Interview, Sarajevo, July 2008.
283 Quoted in: Miettinen 2005b: 5.
284 Presentation of General Leakey at a Geneva-based institute, 2006.
285 U.S. Army Peacekeeping and Stability Operations Institute 2000: 12.

Chapter 4

Kosovo

The case of Kosovo epitomises problems of governing 'international protectorates' and of post-war crime fighting. The empirical picture is a messy one in which numerous international and domestic agencies intermingle in complex ways, often working at cross-purposes. As in Bosnia, military involvement in law enforcement has lacked effectiveness, efficiency and legitimacy. This is only partly the fault of NATO – the UN and its member states arguably carry more responsibility. Crime-fighting in pre- and post-independence Kosovo exemplifies flawed security governance, SSG and SSR.

The first part of this chapter examines the immediate post-war period. The second part discusses the early years of international governance in Kosovo. The third part reveals the travails of crime-fighting around the time Kosovo declared independence. Drawing primarily on interviews conducted in Kosovo in 2007 and 2008 (and a few in 2006), this third part complements the vast literature on international intervention in Kosovo by focusing on more recent events. The chapter also fills a gap by shedding light on dynamics on the ground, which have been neglected due to the propensity of scholars to focus on the strategic/diplomatic level rather than the operational and tactical levels.

NATO Enters Kosovo

In early 1999, NATO waged war against the Federal Republic of Yugoslavia, which by then had shrunk to Serbia (including Kosovo) and Montenegro. The UN Security Council did not approve the war. But the main NATO members argued that diplomacy had failed to stop the persecution of Kosovars by Serbian security forces, requiring a military response.[1] After 77 days of air strikes, Slobodan Milošević gave up. On 9 June 1999, NATO and Yugoslavia signed the Kumanovo agreement, which proscribed the withdrawal of Yugoslav security forces from Kosovo and the establishment of NATO's Kosovo Force (KFOR). This agreement complemented UN Security Council Resolution 1244. The Resolution placed

Kosovo, pending the resolution of its final status, under international administration. It is the main document regulating the governance of this new 'international protectorate'.

On 12 June, KFOR moved into the disputed province. There was much uncertainty over whether the estimated 40,000 Serbian troops, police and paramilitaries would withdraw from Kosovo or try to re-enter the province after regrouping. Yet Milošević complied with the Kumanovo agreement. As Serbian forces withdrew and KFOR entered Kosovo, most Kosovars who had fled the province during NATO's bombing campaign and before returned.

NATO and returning refugees saw a dangerous wasteland. If security was difficult to establish in Bosnia, doing so in Kosovo proved even more difficult. Most of the infrastructure had been destroyed and, following the Serbian withdrawal, no statutory domestic security forces remained in the province. The biggest domestic force was the Kosovo Liberation Army (KLA [UÇK, Ushtria Çlirimtare e Kosovës]) whose around 50,000 members had staged one of the most successful insurgencies in modern history. The KLA was given several months to disarm and disband. Its members largely complied. However, illegal parallel structures reportedly carried out 'policing' tasks,[2] often violating the human rights of minorities as well as of Kosovars in the process.[3] The Serbs had non-statutory security forces, too. The Serb-dominated northern part of Mitrovica was 'policed' by 'bridge-watchers' – toughs wearing plain cloths who inspired fear not only among local Kosovars but also among Serbs.

After the initial euphoria of defeating Serbia, international actors quickly came to realise that war-fighting was easier than crime-fighting. During the first months into the 'peace', up to 50 people were murdered per week.[4] This high rate was due to fighting among different Kosovar factions, as well as inter-ethnic crime. The tables had turned now. Before, Kosovars had been the main victims of violence. The withdrawal of Serbian forces was followed by numerous attacks against Kosovo Serbs as well as other minorities.[5] In Bosnia, the three ethnic groups had 'their' security forces to defend them against attack. In Kosovo, the Serbs had to rely on international forces or on their own devices.

Besides stopping the spree of revenge killings, international forces faced the challenge to apprehend suspected war criminals. This was all but easy. Many Serbian perpetrators had left the province; many Serbs who stayed on were accused by Kosovars of having committed atrocities, yet useable evidence tended to be difficult to obtain; and it was generally unfeasible for Serbs to make a case against Kosovars, given the view, also prevalent among most 'internationals', that the former were the perpetrators and the latter the victims of repression.

Moreover, organised crime was thriving in post-war Kosovo. Some of those indicted for organised crime were also presumed to have committed war crimes and be linked to the most influential political parties in Kosovo.[6] Such presumed overlaps point at the criminalised nature of the Kosovo war.[7] Serbian forces, especially paramilitaries, had preyed upon the civilian population. Many Kosovars, especially those from wealthy families, had paid Serbs to avert repression or to be allowed to stay in business. The KLA, on the other hand, had reportedly bought weapons from drug traffickers.[8] By 1997, it allegedly controlled the heroin trade through Kosovo.[9] When the war ended, criminals (many of whom were motivated by a mix of ideology and business interests), did not cease their illicit activities. Organised crime thus became one of the few thriving activities in Kosovo, with the trafficking of drugs, weapons, cars, cigarettes, alcohol, fuel and human beings.

Whether a post-war security gap opens up greatly depends on the ability of intervention forces to quell or prevent crime. The United Nations Interim Administration Mission in Kosovo (UNMIK), headed by a Special Representative of the United Nations Secretary-General (SRSG), was responsible for overall policy coordination. Several pillars were set up under UNMIK. After changes to the initial structure, by May 2001 there were four pillars. The UN managed pillar I (police and justice) and pillar II (civil administration); the OSCE was responsible for pillar III (democratisation and institution-building); and the EU had the lead over pillar IV activities (reconstruction and economic development).

Governing functions were to be gradually transferred to Provisional Institutions for Self-Government. The mantra, coined in the second half of 2002, was 'standards before status': International actors hoped that improving security and the economy and creating incipient democratic structures would resolve the tricky status issue. The principle of local ownership was circumscribed in important ways, however. In Kosovo, for the first time in history, the UN assumed governing functions in all areas of public life other than the military realm; deployed armed police with executive competencies; and explicitly set itself the task to prevent and disrupt organised crime.[10] International police officers had the power to arrest suspects, international prosecutors to make cases and international judges to impose prison terms. In some domains, the UN shared executive functions with domestic actors. Yet in sensitive areas, the UN had exclusive powers. This was the case with regard to war crimes, inter-ethnic crimes, organised crime, terrorism and property disputes.

During the crucial first few post-war months, a public security gap opened up in Kosovo. In contrast to Bosnia, the UN Police in Kosovo had a strong mandate. Yet as in Bosnia, it deployed late and only slowly increased its presence. It took UNMIK Police two years to reach 90 percent of its agreed strength.[11] Moreover, many CIVPOL officers lacked vehicles, radios and even stationary.[12] In addition, UNMIK was plagued by bureaucratic inertia and a heterogeneous staff coming from countries where law enforcement and criminal justice practices differed markedly (UNMIK Police came from 53 countries). Ten months into UNMIK, "there were still no approved guidelines in force for policing, arrest, or pre-trial detention in Kosovo."[13]

Since UNMIK was unable to fight crime, the military was once again pushed into the law enforcement realm. KFOR was a robust mission that was prepared to fight Serbian forces in a ground war and to protect itself against local acts of violence. At its peak, it numbered 50,000 soldiers, many of whom were heavily armed. Troops came from 30 countries. NATO Headquarters provided strategic guidance to KFOR to enable it to implement the military aspects of the Kumanovo Agreement. Although KFOR's military power was overwhelming, it had never been tested. With tanks, artillery and other heavy weapons at its disposal, KFOR was geared towards protecting Kosovo against any incursion by Serbian forces. At the time, such a move by Belgrade was perceived as possible. Since NATO primarily planned for war and observed the movements of Serbian troops, KFOR did not have much time and resources available to cope with humanitarian and criminal issues within Kosovo.

KFOR's mandate was broader than the one of IFOR/SFOR in Bosnia. The mission in Kosovo was to provide a safe and secure environment so that refugees could return and UNMIK could govern the province. KFOR had to ensure freedom of movement, conduct border patrols and demining operations and support UNMIK.[14] Crucially, UN Security Council Resolution 1244 also stipulated that KFOR was to ensure "public safety and order until the international civil presence can take responsibility for this task."[15] For the first time, a UN resolution gave the military power over public security. In many areas KFOR had full tactical policing authority. This and the avoidance of setting an exit date were improvements over the Dayton agreement.[16]

However, as in Bosnia, major troop contributing nations, especially the US, adamantly opposed subordinating the military to UN command, which led to two separate chains of command.[17] KFOR reported to the Allied Joint Force Command (JFC) in Naples, while UNMIK reported to UN

Headquarters. Thus, even though KFOR coordinated activities with UNMIK, it was not under the authority of the SRSG. NATO was free to decide how deeply it would become involved in law enforcement. KFOR activities in this realm therefore reflected the capacities, priorities and perceptions of troop contributing nations and commanders on the ground. Moreover, the willingness of commanders to support law enforcement depended much on good personal relations between KFOR and UNMIK officials.

After defeating Serbia, NATO now had to establish de facto military governance in those parts of Kosovo where the remit of the UN was small. Quick-impact CIMIC projects and large-scale construction projects became lifelines for many citizens of Kosovo and contributed to economic improvement.[18] CIMIC in Kosovo was partly geared to winning the 'hearts and minds' of Kosovo Serbs who did not regard the NATO soldiers as liberators. Also, KFOR commanders felt compelled to alleviate deprivation and poverty.

Guaranteeing public order proved more difficult. KFOR was as unprepared for this as the UN.[19] During the war, NATO member states and NATO planners, preoccupied with the air campaign and with holding the Alliance together politically, hardly prepared troops for policing tasks. While the short timeframe helps explain this omission, the lack of planning reveals a failure to learn from Bosnia. Law enforcement challenges in Kosovo surpassed those faced in Bosnia since NATO had to substitute for civilian law enforcement and criminal justice agencies. During several months, KFOR soldiers were "the only barrier between the citizen and crime."[20] The presence, in some areas, of UNMIK Police officials acting as advisors for the military did little to civilianise law enforcement.[21]

The way KFOR engaged in law enforcement revealed the mission's heterogeneous structure. In the early phase KFOR was divided into four Multinational Brigades (MNB) and one Multinational Task Force (MTF). In September 2006, KFOR changed its structure to five MTFs. Each MNB/MTF was under the command of a military officer (usually a Brigadier General) of the US, the UK, France, Germany and Italy, respectively. These sectors resembled 'mini-states': Training, equipment, RoE and force protection requirements differed depending on which country held the command.[22] Even within each sector there was no uniform approach because each sector comprised several national contingents (including non-NATO members such as Russia). Also, MTB/MTF and national contingent commanders, who would usually rotate every six months, differed in their peacekeeping and crime-fighting approaches.

The Commander of KFOR was more of a manager than a commander since he had only limited authority over the entire theatre.[23] His ability to coordinate KFOR activities was curtailed by the common practice of KFOR officers to send information and intelligence to their respective capitals before sending it to COM KFOR in Pristina, or to not inform him at all.[24] Moreover, troop-contributing countries imposed caveats on the use of 'their' troops and engaged in micro-management, thus limiting the ability of COM KFOR to respond fast and flexibly to the ever-changing security situation. KFOR officers considered themselves "dual-hatted", serving for KFOR as well as their respective country.[25]

Peacekeeping activities such as the creation of security perimeters around endangered communities, checkpoints along roads and the disarmament of former combatants contributed indirectly to crime-fighting. Yet direct KFOR law enforcement action was unsystematic. For instance, KFOR soldiers at borders focused on intercepting weapons, but were not trained and tasked to carry out customs and excise functions.[26] As KFOR was checking traffic only for weapons, smugglers of various strands operated with impunity.

The ability and willingness of KFOR to stop serious crime varied across sectors. In the Italian sector during the immediate post-war period, former KLA members were allowed to 'police' the streets and offer other governmental services,[27] with inevitable consequences for non-Kosovar citizens. In the US sector, force protection requirements did not allow US troops to 'fraternise' with Kosovo citizens.[28] Some US soldiers also displayed a time-is-money attitude that violated the Balkan tradition of getting to know one another over many cups of coffee. Force protection and a lack of cultural sensitivity prevented the US from understanding local conditions, which is crucial for crime-fighting. Other nations refused to detain suspects or set up prisons at all.[29]

Yet there are also many examples of admirable improvisation. In several chapters of his well-researched book on civil-military relations, Thijs Zaalberg traces the activities of a Dutch battalion posted to the town of Orahovac in southern Kosovo in 1999, where it operated under German command.[30] The Dutch soldiers, specialised in artillery, were unprepared for the situation they faced: They saw war crime sites, armed KLA members taking control of the streets and administrative buildings, and attacks on minorities, especially Serbs. There were no police to speak of, only Kosovar militias and terrified, outnumbered and outgunned minority residents.

The Dutch, with the shadow of Srebrenica over them, tried to establish a modicum of order. In the absence of proper guidance from NATO and the

Dutch Defence Ministry, their commander applied Dutch law, for example when detaining suspects. The Dutch and German commanders interpreted KFOR's mandate of ensuring a safe and secure environment to include tasks such as arresting (often juvenile) Kosovars who torched the houses of Serbs. The Dutch had to learn how to apply heavy-handed measures while at the same time avoiding illegitimate behaviour. On the tactical level this was all but easy. Arsonists, for instance, often managed to escape, benefiting from their superior knowledge of streets and alleyways and their ability to run faster than soldiers with their heavy weapons and armour.[31]

In contrast to IFOR in Bosnia, most KFOR contingents "at least made an effort to stop the anarchy."[32] The Dutch quickly came to understand that the display of military prowess helped to disarm former combatants: When self-appointed local strongmen refused to dismantle barricades or to disarm, the Dutch found that arriving with a howitzer or another large type of weapon led to immediate compliance;[33] Kosovo's 'gun culture' seemed to mean that compliance correlated with the size of the weapon.[34] The Dutch would also try to minimise further inter-ethnic violence, e.g., by returning stolen cars to their owners.[35] Other contingents would rely heavily on military police in their efforts to stabilise Kosovo. Contingents also cooperated with Special Forces flown into Kosovo for targeted operations against suspected war criminals.[36]

One of the many problems encountered by KFOR was the absence of a clear legal framework. Initially, UNMIK decided in favour of the legal system as created in the 1990s. But Kosovars strongly objected to this, arguing that the system had been a tool of Serbian oppression. After several months the UN relented, agreeing to adopt the old Yugoslav legal framework which had been in force before March 1989 when Serbia, by instituting a new constitution, had revoked the status of Kosovo as an autonomous province. Yet this framework lacked provisions against organised crime and war crimes.[37] (Re)-creating an anachronistic framework was problematic symbolically, too: Many Kosovars saw that the UN was not immune to public pressure and many Serbs interpreted the UN's decision as proof of the international community's pro-Albanian stance. Following the u-turn of the UN, "the applicable law in Kosovo became an almost unfathomable combination of old law, international and European human rights conventions, UNMIK regulations and police directives."[38] Traditional conflict regulation mechanisms, which had guaranteed the functioning of society in the absence of reliable state structures, added to this confusion. Prosecution efforts consequently suffered.[39]

Another closely related problem was the absence of functioning criminal justice institutions.[40] Often, KFOR had to release suspects because there were no prisons. KFOR improvised by detaining suspects in makeshift prisons, including tents. There were also no secure courthouses.[41] Most importantly, UN prosecutors and judges arrived late. To empower local actors, the UN allowed domestic judges and prosecutors to deal with specific types of cases. These legal professionals, however, were almost exclusively Kosovars since many Serbian prosecutors and judges had left the province and those who stayed in their jobs faced threats. Sentencing practices therefore discriminated against minorities.[42] The UN recruited an emergency panel of 28 judges to hear the most serious cases.[43] But this was only a stop-gap measure. It took until late 1999 for the UN to replace Kosovar prosecutors and judges with panels made up exclusively of international prosecutors and judges.

The absence of well-functioning police and criminal justice agencies led to human rights violations by KFOR and UNMIK. KFOR, when arresting suspects, often disregarded standard judicial principles because regular soldiers had no law enforcement training.[44] US KFOR soldiers arrested numerous individuals suspected of being involved in serious crime. Some of these individuals were detained for extended periods of time in Camp Bondsteel, which some critics regarded as a precursor to Guantanamo.[45] During the first year in Kosovo, 1,800 detainees were reportedly held at Bondsteel.[46] Even when courts ordered the release of suspects, US KFOR tended to ignore the orders and limited access to detainees by the international Ombudsman, representatives of the Council of Europe, the OSCE and other officials. US KFOR argued that they had evidence of wrongdoing, yet refused to share any evidence.[47] The fate of a few persons detained by US troops remains unknown.[48] Some individuals detained by international personnel were imprisoned for up to six months before facing trial.[49] As KFOR personnel had immunity, suspects did not have access to judicial redress. French troops were accused of violating human rights too. For instance, following violence in Mitrovica in 2000, the French allegedly held detainees under harsh conditions for up to five days.[50] UNMIK, too, broke democratic rules, especially when ordering 'executive detentions', which the OSCE heavily criticised.[51]

From the perspective of KFOR, the absence of a functioning policing and criminal justice system required the use of extraordinary measures.[52] In several cases, KFOR saw that arrested suspects were subsequently acquitted by local courts, which added to KFOR's recalcitrance to cooperate with civilian institutions. One well-known case is the release of a Kosovar accused of murdering three Serbs, including a four-year old child, in front of a small store. However, ethnic bias is only one explanation for the way Kosovo institutions handled the case. Another is "the segmenting and compartmentalization of inculpatory evidence, some of which was classified as military intelligence."[53] Since KFOR classified original alibi claims that contradicted later alibi claims as military intelligence, an international prosecutor was unable to have the acquittal overturned.

The inclusion of non-conventional troops into KFOR only alleviated law enforcement problems, it did not solve them.[54] MNB North included Gendarmes; in the Centre, the British relied on Royal Military Police and military investigators from the Special Investigation Branch; in the East, US Army Military Police operated as a constabulary force; and MNB West included Italian Carabinieri and Spanish Guardia Civil.[55] KFOR also had at its disposal a Multinational Specialised Unit (MSU). The over 300 members of this unit were Italian Carabinieri, French Gendarmes and Estonian ESTPATROL military police,[56] with Italy as the lead nation. As in Bosnia, the unit was allowed to operate theatre-wide. MSU tasks included CRC and the collection of information and intelligence on organised crime.

MSU output in the first years after the war was impressive, with regard to weapons, ammunition, explosives, and contraband goods seized; victims of trafficking liberated; and crime groups identified. However other 'internationals' thought the MSU was a cumbersome partner. UNMIK Police complained that the MSU carried out operations with minimal prior notification of UNMIK and that they did not share criminal intelligence on organised crime investigations.[57] Another problem was the absence of an executive mandate. This meant for instance that MSU intelligence on organised crime could not be submitted directly to court. Furthermore, regular KFOR units were unfamiliar with constabulary forces and therefore underutilised the MSU.

Also, there were turf battles between the MSU and UNMIK's Special Police Units (SPUs) that additionally hampered the effectiveness of the MSU. The SPU included formed police units from constabulary forces. Their task was to support regular UNMIK Police and also KFOR through activities ensuring public security. Their mandate and structure made the SPU similar to the MSU, which created much friction. Sometimes, writes Robert Perito, the MSU

> would turn over suspects and contraband to the UNMIK police but not detain the individuals or collect evidence in a manner that could be admitted in court to obtain convictions. For their part, the UNMIK police, particularly the

Special Police Units, had little incentive to cooperate with the MSU, considering their redundant capability and the difficulty of communicating via KFOR's chain of command.[58]

KFOR's crime-fighting role after the war is ambiguous. On the one hand, KFOR became deeper involved than had been the case with IFOR and the first SFOR rotations in Bosnia. However, this was not so much a result of institutional learning from Bosnia. Rather, the near-complete absence of international and domestic policing and criminal justice structures compelled the military to do something. Also, many interventions violated human rights. Moreover, KFOR involvement varied across sectors. Unsystematic or no law enforcement – by KFOR and other international actors – led to many crimes being committed with impunity. Numerous people died in ethnically motivated revenge attacks; houses were destroyed or emptied of their inhabitants; the smuggling and trafficking of people and goods was conducted without much interference; and many suspected war criminals were not apprehended.

NATO in an International Protectorate

After 1999 there were signs that Kosovo was becoming more stable. In 2001 the murder rate was down by 50 percent, arson by 58 percent, and looting by 73 percent.[59] However, a decrease in serious crime reflected the fact that Kosovo was no longer as multi-ethnic as it used to be. The United Nations High Commissioner for Refugees (UNHCR) reported that by February 2000 around 820,000 persons, almost all of them Kosovars, had been officially repatriated. 230,000 Serbs, Gypsies and others, by contrast, had left the province.[60] Also, while the number of attacks on minorities (as well as internecine violence among Kosovar factions) declined, minorities were far from safe.[61] Province-wide riots in March 2004 revealed the inability of international actors to control violent crowds. Less visible forms of serious crime, especially organised crime, were present, too, or even increased.

Crime-fighting was difficult for several reasons. International actors faced the continuing dilemma of how to cope with former combatants. The DDR of KLA fighters proceeded slowly. Many rank-and-file members handed in their weapons and some found jobs. However, many former combatants kept their weapons and some became involved in crime or, having profited during wartime, continued to conduct illicit business. At the same time, many former KLA commanders secured their formal and informal domestic power base by morphing into politicians and businessmen.

International actors tried to channel non-statutory security forces into new institutions. One was the Kosovo Protection Corps (KPC), the de-facto successor of the KLA. Some members of this incipient army were allowed to keep small arms for specific purposes, such as protecting compounds. Moreover, in 1999 the Kosovo Police Service (KPS) was created (it was later renamed Kosovo Police). Its members were trained at the police academy in Vushtrri, which was run by the OSCE and which initially used a curriculum developed by ICITAP.[62] The international police commissioner (head of UNMIK Police) had authority over both the international police as well as the KPS. A quota system applied, ensuring the representation of Serbs and other minorities. By 2004, the KPS had reached its full strength, employing around 7,000 officers. In addition to normal police patrol units, the KPS included units focusing on organised crime, forensics, close protection, CRC and other sensitive areas.

The ability of the KPS to fight serious crime was curtailed by the fact that crucial areas of crime-fighting remained the domaine reservé of internationals. Also, many officers feared going after criminals and the force suffered from corruption and criminal collusion.[63] Moreover, despite the quota system, the KPS found it difficult to operate in minority areas. With around 85 percent of its members being Kosovars, Serbs and other minorities perceived the KPS as biased, an impression reinforced by the UN's allowing former KLA members to constitute half of the original KPS cadre (in total, this cadre was 4,000 strong).[64] Last, the KPS did not possess the manpower, equipment nor intelligence capabilities it would have needed to challenge the often well-equipped, fast-moving and well-connected criminals.

UNMIK suffered from shortcomings, too. The UN managed to increase the number of international police officers as well as prosecutors and judges. But these were still thinly spread over the province. Moreover, UNMIK tended to use the SPU for tasks other than CRC.[65] Maintaining public order remained difficult, not least because in 2002 UNMIK began to clamp down more systematically on major offenders, a move that was facilitated by the creation of the Kosovo Organised Crime Bureau (KOCB).[66] The main criminal suspects were former KLA members who later joined the KPC.[67] Some of these were also members of the Democratic Party of Kosovo led by Hashim Thaçi, a former KLA leader. Accusations included war crimes, organised crime and attacks on members of Ibrahim

Rugova's Democratic League of Kosovo. Arrest operations always carried the risk of triggering violent demonstrations.

Coordination between UNMIK and KFOR remained difficult, and depended on personal relationships.[68] UNMIK established regional coordination offices headed by administrators, trying to ensure that these quasi-governors came from the same country as the respective MNB/MTF commander in order to minimise cultural friction and language problems.[69] In Pristina, decision-makers' ability to empathise mattered, too. COM KFOR Mike Jackson and SRSG Sergio Vieira de Mello, as well as COM KFOR Klaus Reinhardt and SRSG Bernard Kouchner, got along well. But sometimes, KFOR and UNMIK personnel would not trust one another. In one case involving a high-level criminal in 2002, KFOR did not contact UNMIK Police because it feared its intelligence-gathering methods and sources would be revealed.[70] KFOR generally mistrusted the heterogeneous UN mission, and all non-military actors in general, due to concerns of corruption and collusion with criminals.[71] A lack of cooperation sometimes would lead to situations whereby KFOR raided brothels without informing UNMIK Police, who were investigating the same brothels.[72]

Weak policing implied continuing KFOR involvement in law enforcement, including the arrest of individuals indicted by the ICTY for war crimes.[73] But military crime-fighting reflected national priorities and the role of individuals. General Reinhardt, despite his close relations with Kouchner, was adamant that the German contingent, one of the largest in Kosovo, would not become mired in policing tasks. This stance reflected the historically motivated German uneasiness with the blurring of civilian and military functions. By contrast, COM KFOR Marcel Valentin underlined in spring 2002 that KFOR's main task would be to fight organised crime.[74] Another active crime-fighter was the Italian COM KFOR Fabio Mini. He was particularly concerned about criminals within the KPC. Moreover, in a 2003 report he underlined that he wanted KFOR to lead the fight against organised crime, arguing that the smuggling of weapons, drugs and human beings, as well as extremism, terrorism and money laundering, constituted a threat to a safe and secure environment. He acknowledged difficulties of using military intelligence for criminal prosecution purposes, but said that he and the head of the UNMIK Justice Department had tried to make the best use of military intelligence.[75] These views reflected experiences with efforts against organised crime in Italy.

To cite another example of divergent approaches, US forces relied on heavy equipment and weaponry against violence that might endanger troops and threaten a safe and secure environment. This stance was counterproductive when it came to stopping the smuggling of weapons into and through Kosovo (stopping weapons smuggling gained new urgency by the outbreak of near-civil war in Macedonia in 2001, as well as an ethnic Albanian insurgency in the Southern Serbian Preševo area).[76] According to a British military officer, the US would dispatch heavily armed and very visible patrols to border zones, but fail to arrest any weapons smugglers. The US commander then accepted a British offer of support. British Special Forces would hide in difficult terrain. After a few days, the soldiers observed a smuggling operation, the members of which were subsequently arrested.[77] In cities and villages, in order to reassure ethnic minorities, British forces applied lessons from Northern Ireland, carrying out, for instance, foot patrols whenever possible.[78]

KFOR not only struggled to detect illicit activities, but also had difficulties in ensuring the prosecution of offenders. According to a former senior UNMIK official, cases were lost whenever the military stepped in.[79] Up until 2002-2003, KFOR would still find large weapons caches. Soldiers would arrest those presumed responsible and put the weapons on a truck. But they often failed to preserve the crime scene and to secure evidence. Evidence-gathering was insufficient with regard to inter-ethnic crime, too. One of the most spectacular attacks in post-war Kosovo was the bombing of a KFOR-escorted bus carrying Serbs on 16 February 2001 from Niš to Gračanica, resulting in the death of 11 passengers and the injury of 40 others. KFOR intelligence led to the arrest of three suspects. However, the intelligence could not be used in court.[80]

KFOR's relations with civilian actors thus remained problematic even after the immediate post-conflict phase. One former UNMIK Police officer recounts giving five radios to KFOR because KFOR was not listening to police communication and therefore was unaware about crime problems.[81] A UN official working on minority returns after the war said that KFOR failed to inform his agency of the locations of Blue Zones and Red Zones. In Blue Zones, KFOR would evacuate the population in case of an emergency. In Red Zones, KFOR would hold the ground. The failure to share this information made it more difficult to plan for contingencies, according to the official.[82] The OSCE found KFOR reluctant to evict individuals who were illegally occupying property, presumably because KFOR feared instability.[83]

Flawed cooperation between KFOR and UNMIK was particularly visible in Mitrovica. In February 2000, for instance, French KFOR troops repeatedly failed to relieve overwhelmed UNMIK police contingents. The first UNMIK SPU did not arrive in Mitrovica before April 2000. But even after they arrived, the French generally did not draw on the SPU in their violent encounters with radical Serbs and Kosovars, and even prevented the unit from crossing the bridge over the river Ibar that divided the two communities.[84]

The civil-military gap was only partly filled by the MSU. Carabinieri gathered information on human traffickers, raided sites where victims and traffickers worked and turned suspects over to UNMIK.[85] The constabularies also contributed to CRC. Typically, riot police of the KPS would constitute the first line in case of violent public disorder. UNMIK Police would be in the second line. In case this second line would not hold, the MSU would step in. In case of full-scale escalation, regular KFOR units, holding the fourth line of defence, would intervene.[86] However, commanders of regular KFOR forces often failed to leverage the advantages of the MSU. Moreover, the MSU were not embedded in a Kosovo-wide strategy against large-scale emergencies or organised crime and therefore did not receive proper guidance. Cooperation was an issue, too, with even the Guardia di Finanza experiencing difficulties. One of their officers recalls that the Guardia di Finanza was keen to obtain access to the database of the Carabinieri which, however, proved uncooperative.[87]

The problems to cope with violence dramatically came to the fore from 17-19 March 2004.[88] Following allegations that Serbs had caused the drowning of Kosovar children in the river Ibar, over 50,000 people participated in 33 major riots taking place across Kosovo for three days. The violence led to the death of 19 people and injuries to over 1,000 others, to the displacement of around 4,500 people and to the destruction of hundreds of houses as well as dozens of Orthodox churches, some from the Middle Ages. The failure of UNMIK and KFOR to protect people and property has tainted international legitimacy and credibility ever since.[89] Despite indications that violence would flare up, all international actors were taken by surprise. Once the violence had erupted, it was unclear who was responsible and who would give and enforce orders, as responsibility was divided between KFOR, UNMIK Police and the KPS.[90]

The violence was partly orchestrated.[91] But instead of facing a military adversary – the task NATO was prepared for – KFOR troops faced crowds composed partly of women, adolescents and even young children. While some demonstrators carried military weapons, most used sticks, stones, Molotov cocktails, or their bare hands to attack members of 'the other' ethnic communities as well as domestic and international security forces.

The absence of a KFOR contingency plan for large-scale riots and disparate responses proved disastrous. Outnumbered German troops made room for rioters who subsequently destroyed Serb houses and churches in

Prizren. The French evacuated Serb inhabitants of the village of Svinjare, yet did not stop the destruction of their village. In Mitrovica, French KFOR worked against, not with, UNMIK Police and the KPS.[92] Yet there are also positive examples of KFOR responses. 700 troops from Sweden and other countries prevented a mob several thousand strong from getting to Gračanica and its medieval church, one of the most important Orthodox monuments in the Balkans. The soldiers, assaulted with sticks and stones, held the line, fighting "a medieval battle", while at the same time trying to respect the principle of proportionality, avoiding civilian casualties.[93]

There are various reasons for KFOR failures during the March 2004 riots. National caveats and RoE prevented a harmonised approach. According to one journalistic account, only 17 out of 55 units were allowed to engage in CRC and no KFOR officer kept track of other activity bans imposed by capitals of troop-contributing countries. A Swedish officer said that some units "were probably not allowed to stay out after five, P.M."[94] The RoE governing German troops barred the Germans from using their weapons against civilians, except in extreme circumstances. Troops did not have proper equipment to disperse crowds without causing massive casualties – as in Bosnia, assault rifles proved of little value against stone-throwing teenagers. Also, there was little mobility between the sectors, preventing the reinforcement of troops across MNB boundaries. COM KFOR did not have sufficient 'battle space' information and was hampered by the autonomy of the MNB. The fact that KFOR was taken by surprise also indicates a lack of prior intelligence gathering, analysis and early warning mechanisms.

NATO was reluctant to publicly admit that it had failed to contain the riots.[95] Still, NATO members tried to rectify shortcomings. For instance, German troops were now allowed to use tear gas in order to disperse crowds. Also, troops received more training in CRC. Moreover, KFOR worked towards better information and intelligence gathering and exchange, and the position of COM KFOR was bolstered. Furthermore, mobility of the MNBs/MTFs across sectors was enhanced, allowing troops in one sector to aid troops in another one. The creation of a Tactical Reserve Manoeuvre Battalion, placed under the direct command of COM KFOR, was a major element of the new force structure. Another was the better use of KFOR assets such as helicopters and bulldozers that had partly been idle during the riots.[96]

Another consequence of March 2004 was that KFOR, as well as other international actors, became more circumspect when cooperating with domestic institutions. Kosovar politicians as well as the KPS were seen as having failed to stop the riots. While many KPS officers performed bravely, others allegedly went so far as participating in the riots by throwing petrol bombs.[97] The riots thus exposed the risks of domestic ownership.[98] In the months and years prior to March 2004, KFOR had cooperated closely with the KPS. Following the riots, it scaled down such cooperation, no longer seeing the KPS as a reliable partner.[99] (By 2007, this stance had again been reversed, as shown further below.)

KFOR responded to another type of criticism as well. After the war, KFOR and other international missions contributed to a boom in human trafficking in Kosovo because of increasing demand for commercial sexual services, which often were not offered voluntary. There were brothels in Kosovo and Macedonia, serving international personnel on leave from duty in Kosovo and also 'internationals' stationed in Macedonia. First, international organisations turned a blind eye to the problem[100] – human trafficking was not even mentioned in military intelligence reports.[101] A zero-tolerance policy on trafficking, institutionalised at NATO's Istanbul Summit in 2004, led troop commanders to control their troops more tightly and to designate notorious bars and hotels off-limit.[102] As law enforcement pressure grew, the industry went underground and also declined. Moreover, traffickers reduced risks through lower levels of violence and exploitation and by using more domestic victims.[103] Such changes were only partly due to international zero tolerance policies – the scaling-down of the international presence contributed more to reducing the demand for commercial sex.

NATO and Serious Crime in Kosovo Before and After Independence

International actors interpreted the March 2004 riots as a sign that the 'standards before status' policy had failed. In late 2005, therefore, major powers decided to resolve the status question. Negotiations were held in 2006 and 2007, yet failed to reach consensus between Serbia and the Kosovar leadership in Pristina. The limbo ended on 17 February 2008, when the Kosovo Assembly declared independence.[104] Ever since, the Serbian government and Kosovo Serbs have tried to ensure that the North of Kosovo (dominated by Serbs) and Serbian enclaves in other parts of Kosovo (where most Kosovo Serbs live) retain their links to Belgrade. Much has been written about Kosovo's road to independence and the role of major powers.[105] This section focuses on the under-researched fight against serious crime during this period.

Types of Serious Crime

Assessing serious crime in Kosovo is difficult because of a lack of reliable primary data,[106] the difficulty to obtain confidential reports outlining crime problems and the tendency of interlocutors to overstate or understate serious crime in order to promote institutional or personal interests. The following overview is therefore sketchy.[107]

One of the main problems affecting Kosovo has been organised crime. One scholar writes that Kosovo's crime scene has been dominated by around a dozen clans headed by either former KLA members or persons close to the KLA.[108] The German Federal Intelligence Service (Bundesnachrichtendienst, BND), in a report from 2005, states that Kosovo was divided into three organised crime zones controlled by former KLA leaders with close ties to ethnic Albanian leaders in Kosovo and also Albanians whose influence stretched into Southern Serbia and Macedonia. Around 20 criminal groups supposedly worked for the masterminds of organised crime.[109]

According to one estimate from 2007, organised crime revenues equal more than one quarter of the GDP of Kosovo.[110] Proceeds from drug trafficking probably have exceeded the value of revenues from all other crimes. Kosovo has been a crucial transit zone for heroin shipped from Afghanistan and Turkey via the Balkans to Western Europe, and served as a main hub for organising the drug trade.[111] According to an UNMIK Police officer interviewed in 2008, each week 200-300 kg of heroin are smuggled through Kosovo destined for Switzerland alone (a country where around every tenth Kosovar resides).[112] Kosovo has also become a transit point for cocaine and other illicit drugs. There are even reports of opium cultivation and heroin laboratories in Kosovo,[113] as well as cannabis fields possibly protected by landmines.[114] According to the UN, the drug trade in Kosovo "appears to be well organised, with perhaps five regional strongmen controlling corners of the territory and distributing to diaspora clan members in specific destination countries."[115]

While authorities have seized only relatively small amounts of drugs in Kosovo, the iceberg has been believed to be very big. The main indicators for this are large seizures of drugs in Western Europe coming from Kosovo and numerous intelligence reports on drugs. One could ask why drug traffickers would use Kosovo as a transit country if bringing drugs, e.g., via the highway linking Sofia and Belgrade, would be faster. Yet some of the actors that had established networks in the 1990s were still based in Kosovo or maintained close links to Kosovo. Weak policing especially in the North and also along the border with Macedonia is conducive to trafficking as well.

From the rugged territory of northwestern Macedonia, smugglers and traffickers have conducted lucrative cross-border trade into Kosovo.[116] Insignificant seizures therefore point at weak intelligence-led policing (and also, possibly, the quick transshipment of drugs instead of long storage, making detection more tricky), rather than an insignificant drug trafficking industry.

Human trafficking continued as well. Several years into the 'peace', human trafficking had declined and also been pushed underground. Yet the industry had not altogether disappeared. Women, including some from countries such as Moldova, were reportedly exploited in Prizren in brothels along the Pristina-Skopje highway, and elsewhere in Kosovo.[117] By late 2008, an estimated 200 brothels were still operating in Kosovo.[118] Another criminal branch has been human smuggling, with Kosovo serving as a transit zone for people smuggled further West. By late 2008 Kosovo still had no visa regime, leading migrants to come to Kosovo from Turkey, African countries and elsewhere, many of whom arrived without valid papers.[119]

Another lucrative criminal activity in Kosovo has been the trafficking of weapons. The combined trafficking of various goods in Kosovo is a legacy of the war and has survived the war. After the war, arms smuggling networks diversified, selling weapons to countries in the region and beyond (as the Kosovo market was saturated).

In addition, criminals used Kosovo to smuggle timber, cigarettes, cars and fuel. The fuel price differential between Serbia and Kosovo, for instance, led to the smuggling of fuel from Serbia. Only when Serbia, in 2008, imposed VAT at the fuel pumps, did this price differential diminish and smuggling decline. But even then, in the North of Kosovo smugglers and traffickers have had relatively free reign due to a lack of international and domestic law enforcement. Following the declaration of independence, a Serbian mob destroyed two border posts in the North, leading to a temporary increase in smuggling.[120] There were also allegations of illicit fuel pipelines linking Kosovo and Montenegro.[121]

Inter-ethnic crime also continued to preoccupy international actors, although incidents were sporadic and relatively small-scale. By 2008, it was possible again to wander the streets of Pristina and speak Serbian. But elsewhere, it was still not perfectly safe for a person from one ethnic group to wander into an area dominated by 'the other' group. For instance, Serbian shepherds crossing the boundaries of Serbian enclaves ran high risks.[122] Moreover, individuals returning to their houses were not safe. And in Mitrovica, numerous incidents, some of them costing lives, underscored that Kosovo was still a place where sparks could cause big fires.

Other forms of political violence also preoccupied security forces, including war crimes cases. By early 2009, UNMIK had handed over to the European Union Rule of Law Mission in Kosovo (EULEX) all files on investigations. Of the 250 files on criminal cases, some 50 concerned war crimes.[123] Another objective of 'internationals' was counter-terrorism. Kosovo has been one of the sites of the US 'war on terror'. Washington was worried, for instance, about Kosovars studying at religious schools abroad.[124] Some of the violent groups based in Kosovo or having links to Kosovo were presumed to be well-armed. At least one of what a confidential intelligence report produced by UNMIK called "Kosovo Albanian terrorist groups" was believed to possess anti-aircraft missiles.[125] Illicit non-state armed groups that were partly politically motivated were cause of much international worry, not least due to their capacity to attack international personnel.

It is important to note that no neat distinctions between different types of serious crime in Kosovo can be drawn, as the same actors could commit several crimes. According to a UN intelligence report, there are ties between drug traffickers, weapons dealers and terrorist groups operating in Kosovo.[126] Some weapons and drugs traffickers, for instance, were believed to share their smuggling routes and couriers to import and export weapons and drugs to and from Western Europe. Moreover, economic and political crime overlapped. Many acts of inter-ethnic violence, including the March 2004 riots, may have been instigated by criminals.[127] Criminals can benefit from peace operations since intervention forces stem the escalation of hostilities to a point where trade becomes impossible.[128] Yet smugglers and traffickers equally have an interest in flaming up tension. Inter-ethnic violence, especially in Mitrovica, obscured inter-ethnic criminal cooperation behind the scenes,[129] focused the attention of security forces on peacekeeping instead of policing and allowed criminals to make money. According to (unconfirmed information), during the March 2004 riots trucks carrying heroin and cocaine crossed the Kosovo border/boundary line.[130]

Serious crime in Kosovo has undergone transformation. After the brutal post-war period when former fighters and criminal groups staked their claims, subsequent years saw relatively few reported incidents of violence related to organised crime. Even when taking into account underreporting (which may be higher in Kosovo than elsewhere), the murder rate has dropped significantly in Kosovo, by 75 percent in five years, according to the UN.[131] This can be read as a sign of criminals' delineating territorial and functional divisions of labour.[132] Moreover, ethnic Albanian trafficking groups used to be notorious for their use of violence against criminal rivals, trafficked women and children and anyone standing in their way. More law enforcement pressure, inside and outside of Kosovo, has led traffickers to diversify into other activities and to reduce levels of violence, thus reducing the risk of exposure.

The transformation of crime is most obvious when looking at the increase in business crime. This increase, in turn, indicates criminal state capture. International institutions and observers argue that criminal networks in Kosovo "extend to various socio-economic sectors and into politics".[133] An UNMIK official working in the Criminal Intelligence Unit (CIU) was surprised to see, when taking up the new position, that many individuals in senior political positions were accused of having committed crimes.[134] One journalist argues that political parties in Kosovo resembled organised crime networks, as shown by the fact that politicians were living in multi-million dollar houses.[135] One UNMIK official said: "When we talk of organised crime in Kosovo, we are very much dealing with politicians, [and] ministers."[136]

An important role in Kosovo has been played by what the German Federal Intelligence Service calls "multifunctional persons".[137] Such individuals are entrenched in politics, business and the security forces in Kosovo. They have occupied senior official positions themselves or have been close to powerful officeholders, and have enabled organised crime groups to operate. Investigations have generally failed to disclose links between organised crime and politics,[138] and to produce incriminating evidence against 'multifunctional persons' that courts need to prosecute crimes such as the hiring of hit men, the corruption of public officials and money laundering.[139] Besides shortcomings of international crime-fighting, prosecution lagged behind because, paradoxically, prosecution depended on support from the same people in positions of power who might be the target of prosecution. Moreover, few witnesses dared to speak out and many of those who testified were threatened or killed.

At the time of independence, Kosovo thus resembled Bosnia at the turn of the millennium: While more traditional forms of organised crime continued, these were complemented and partially substituted by business crimes. While harder to detect than the former, their societal impact is significant. Privatisation fraud, tax fraud and money laundering have deprived Kosovo institutions of much-needed capital.[140] Such crimes have been complemented by credit card fraud, Bingo fraud, cyber crimes and other illegal activities. Numerous signs pointed at the dodgy nature of capitalism in Kosovo. For example, the large amounts of money deposited in banks, the impressive building activity and the large number of big banking institutions can be explained neither by remittances from abroad nor legal economic activities in Kosovo.[141]

An increase in business crime has gone hand in hand with starker social stratification. As reckless and fraudulent capitalism took hold, personal greed undermined traditional redistribution mechanisms that had allowed even weak members of ethnic Albanian society to survive the discrimination practiced during Milošević's Yugoslavia. Organised crime thus partly reflects a change in values.[142] This transformation has been of little benefit to most Kosovo citizens.

Five Problems of Crime-Fighting in Kosovo

The following sections examine crime-fighting in Kosovo. Since KFOR activities in the law enforcement realm cannot be isolated from the activities of civilian actors, the latter are discussed as well. The analysis reveals five features, all of which are problematic.

First, Kosovo has seen paramilitarisation across the board. The military has been policised, while police forces have been militarised. Second, KFOR involvement has often been direct. As in Bosnia, this defies the official mantra that the military merely supports the police. Third, international actors have failed to coordinate crime-fighting activities, duplicated one another, engaged in turf battles, blamed each other for failures and claimed success for their own respective institution. Fourth, crime-fighting by 'internationals' has not been effective. Fifth, counter-crime activities have been conducted in a largely unaccountable manner. There is much empirical and analytical overlap between these problems. But for the sake of clarity, they are discussed separately.

1) Policisation and militarisation. One of the major lessons learned from the March 2004 riots is the need for CRC capabilities. Subsequently, regular KFOR units, who at home had been trained to fight wars, received CRC training within their respective MTF. As independence drew closer, all MTFs had CRC capabilities. Troops received much of their CRC training in Kosovo, although some troops had also received CRC training before their deployment. Some troop-contributing nations had advantages in this field. As Kosovo became more stable, the US deployed mainly the National Guard. Officers of the National Guard emphasised that the National Guard is a good fit for Kosovo since troops are used to interacting with the local population and with civilian institutions.[143]

Some of the 'regular' peacekeeping activities are indistinguishable from crime-fighting. By deterring violence through patrols and through the display of force, KFOR prevented inter-ethnic crime. One of the most important services provided by KFOR to minorities was to accompany travellers. In 2007, for example, US troops escorted Serbian secondary school children who were travelling from the enclave where they lived to a monastery.[144] Such activities ran counter to the professed view that soldiers should not "escort kids to kindergarten" (Condoleezza Rice). KFOR also participated in go-and-see visits, protecting persons who were considering a return but first wanted to inspect their houses.

KFOR support of crime-fighting was partly inadvertent. Ever since moving into the province, KFOR established checkpoints where vehicles and their drivers and passengers were searched. The primary aim was to detect weapons and weapons smugglers, as well as wanted persons. Weapons clearly were a threat to a safe and secure environment. KFOR variably characterised weapons smuggling as organised crime or as a military activity.[145] Yet no matter how the problem was constructed, KFOR accepted that checking the weapons trade was clearly within its mandate. Yet often, soldiers would not find weapons but drugs and other contraband. The likelihood of coming into contact with smugglers was particularly high in border zones. KFOR patrolled Kosovo's borders, especially the one with Macedonia, but also the boundary line/border between Kosovo and Serbia. In one incident in January 2008, KFOR, using aerial surveillance, observed people with mules in a border zone. After apprehending the men, KFOR found that they had been trying to smuggle coffee, not weapons (the smugglers were then handed over to the KPS).[146] Activities clearly within the military mandate thus spilled over into the policing realm.

KFOR also had special teams used for operations requiring particular skills and technology. The most secretive of these was an Intelligence, Surveillance and Reconnaissance (ISR) unit, which included British Special Forces. The unit was based at Film City, KFOR's headquarters near Pristina. It was intelligence-led, operating assets such as drones and observing suspects. ISR members would often wear civilian cloths and would conduct highly clandestine surveillance operations.[147] ISR members would limit themselves to observation, leaving actual arrests to SWAT teams of KFOR or UNMIK Police.

ISR focused on persons accused of serious crime. These persons were put on a targeting list, also called flip book. ISR members, G2/J2 personnel, the MSU, UNMIK Police and other intelligence-led military and civilian institutions had access to the list (except for the KPS, which revealed a lack of trust in the integrity of domestic security forces). When KFOR saw wanted persons it was obliged to arrest them. Most of the individuals listed presumably were suspected war criminals and persons suspected of having committed murder and other grave crimes after the war.

KFOR commanders understood that any threat to a safe and secure environment was best countered through intelligence-led work. As a consequence, military intelligence personnel assumed a crucial role within KFOR. J2/G2 officers would write reports for COM KFOR and MTF commanders. Intelligence officers also exchanged information and intelligence with Liaison and Monitoring Teams (LMT, see below). Moreover, they closely liaised with UNMIK Police and the KPS. Crime-fighting is not the prerogative of military intelligence. But in Kosovo, risks emanating from criminals were inseparable from risks to military security. Military intelligence officers therefore could not afford to ignore drug traffickers and others the military professed it was not particularly interested in.

At KFOR headquarters, the main institution responsible for collecting and analyzing information and intelligence was the Joint Intelligence Operations Center (JIOC). The JIOC brought together the various intelligence-led actors within KFOR, including the MSU (see below). Representatives of UNMIK participated in meetings, too. ISR, although not formally part of the JIOC, would conduct operations to support the JIOC. While most internationals working in the field of intelligence saw the JIOC as valuable, intelligence was exchanged mainly informally, outside of institutions (see further below).

A crucial role was played by the National Intelligence Cell (NIC). Each of the so-called Quint nations (the US, UK, France, Italy and Germany), the most influential countries in Kosovo, had a NIC, as did around a dozen other countries. The NICs were not official KFOR assets. Much of the intelligence gathered by the NIC was collected at the MTF level, by troops from the country of the respective NIC. The NICs reportedly were at the centre of many intelligence-led activities and – as shown below – were much criticised for not sharing intelligence.

Military police were also important in post-war Kosovo. A few troop-contributing nations, especially Italy and France, had constabulary forces that complemented their regular military forces. Other countries had to improvise. In their home countries, the military police would enforce discipline among troops and also conduct initial investigations into accidents and crimes involving military forces, before handing over cases to civil police forces. In Kosovo, the absence of a functioning civil police and criminal justice system pushed the military police much deeper onto civilian turf than would have been possible at home.

KFOR elements focusing on CIMIC inadvertently contributed to crime-fighting, too. Across Kosovo, as one of the responses to the March 2004 riots, KFOR established LMTs. Similar to the LOT houses in Bosnia, the task of the LMT was to find out about the needs of the local population. By late 2008, LMTs staged around 600 patrols a day.[148] Consisting of small groups of soldiers, the LMTs were to win ‘hearts and minds’. LMT personnel would help improve living conditions through quick-impact projects and support for larger construction and sustainable livelihood projects. In contrast to Bosnia, LMTs were based in military camps instead of rented houses, mainly due to concerns for force protection. By late 2008, there was only one team, in Orahovac, that lived permanently within a community.[149]

Crime-fighting was not an official task of the LMT. However, the LMTs were to collect information, serving as the ‘eyes and ears’ of MTF commanders.[150] Frequently, LMTs came across allegations and evidence of crime.[151] LMT reports were therefore of interest to intelligence-led actors. In at least two MTFs, KFOR officers confirmed that LMTs gathered information about possible illegal activities while conducting CIMIC projects.[152] The LMT thus de facto, although not officially, contributed to intelligence-led operations against serious crime;[153] the LMT is one more example of the blurred line between CIMIC and crime-fighting. To be sure, LMTs, trained in CIMIC rather than crime-fighting, were not necessarily well-informed about crime. In one case, an UNMIK official asked a LMT for information about crime in an area that everybody – except the LMT – knew was badly affected by crime.[154]

One of the most important KFOR assets in the fight against serious crime was the MSU. As shown above, the deployment of the MSU to post-war Kosovo had been fraught with problems. Around the time of independence, the MSU had improved its performance in filling the gap between regular military forces and civilian actors. In Pristina, MSU members were directly responsible for security. Moreover, COM KFOR apparently relied a lot on the intelligence-collection capabilities of the MSU. The MSU served as the expert consultancy authority for COM KFOR on crime and counter-terrorism.[155] ISR members relied on the MSU as well, occasionally asking the constabularies for human intelligence (HUMINT) material.[156]

For collecting information and intelligence, the MSU used several methods. Covert observations were one method, quick-impact CIMIC projects were another. Concerns about the instrumentalisation of development projects for security purposes notwithstanding, the MSU exchanged material aid for information and intelligence.[157] Yet most commonly, the MSU would collect open-source information while on patrol. According to the MSU, it was able to present itself as a reliable partner of the local population and understand the public mood because it talked to citizens on the street and had a posture less martial than the one of regular KFOR units.[158]

A major task of the MSU was to support CRC. MSU members were to be deployed in situations where the KPS and SPU could no longer control the situation. Moreover, the MSU trained riot police of the KPS and UNMIK, and also sent CRC instructors to the MTF to improve the capabilities of regular KFOR troops in this area.[159]

The policisation of KFOR occurred simultaneously with the militarisation of police forces. UNMIK Police had units that were trained and equipped for tasks beyond the remit of normal police forces. For CRC, UNMIK Police deployed the SPU. On several occasions these units intervened in riots (their legitimacy was much undermined when, in February 2007, UNMIK riot police from Romania unintentionally shot dead two demonstrators with rubber bullets at a rally in Pristina[160]). UNMIK also drew on SWAT teams for high-risk operations. Team Six, with elite police forces from different countries, stood permanently ready for high-risk arrest operations. One UNMIK Police officer said that special teams were mainly preoccupied with arresting 'ordinary' criminals such as murderers, not so much members of organised crime groups.[161] This indicates that KFOR/MSU was deeply involved in the arrest of the latter. Some UNMIK Police officers were from constabulary forces. In at least one case, UNMIK designated a constabulary officer to be the liaison officer with KFOR.[162] Military-police relations were thus, in some cases, 'militarised' on both sides.

The trend toward paramilitarisation was not limited to international forces. A major objective of international security assistance was to improve the CRC capabilities of the KPS. KPS riot units received training from UNMIK Police as well as from units within KFOR, particularly from the MSU but also from Military Police. Preparations for CRC inevitably forged close, direct links between KFOR and the KPS. Since the KPS constituted the first line of defence and KFOR the third, KFOR needed to know what the first linc was doing.[163]

To build domestic capacity for high-risk operations and intelligence-led work, the KPS received surveillance equipment as well as information and intelligence from UNMIK and KFOR. Moreover, international actors sponsored the creation of domestic SWAT teams (such as the First Intervention Team) tasked with arresting dangerous suspects and liberating hostages. On the regional level, platoon-sized Regional Operational Support Units stood ready for CRC as well as high-risk arrest operations.

Capacity-building forged particularly close relations between the KPS and the MSU: The latter taught the former skills in CRC, shooting, forensics, close protection and other areas. To facilitate cooperation, the MSU had a permanent liaison officer within the KPS. Unlike the constabularies in Bosnia, the MSU in Kosovo did not train the domestic police in wiretapping.[164] This is because the fight against organised crime was not explicitly within the remit of the MSU and UNMIK Police had executive powers in this area. However, COM KFOR could call on the MSU to support efforts against organised crime.

KPS officers saw the MSU as a crucial partner and mentor. One officer said that the MSU was always willing to help. When the KPS needed information and intelligence, the MSU would collect and share it.[165] The MSU supported the KPS also by organising helicopter rides for aerial surveillance and by installing MSU equipment (including surveillance equipment) at the KPS Headquarters. Moreover, the MSU was often present when the KPS arrested local strongmen. It must be noted that although the MSU cooperated closely with the KPS, it often did not inform the KPS beforehand about operations, due to fear of leaks.[166]

International capacity-building not only facilitated the paramilitarisation of the KPS, but also of the incipient Kosovo army. International actors, after the war, had seen the creation of the KPC as a way of providing jobs to former KLA combatants and also as a force for stability. In 2008, the KPC was replaced by the Kosovo Stability Force (KSF). Since NATO was to deter any external military threat, the 2,500 strong KSF was limited to disposing of explosives and responding to civil emergencies. Pending potential contributions to peacekeeping operations elsewhere, the KSF's remit was thus domestic. According to a leading Kosovo politician, the KSF was to protect "the internal safety of people and property in Kosovo."[167] This job description again illustrates the blurred distinction between internal and external security and between policing and military work.

2) Direct involvement of KFOR in crime-fighting. After the stormy immediate post-conflict phase, international actors agreed that KFOR should scale down its law enforcement activities. However, dynamics on the ground around the time of independence reveal the travails of the military's handing over responsibility to the police. Even though KFOR was no longer as deeply and directly involved in crime-fighting as had been the case right after war, involvement continued to be substantial.

For some high-risk arrest operations, regular KFOR units created an outer security cordon, leaving the actual arrest to UNMIK, KPS SWAT teams, or the MSU. This was the role that KFOR preferred, in order to minimise risks for troops and to underline police prerogatives. But in some cases KFOR teams would make the arrests themselves and then turn over the suspects to the police. Autonomous KFOR arrest operations were directed at those suspected of keeping or selling explosives, weapons, or drugs, as well as at suspected war criminals.[168]

At borders, regular troops made direct contact with suspected criminals, too. On the MTF level, KFOR tried to ensure that the KPS or the Border and Boundary Police would accompany troops on patrol.[169] Yet due to the weakness of these forces, many patrols consisted of soldiers only. In at least one MTF, KFOR, in late 2008, remained highly active in securing the border against smuggling not only of weapons, but also of drugs and human beings.[170]

KFOR also had a policy of putting up checkpoints jointly with the police. But many checkpoints were manned by KFOR alone because UNMIK Police and the KPS did not have enough officers. At checkpoints, KFOR would try to seize guns, drugs and other contraband.[171] In late 2008, KFOR continued to patrol towns and rural areas. In case the patrols came across anyone suspicious, they would control documents and call the police.[172]

At the centre of KFOR's crime-fighting efforts were the MSU. By late 2008, the MSU, still around 300 strong, were composed of Italian Carabinieri and French Gendarmes, at a ratio of roughly three to one. One MSU activity was to operate checkpoints. The main purpose was to confiscate weapons. But personnel would also come across drugs and other smuggled goods, as well as minor offences, and then inform the KPS. At one checkpoint in late 2008, the MSU stopped around a dozen cars within 1.5 hours.[173] Moreover, the MSU searched specific sites in various parts of Kosovo. Troops would often arrive early in the morning, enter a house and seize weapons, ammunition and any contraband they would find.

The MSU would also conduct arrests. Targets could be Kosovo officials, including police officers. The MSU would take strict force protection measures especially in cases where suspects might be armed. As in Bosnia, domestic police appreciated MSU involvement in arrests, since it allowed the KPS to say that 'internationals' had ordered the arrest.[174] This trick was used especially by KPS officers who knew the target of an arrest operation and consequently had to fear retaliation. Suspected war criminals were among the persons arrested by the MSU.[175]

KFOR continued to be directly involved in crime-fighting for several reasons. One was the nature of serious crime in Kosovo. As mentioned above, sometimes the same person was suspected of having committed inter-ethnic crime and organised crime, of threatening a safe and secure environment and of posing threats to KFOR. This created much overlap between military and civilian institutions.[176]

One example was overlap between the work of the SPU and the MSU in CRC. Another example are the JIOC and the CIU. The first has been dominated by the military and has had more material resources. The CIU, in contrast, has been dominated by civilian law enforcement experts, such as police officers seconded by the German Federal Criminal Office and others with much law enforcement experience. It was created in 2000 and comprised officers from the Quint countries.[177] The CIU "was meant to pool police information on organised crime with relevant KFOR intelligence, perform analysis, spot trends and recommend targeting strategies that would make best use of scarce police resources."[178] One of its outputs has been the bi-annual, confidential Strategic Threat Assessment. For logistical reasons, the CIU was housed within KFOR Headquarters; it had regional offices as well. The two institutions were tasked with analyzing and sharing information and intelligence about risks and threats. Whether these were of a military, criminal, or terrorist nature was often impossible to say.

The expression 'safe and secure environment' offered poor guidance for delineating military from policing work, since it could be interpreted narrowly or broadly. For one EULEX official, the expression meant everything and nothing.[179] Whether the military interpreted its mandate narrowly or broadly hinged not least on military perceptions of the scale of serious crime. Some KFOR officers agreed that Kosovo was a haven of crime, whereas others disputed this assessment. One MTF officer, for instance, complained about what he regarded as an exaggeration of crime problems in Kosovo and resulting information overload: If a minor crime occurred in a far-away part of Kosovo, he would have a file on his desk the next day. The same officer also described smuggling and trafficking as small-scale rather than industrial.[180] Critics of KFOR argued, of course, that the military was downplaying crime to justify what critics saw as military complacency.

Shortcomings of police forces, discussed further below, equally pushed KFOR into the law enforcement realm. KFOR had more manpower and equipment than international and domestic police. By early 2008, around 16,000 troops remained (from 24 NATO and 10 non-NATO nations). UNMIK police, in contrast, had around 2,000 officers, most of them SPU standing ready for CRC, and around 400 officers monitoring and advising the KPS.[181] After the proclamation of independence, UNMIK downsized and largely confined itself to a monitoring role, thus further reducing its ability to effectively coordinate KFOR-KPS relations on the operational level.[182] For example, while there was much functional overlap between the MSU of KFOR and the SPU of UNMIK, the former was better able to quickly deploy troops, e.g., by using helicopters.[183]

KFOR therefore had no choice but act alone, or jointly with the KPS. UNMIK Police was supposed to coordinate KFOR support to law enforcement. This arrangement resembled the one in Bosnia, where the EUPM had placed itself between EUFOR and Bosnian police forces. However, UNMIK Police was stretched too thin to always be between KFOR and the KPS. For instance, in early 2008 no UNMIK Police officer was permanently based in Camp Bondsteel, the largest military base in Kosovo.[184] Moreover, the KPS did not need permission from UNMIK to draw on KFOR support for high-risk operations.[185] Hence, UNMIK tended to be sidelined, watching the forging of close relations between an international military mission and a domestic police force. On many occasions, KFOR would lend support to the KPS without UNMIK Police being present.[186] Neither KFOR nor the KPS saw the relatively marginal role of UNMIK Police as a problem. The KPS underlined that UNMIK was well informed about its activities.[187] For KFOR, the frequent absence of UNMIK police was not a problem either. One officer argued that KFOR did not need another level of bureaucracy.[188]

In addition to the weaknesses of UNMIK, close military-police relations also resulted from KPS dependence on KFOR. In at least one MTF, the KPS asked for support in almost all cases.[189] KFOR complied with many demands for help. At the same time, however, it treated carefully when cooperating with the KPS, due to the military's reluctance to share information and intelligence about targets and operations. KFOR feared compromising force protection and operational success because of police corruption and mismanagement, therefore confining cooperation with the KPS to non-sensitive topics. Also, KFOR, before and after independence, had to be status-neutral. Overly close relations with the KPS could have been construed as a de-facto recognition of Kosovo by all NATO member states.[190]

Another explanation for KFOR's continuing direct involvement in law enforcement is military activism. As argued in the first part of this publication, this explanation underestimates fear of military mission creep. In Kosovo, there is little evidence of the military trying to do too much; instead, it was often accused of doing too little. The MSU are an exception, however. The force proactively placed itself within civil-military grey zones and eagerly produced output such as checkpoints, patrols, raids and investigations. As shown below, international civilian representatives complained about this activism. Moreover, there is not much evidence that constabulary output has led to impressive outcome, or that it has had any strategic impact.

KFOR's direct involvement in crime-fighting thus resulted from several factors. Functional needs to draw on military assets (including surveillance technology such as drones and helicopters with thermal vision and Signal Intelligence [SigInt] capabilities) played a role. The relative weakness of international and domestic civilian institutions was important, too. Moreover, while many KFOR officers were reluctant recruits, the MSU were rather proactive. Hence, law enforcement in Kosovo did not so much reflect a strategic plan attributing clear roles to particular actors. Rather, it resulted from a mix of functional requirements and institutional preferences.

3) Cooperation problems, turf battles and blame-games. Another problem of crime-fighting in Kosovo pertains to cooperation and coordination. Kosovo perfectly illustrates the difficulty of creating sound security governance and SSG systems. Both KFOR and civilian institutions have tended to protect their turf vis-à-vis other institutions, blame each other for failures and claim success for themselves.

International actors usually explain the lack of systematic crime-fighting by pointing at domestic actors.[191] Problems pertained to a lack of personnel, material, logistical and financial capacity, as well as insufficient laws and regulations, witness protection and accountability. Many have hailed the KPS as an example of successful institution-building. Indeed, the creation of a new police force from scratch was impressive. By 2008, the KPS employed around 6,000 officers and was responsible for around 80 percent of law enforcement in Kosovo.[192] However, the KPS was still unable to run sophisticated counter-crime operations.[193] It also often mishandled human trafficking and other cases.[194] Furthermore, allegations abound of KPS corruption and criminal collusion. According to one KFOR officer, the

KPS often did not follow up when informed about possible smuggling operations in border areas because of close links between local smugglers and some KPS officers.[195] In fall 2008, around 1,400 Kosovo Police officers were under investigation, some for corruption.[196]

Adding to these problems were KPS operations in Serb-dominated areas. In one enclave, Serbs complained that an all-Kosovar SWAT team raided a house, using excessive force in order to frighten Serbs.[197] One of the minority concerns about the KPS was that many officers were former members of the KLA. After independence, many Serb officers left the KPS, making the force even more vulnerable to charges of ethnically biased policing. Serbs complained about harassment by the border police as well.[198]

While domestic actors accepted some of the blame, they also pointed at problems affecting international missions. Indeed, the 'international community' was all but unified. Many international and domestic political actors, as well as most Kosovo citizens, had a negative view of UNMIK. One Kosovo journalist says that the UN administration in general has been a failure, but particularly so with regard to the rule of law.[199] The presence of organised crime, the risk of inter-ethnic violence, the failure to arrest and prosecute wanted war criminals and the merger of crime and politics were cited as clear evidence that UNMIK had failed to establish rule of law.

Since the beginning of the mission, UNMIK had suffered from a lack of pre-deployment planning; heterogeneous personnel, with some staff coming from countries in which human rights violations and corruption were the norm;[200] underinvestment in the domestic criminal justice sector;[201] quick rotations of international personnel;[202] inflated international salaries; arrogance and aloofness of some UNMIK staff;[203] collusion and corruption;[204] the failure to document lessons learned; insufficient information and intelligence sharing; the export of a confusing mix of common and civil law; and the inability to ensure a stable supply of electricity, an affordable telephone system and other services. In Kosovo, the UN and its member states repeated many of the mistakes made in Bosnia.

Critics have charged UNMIK with sacrificing justice and the rule of law to superficial stability. According to this view, UNMIK officials, during their short rotations, did not crack down on serious crime for fear of causing instability and tainting their careers.[205] Since many suspects held official posts and were regarded by citizens as war heroes, there was a risk that arrests would cause domestic upheaval as well as casualties among international personnel. International decision-makers were therefore reticent to take any chances. Some 'internationals' went even further than avoiding conflict by going so far as forging dubious friendships. Former COM KFOR

Fabio Mini criticised this penchant as follows: "It is extremely frustrating for law enforcement personnel to spend their working day collecting evidence against leading criminals and then to find themselves invited together with them to a social event in the evening – something that happened to me on several occasions."[206] Some Kosovo strongmen skilfully played the social card, presenting themselves as mediators between the international community and Kosovo institutions and citizens.[207] Carla del Ponto, the ICTY Chief Prosecutor, complained about a lack of support from international officials in Kosovo in investigating former KLA fighters.[208] Many international officials argued that the arrest of high-level targets was not a technical problem, but one of political will (see also below).[209]

In response to its critics, UNMIK argued that this was the first time the UN had to govern an entire territory, and one in which institutions had to be created from scratch, and that member states were divided over the status of Kosovo. To salvage its reputation, UNMIK officials engaged in much spin-doctoring but failed to conceal crime-fighting failures.[210] One indicator of failure was the relatively low number of cases successfully prosecuted by UNMIK.[211] Among the main beneficiaries of the failure to indict and convict were the instigators and perpetrators of the March 2004 riots.[212]

The weakness of UNMIK pushed KFOR into a precarious law enforcement role. More specifically, KFOR charged UNMIK for insufficient exchange of information and intelligence. For instance, shortly before independence, some KFOR officers felt that UNMIK police did not properly share information with KFOR about contingency plans in case the declaration of independence spilled into violence.[213]

However, KFOR was on thin ice when criticising other international missions, being the object of much criticism itself. Critics pointed to the ineffectiveness of military crime-fighting and to accountability problems (see below), and also complained about military failures to share information and intelligence. Critics cited, for example, the alleged practice of KFOR commanders to first refer back to their national capitals after being asked for intelligence or support, and governments denying some such requests. More generally, one UNMIK official said KFOR suffered from a culture of secrecy that impeded sharing information with civilian institutions.[214] One EULEX official, despite having the highest security clearance from NATO, often did not receive material that was crucial for the official's work.[215]

Law enforcement continued to suffer due to these civil-military coordination problems. In early 2008 Serbian protesters occupied a court house building in northern Mitrovica as part of their refusal to submit to Kosovo institutions. UNMIK Police went into the building to evict the protesters. In the ensuing violence, one Ukrainian UNMIK Police officer was killed and several others wounded. KFOR soldiers, supporting and partly substituting CIVPOL officers in the melée, were wounded as well. The events once again revealed how quickly protests could turn into violent mob action and escalate even further, posing a military threat with the potential for 'protesters' to use hand grenades and automatic rifles. Given this escalation potential, smooth cooperation was essential. However, according to one UNMIK Police officer, UNMIK's pre-intervention intelligence-gathering was inadequate. Moreover, the decision to raid the court house was made in Pristina without even consulting the UNMIK police commissioner in Mitrovica or properly integrating KFOR into the planning process. The officer, who was present when his police colleague was killed, described UNMIK as incompetent.[216] One KFOR officer corroborates this impression, saying that KFOR had overestimated the capacity of UNMIK Police to control riots.[217] However, CIVPOL officers criticised KFOR for not sharing their Operational Plans with UNMIK.[218] No matter who carries the most responsibility: The events in March 2008 undermine claims that international actors had learned much from the riots that occurred in March 2004.

The troubled relationship between UNMIK and KFOR cast a shadow over the relationship between KFOR and EULEX, after the latter deployed to Kosovo in late 2008.[219] EULEX resented the deep involvement of KFOR in law enforcement. It tried to curtail the military's role in this field and place itself in between KFOR and Kosovo institutions.[220] Using CIVPOL to coordinate military support to domestic law enforcement institutions was the model developed in Bosnia. But it had taken time in Bosnia for this model to evolve, and in Kosovo conditions after independence were not conducive to a proper delineation of responsibilities. In fact, KFOR and EULEX, in early 2009, trained intensively for CRC scenarios, revealing the continuing dependency of civilians on the military.[221]

Cooperation problems, turf battles and blame games affected relations not just between international military and civilian missions. Around the time of independence, all international institutions jockeyed for influence, money and reputation. While everybody professed to be cooperating with others, behind the scenes competition and charges of wrong-doing reigned. One example is the relationship between UNMIK and EULEX during the transition phase (or, to use the official term, the 'reconfiguration' phase).[222] In late 2008, as EULEX began to replace UNMIK, EULEX officials were frustrated by UNMIK. According to one EULEX police officer, UNMIK was doing everything it could to make life difficult for EULEX.[223] From the perspective of UNMIK, the situation was different. For instance, one UN official said that EULEX wanted to take over UNMIK cars while at the same time asking UNMIK to remain fully deployed during the transition phase.[224] In some ways, the transition from UNMIK to EULEX resembled the chaotic transition from IPTF to EUPM in Bosnia.

EULEX was adamant that it would enforce the law irrespective of political considerations. Representatives also underlined that the mission better integrated police and criminal justice components and that more staff would work on investigations into serious crime than had been the case under UNMIK.[225] However, EULEX, too, had to balance a forceful approach with the politically imposed requirement to maintain stability in Kosovo. When EULEX officials explained to decision-makers in Brussels and in national capitals that going after criminals might cause international casualties, the decision-makers shifted into lower gear.[226]

There were also concerns that information and intelligence collection and sharing would not improve much under EULEX, or that problems might increase. After all, under UNMIK, a few countries had dominated institutions such as the CIU (renamed under EULEX to EU Office for Criminal Intelligence). This practice was maintained to some extent – selection for sensitive posts was based on merit. Still, EU practices made it difficult to marginalise intelligence institutions from countries such as Bulgaria that elicited little trust among officials from old EU member states.[227] Another concern was that EU member states had more direct stakes in Kosovo than UNMIK contributors such as Nigeria or India, leading to even more politicised law enforcement as European capitals would try to exert direct influence.[228] Also, balancing the different elements of EULEX was not easy. For example, EULEX prosecutors and judges were unhappy about what they regarded as a mission dominated by police.[229]

One type of actor around whom criticism converged were intelligence-led institutions. Many KFOR, UNMIK and EULEX officials complained that the NIC served primarily perceived national needs. Information and intelligence allegedly were not properly shared with other nations, COM KFOR, the JIOC and UNMIK, especially the CIU. This was problematic especially for UNMIK since the CIU was only an analysis unit, lacking the capacity to collect information and intelligence.[230] National intelligence officials operating the NICs allegedly fed material to their respective capitals first.[231] Often, intelligence reports would never make their way back to Kosovo. One intelligence official said that he used to work five metres away from a NIC representing the official's country and that he had the same security clearance as the officers who worked in that NIC, but did not know what they were doing because of what the official regarded as "paranoia" on the part of the NIC officials. Reports given to the NIC by the official would sometimes not be given back because the NIC had increased security levels for the reports; as a consequence, the official always made a copy.[232]

Officials from foreign intelligence services seemed to play the most problematic role. A scandal in November 2008, when agents of the BND (Bundesnachrichtendienst [German Federal Intelligence Service]) were arrested,[233] indicated the scale of involvement of foreign services, and the lack of caution by these agents showed the leeway services felt they had in Kosovo. According to one press report, in late 2008 the BND alone had eleven agents rotating in and out of Kosovo. Some missions were so secret that neither the official BND representative nor the German ambassador was informed.[234] Some critics also alleged that governments and their secret services protected from arrest, or even paid, suspected criminals who were providing information about crime abroad. According to one official with many years of experience in Kosovo, much was known about major criminal suspects, but the Embassies of powerful countries and foreign services interfered with the work of international and domestic police. Asked whether it would be possible to arrest major criminal suspects without military support and what the official saw as political interference, the official estimated it would take around two months, if the police were only allowed to do their job.[235] One study singles out the US as the country hampering European law enforcement efforts.[236] Alleged interference in law enforcement by any foreign government or service, if true, would not only be legally problematic, but – short-term information advantages notwithstanding – in the long run would also undermine crime-fighting in Kosovo and abroad, by allowing criminals to use Kosovo as a safe haven.

Another institution that drew criticism was the MSU. One KFOR officer complained about Carabinieri weapons-harvesting operations,[237] saying that raids turned the local population against KFOR. Moreover, from his point of view, MSU operations were not effective, since "searching for weapons in Kosovo is like digging sand on a beach with a tea spoon." His main concern was that he was not informed well in advance about MSU operations. Therefore, in one recent case, when he learned that an MSU operation was about to take place, he vetoed it. He also said that if the MSU staged an operation without his approval and things turned violent, if asked for support he would be reluctant to send reinforcements. Communication was difficult, he said, as regular KFOR units and the Carabinieri would often talk past each other. Such tension mirrors disputes that occurred in Bosnia.

As shown in the previous chapter, LOT house personnel resented raids by the IPU. In both Bosnia and Kosovo, contingents have been weary about encroachments on their Area of Responsibility.

Many civilians were similarly unhappy about the MSU. One EULEX official said that MSU operations would have to be curtailed, stating that it was not normal that MSU members were raiding houses at dawn, only to then hand over an AK-47 to the KPS; this had to stop. The official argued that operations were motivated by personal interests: Incoming commanders felt obliged to seize at least as many weapons as their predecessors in order to further their careers.[238] A Guardia di Finanza official working for UNMIK complained that the Carabinieri did not properly support efforts to investigate irregularities.[239] Several security observers and practitioners argued that information gathered by the MSU was not shared with other international actors in Kosovo, but instead went straight to Rome. The MSU was thus seen as an Italian instrument against ethnic Albanian organised crime in Italy.

It must be noted, though, that many KFOR officers appreciated the work of the MSU. One senior officer described the force as fundamental for security in Kosovo.[240] Also, MSU officers defended their activities as necessary.[241] They argued that since 1999 they had seized significant amounts of weapons and other contraband and arrested many criminal suspects. Moreover, MSU officers argued that disputes between the MTF and the MSU were an old story, resulting mainly from the fear that constabulary operations would endanger regular troops. It was inevitable to break doors if residents did not open after two requests and absurd that LMT would then offer to repair the damage. MSU officers also dismissed the accusation that the MTFs were not properly informed before operations, arguing that the MSU G3 (Operations) officer liaised with the MTF before an operation.

Blame-games spared nobody in Kosovo. Some observers argued that business fraud was not least a consequence of international pressure for the rapid privatisation of state assets. According to one Guardia di Finanza official, Italy tried to institutionalise proper mechanisms against fraudulent privatisation practices such as the use of front companies that 'outbid' one another. But one agency of a major donor government, according to an official, obstructed such attempts, fearing that it would slow down privatisation.[242] Efforts against human trafficking similarly exemplify that international intervention is incoherent and marked by institutional competition, duplication and moral hazards. As in Bosnia, counter-trafficking efforts did not so much reflect the interests of trafficked persons and other vulnerable groups, but rather the priorities and biases of the most powerful donors and implementing agencies.[243]

By winter 2008/2009, many practitioners and observers in Kosovo were frustrated about the slow political, security and economic progress in Kosovo. Few people approved of the performance of their own institution and, even more so, the performance of other institutions. Indeed, shortcomings are discernible everywhere. All critics were therefore sitting in a glass house.

4) Problems of effectiveness. International counter-crime efforts often boiled down to issues of effectiveness. By mid 2009, Kosovo had not yet reached the stage of Bosnia. In Kosovo, smuggling and trafficking were still pervasive, many suspects (including suspected war criminals) were at large and inter-ethnic crime continued.[244] The continuing presence of serious crime in Kosovo indicates that success has been tactical, not strategic. While military and civilian actors have produced much output and some outcome, there are few signs of policy impact.[245]

KFOR carries some responsibility for law enforcement failures. Kosovo citizens would be better off if KFOR had been a better crime fighter. Many civilians were weary about military encroachment on law enforcement turf and said that the military was not good at police-type tasks. However, the need for military support was acknowledged. One UNMIK Police officer said: "As a police officer, I do not like military involvement in policing. But here in Kosovo, only the military has the means required for some operations. Yet they are the wrong branch since they do not have the training."[246]

In a way, KFOR was 'damned if it did and damned if it did not'. Often, the mission was criticised for interpreting its mandate too narrowly. As shown above, KFOR tended to ignore the smuggling and trafficking of goods other than weapons, saying that crime-fighting was not within its mandate. The ICG writes: "KFOR's approach to providing a secure environment for UNMIK's work is minimalist. It has mostly not helped to get convictions against extremist and organised crime groups."[247] One EULEX official said that the JIOC had contributed little to prosecuting those committing serious crime.[248] There were even doubts about KFOR's readiness in case of renewed large-scale inter-ethnic violence. KFOR was adamant that it had learned the lessons of March 2004. However, continuing problems with intelligence exchange and national caveats raise the question of whether KFOR would be able to cope better with large-scale riots.[249]

Whether civilian actors would be able to do so was even less certain, to be sure. Plans to scale down NATO's presence in Kosovo to a minimum, as discussed in summer 2009,[250] therefore caused much anxiety, not least among those Kosovo citizens fearing a renewed outbreak of violence.

When KFOR did get involved, problems arose. For instance, in 2007, according to one UNMIK official, KFOR destroyed a crime scene in northern Kosovo after a shooting incident.[251] Often, KFOR failed to collect evidence that could be used in court. As shown above, one rather unpopular actor among 'internationals' was the MSU. Critics argued that the MSU had not been very successful in arresting major criminals and in dismantling organised crime networks. One EULEX official emphasised that MSU operations had not greatly contributed to prosecutions.[252] Another EULEX official stated that he could not think of any major case that had been solved thanks to the MSU.[253] Also, critics argued that assets seized by the MSU had become less impressive over time. Indeed, when asked about major weapons seizures in 2008, the MSU mentioned the confiscation of six new pistols.[254] Some activities of regular military forces similarly smacked of military activism. In 2005, KFOR tried to stop illegal wood-cutting,[255] mirroring simultaneous efforts by EUFOR in Bosnia. As in Bosnia, many loggers were local residents who had no other means of income. KFOR efforts to protect trees were not sustainable; the efforts were largely symbolical.

When discussing shortcomings of KFOR, several caveats are in order. First, failures resulted partly from the cooperation problems discussed above. An UNMIK Police officer stresses that Kosovo has received much funding, but that the money was not spent systematically because too many actors were involved.[256] Many vulnerable people have fallen through the cracks of the international security architecture. Around the time of independence, returning refugees could count on no one institution to protect them from potential attack. KFOR would at times see protection as being underneath the threshold of military responsibility. The police would intervene only after a crime occurred. And other agencies did not have the means and mandates to deter any attacks. One Serbian refugee who contemplated a return to Kosovo asked an UNMIK official who would ensure his security. The official had to respond: "Nobody".[257]

In another example, fuel smuggling was thriving in northern Kosovo, until Serbia began to levy taxes at the gas pump. Smugglers could easily walk around KFOR roadblocks, or even pass through them. After all, soldiers were not trained in detecting false documents,[258] and KFOR did not feel that acting against smugglers was within its mandate. While KFOR checked the papers of trucks passing through the North, it did not carry out regular customs controls.[259] By late 2008, KFOR officers spoke of numerous illegal fuel stations in the North. But one senior officer said that KFOR would not interfere with smuggling. Sometimes KFOR would provide information to the police, but not always since KFOR assumed the police had their own informants.[260] Yet, in 2009, policing was fraught with problems in the North.[261] UNMIK police was waiting to be replaced by EULEX. As UNMIK was downsizing it did not have the capacities to stop smuggling so it delegated responsibility to the municipalities in the North and to the KPS. One UNMIK Police officer said that no proper investments had been made for two years to ensure an effective UNMIK Police.[262] EULEX, up until early 2009, was unable to operate in the North since Serbs did not endorse the mission. The Kosovo police did not stop the smuggling either since it was split along ethnic lines. Smugglers were thus able to exploit the absence of institutional leadership on the part of security actors.[263] By summer 2009, the situation had somewhat improved, as EULEX increased its presence.[264]

Such examples underline that if police had been stronger, KFOR would have needed to become involved less often and not as directly as it did. KFOR would also have needed to be less concerned about intelligence leaks or prosecution failures. The fight against some types of serious crime, especially organised crime, requires intelligence-led policing techniques. One UNMIK Police officer underlines that discovering evidence of crime has become more difficult: "The times when road blocks were effective are over. The criminals are not stupid. Now we need more sophisticated methods, such as surveillance and wiretappings."[265] In Kosovo, the military had trouble shifting from disruption strategies to the dismantling of illicit networks through intelligence-led policing.[266] But the same holds true for UNMIK. Not until 2005 did UNMIK reach a conviction (in a drugs case) that depended heavily on the tapping of telephones.[267] The shift to business crimes in Kosovo makes intelligence-led policing even more urgent. Yet intelligence-led policing in protectorates faces the problems of the large number of actors involved, short rotation periods and other challenges. One UNMIK Police officer emphasised that fighting white-collar crime is difficult enough in stable countries, but is even more difficult in Kosovo and other war-torn countries.[268]

From a broader perspective, any security force, including the military, can only do so much against crime – local law enforcement is not sufficient for crime reduction. Organised crime has thrived in Kosovo not least because of domestic crime-fighting failures by states deploying personnel to international missions in Kosovo. These states have done little to allow witnesses from Kosovo testifying in criminal cases to permanently settle abroad,[269] or to reduce demand for illicit goods supplied by Kosovo criminals. Kosovo has received much more international economic assistance than any other war-torn country.[270] It also probably has had the highest per capita number of security personnel in the world.[271] Unimpressive policy impact is only partly a result of unsystematic law enforcement in Kosovo; it also reflects regional and global conditions conducive to crime in Kosovo.

Last, it is important to note that KFOR has saved many lives in Kosovo and suffering casualties in the process. Moreover, intelligence-gathering, raids and the creation of security perimeters, although not effective in all cases, did lead to the arrest of suspects. Yet gauging military effectiveness is difficult because of the lack of primary data on serious crime; the fact that KFOR and police forces undertook many operations jointly; and the secrecy provisions prohibiting the military to publicise success based on the fear of revealing operational methods and sources. More is known about failure than success since failure attracts public scrutiny. Yet even though evidence for military success is hard to come by, it seems fair to say that Kosovo would be worse off if KFOR had not contributed to the fight against serious crime.

5) Problems of accountability. One of the main problems of international involvement in Kosovo and of crime-fighting in particular has been a lack of accountability. All international actors in Kosovo, not only KFOR, have at times operated in ways that were problematic from a democratic accountability point of view. Accountability deficits have manifested themselves in various ways.

One accountability deficit was the operational leverage given to international security forces. The commander of the MSU, for instance, needed permission only from COM KFOR to raid a house in Kosovo. In Italy, in contrast, the Carabinieri need a court order for such an operation. One critic consequently accused the MSU of operating under their own law in Kosovo.[272] An academic observer wrote in 2002 that in Kosovo, the Carabinieri tended "to act independently and have been reluctant to submit to the law as it is enforced by the UN."[273]

Also, the sudden influx of a large number of wealthy foreigners has been problematic for accountability. The large international presence has distorted the economy (driving up prices, for instance) and sustained small-scale fraud (for example, by creating demand for grey and black market goods such as pirated CDs and DVDs). Worse, 'internationals' allegedly engaged in large-scale fraud and human rights violations.[274] With regard to (forced) prostitution, an industry fuelled mainly by domestic clients, NATO's 2004 zero tolerance policy was a major step forward. However, the policy did not completely sever the link between foreign deployment and prostitution (which in unstable environments is often equivalent with trafficking). Well into 2008, some contingent commanders had not been informed about the problem of trafficking, indicating gaps in pre-deployment training. Moreover, while troops were under much tighter control than ever before in Kosovo, some allegedly continued to visit prostitutes while on leave in neighbouring countries.[275]

Prosecuting 'internationals' has been difficult. KFOR soldiers and other international personnel generally had immunity from domestic prosecution. The main responsibility in case of wrong-doing was with the home country government. Governments often simply withdrew international personnel accused of breaching laws and norms from Kosovo, without prosecuting the individuals involved.[276] According to one UNMIK Police official, every time UNMIK Police found out that an international was implicated in an offence, the UN either simply terminated the contract, or the person was withdrawn by his or her government.[277]

Moreover, there has been little oversight of foreign intelligence services operating in Kosovo. Control was merely indirect, by government branches at home. But parliamentary committees and other oversight actors generally did not have the means or mandates to scrutinise the activities of intelligence services abroad. By 2008, international actors pushed for the creation of a Kosovo intelligence agency. The lack of accountability of foreign intelligence services undermined the call for the integration of the various quasi-intelligence services linked to political parties into one single, democratically accountable Kosovo intelligence agency.[278]

The lack of accountability further manifested itself in informalisation. The formal SSG architecture in Kosovo has been highly complex. Yet for pragmatic or parochial reasons, security actors often cooperated informally, bypassing official channels. Informalisation has forged close links between nominally separate institutions. For instance, in some MTFs there was close cooperation between the LMT and J2 intelligence officers, even though these two KFOR elements were formally separate. In one case, a MTF J2 officer and the head of the LMT in this particular MTF were close friends and exchanged information and intelligence.[279] CIMIC operations were thus imbued with the spirit of intelligence.

According to one KFOR officer, "what is important is who is meeting who at a barbeque."[280] A EULEX intelligence official stresses that "sharing only happens through personal contacts." The JIOC, for instance, would share information and intelligence with the CIU, but only through one person, a military officer reporting only to the SRSG. The official interviewed was on good terms with this officer and could go to his office when he needed any material.[281] Individuals constantly feared being left out of the loop, leading them to develop personal networks of acquaintances. These networks complemented the official channels, such as JIOC meetings. Often, these networks were composed of officials from the same country. One German KFOR officer said that he regularly met with German UNMIK officials.[282]

Informalisation thus much accelerated the blurring of functional distinctions between the military and police. By late 2008, the KFOR database included around 65,000 reports on various issues, including serious crime. Many of these reports were of interest to the police. Yet formal sharing was bureaucratically cumbersome. As a consequence, KFOR and the police (mainly UNMIK and EULEX) established informal relations that allowed the police to draw on the knowledge of the military.[283] One EULEX official underlined that EULEX, KFOR and the MSU exchanged a lot of information and intelligence informally.[284]

Institutions help to build trust.[285] But in the murky world of intelligence and law enforcement, trust is built largely outside of formal institutions. A former US intelligence officer underlines that their culture forces intelligence agents to be suspicious towards one another.[286] This is especially the case when many countries with divergent interests, as well as divergent police, military and intelligence cultures, govern post-war territories. While partly necessary for pragmatic reasons, informal cooperation exacerbates problems of accountability. For instance, very little is known about US counter-terror operations in Kosovo, which are conducted secretly and partly informally. Similarly, the process whereby suspects were included on crime target lists is unclear to outsiders. Both KFOR and UNMIK added information to the list, but apparently in a rather informal manner.[287]

Besides the issue of trust, the informal sharing of information and intelligence by international actors was also a consequence of the fact that national laws of foreign countries prohibited the sharing of sensitive material (gathered, for instance, through SigInt). Such prohibitions affected sharing among institutions of the same donor state as well as among institutions of several donor states. The separation of responsibilities among police intelligence cells, military intelligence cells, national intelligence services and foreign intelligence services reflects norms of democracy and is also warranted for reasons of effectiveness (the availability of separate channels of information enables better verification of incoming information). However, these separations of powers have made intelligence cooperation in Kosovo (and in other places where international intervention has occurred) cumbersome. Restrictions also led to situations where intelligence-led institutions cooperated on shaky legal ground, or possibly outright illegally.[288]

The lack of accountability and oversight of the international security sector in Kosovo says much about the nature of modern protectorates. Domestic actors are not able and/or permitted to exercise oversight functions. At the same time, the large number of international actors makes it difficult to attribute responsibility for wrong-doing and failure; instead, there are blame-games. For instance, the international intelligence architecture in Kosovo is composed of JIOC, MSU, G2/J2, NIC, ISR, CIU, UNMIK Police, foreign intelligence services, foreign law enforcement liaison officers and many others. If saying who is doing what is difficult, saying who failed exactly where, when, why and how is impossible. Blurred divisions of labor, whether necessary and deliberate or a result of uncontrolled growth and competition, undermine accountability and oversight. Furthermore, international actors have not been willing to submit to greater scrutiny. Fostering accountability does not require radical measures such as abolishing the convention of immunity of international personnel from domestic prosecution. And secrecy will always be needed, to deprive criminals of information advantages. However, the 'international community' in Kosovo has generally failed to adhere to the same standards and norms that domestic actors are expected to comply with.

Conclusion

To what extent has NATO met criteria of effectiveness, efficiency and legitimacy in post-war Kosovo? The previous chapter showed that 'internationals' partly failed in fighting serious crime in post-Dayton Bosnia. The same can be said about post-war Kosovo. There have been problems on the security governance and SSG levels, and this has had repercussions for internationally-sponsored SSR efforts. The next, final chapter, summarises the empirical findings of this chapter and compares NATO activities to an ideal-type strategy for military support of law enforcement in war-torn countries.

Notes

1 The term Kosovar here connotes a Kosovo Albanian.

2 Lorenz 2000: 131. See also Zaalberg 2006: 310, 323, and chapter 12.

3 Interview with Kosovar tortured by unofficial 'police' after the war, Geneva, September 2006.

4 Jones et al. 2005: 49.

5 UNHCR and OSCE 1999.

6 Stefanova 2004: 271-272 and 275 (footnote 11).

7 Kaldor 2005: 155-159; Mueller 2004: 96-97.

8 Mappes-Niedieck 2003: 106; Ulfkotte 2005: 233-234; The Times (of London), Drugs Money Linked to Kosovo Rebels, 24 March 1999; UNODC 2008: 52; Montanaro-Jankovski 2005: 19.

9 Teran 2007: 9.

10 Holt and Boucher 2009: 24.

11 Robert Perito, in: Wilton Park 2004: 97. On the causes of this failure, see Perito 2004: 204-207. See also Rausch 2006: 149; Perito 2008: 59-60.

12 International Crisis Group 2000c.

13 Lorenz 2000: 139. On the reasons for UNMIK's failure in the first years after the war, see Stefanova 2004. To be fair, governing Kosovo was an enormous challenge, and the UN had little time to prepare since it was expected that the OSCE would take on this task. However, this solution was blocked by both Moscow and Belgrade (Perito 2004: 183). Moreover, UN pre-deployment training and post-war planning during NATO's war was not feasible since it would have signalled approval of the bombing campaign.

14 Perito 2004: 186.

15 UN Security Council Resolution 1244, 10 June 1999, paragraph 9 d.

16 Dobbins et al. 2008: 83. Another improvement in comparison to Bosnia was the territorial congruence of military and civilian sectors.

17 On the failure to learn from Bosnia in this regard, see International Crisis Group 1999c: 9-10.

18 See Zaalberg 2006: chapter 13. Post-war CIMIC projects continued the war-time military involvement in relief work (for a critical perspective on the latter, see Pugh 2000).

19 On the causes of this failure, see Zaalberg 2006: Part IV.

20 International Crisis Group 1999d: 1.

21 On this arrangement, see Cockell 2002: 488.

22 For an analysis of divergent law enforcement approaches, see Cockell 2002: 489-490. On divergent CIMIC approaches, see Mockaitis 2004.

23 Zaalberg 2006: 332.

24 It must be noted, though, that KFOR J2 often refused to share intelligence with intelligence officers of national contingents (personal communication by former KFOR officer, April 2009).

25 Sowers 2005: 387.

26 International Crisis Group 1999d: 3.

27 Zaalberg 2006: 333-334 and 382.

28 Mockaitis 2004: 14-17.

29 Rausch 2006: 128.

30 Zaalberg 2006: Part IV. See also Sion 2006.

31 Zaalberg 2006: 312.
32 Zaalberg 2006: 315.
33 Zaalberg 2006: 309.
34 For a problematisation of Kosovo's alleged 'gun culture', see Small Arms Survey 2005.
35 Zaalberg 2006: 323.
36 Susanne Koelbl, "Gegen das Böse kämpfen", in: Der Spiegel 31, 24 September 2001: 42; Zaalberg 2006: 356-367.
37 Bernabéu 2007: 85.
38 Perito 2004: 207-208. See also Lorenz 2000; Rausch 2006: 41 and 51.
39 For an example, see Rausch 2002: 16, footnote 16.
40 Naarden and Locke 2004.
41 Rausch 2006: 26.
42 Bernabéu 2007: 86; Rausch 2006: 86-87 and 145.
43 International Crisis Group 1999d: 5.
44 On legal obligations of KFOR, see Cerone 2001.
45 Council of Europe 2006: 16; interview with a former senior UNMIK official, Southern Germany, September 2008. Contingents from some other troop-contributing countries handed suspects over to US KFOR (Baldwin 2006: 497).
46 Zaalberg 2006: 336.
47 Baldwin 2006: 497.
48 Interview with a former senior UNMIK official, Southern Germany, September 2008.
49 Rausch 2002: 28, footnote 32.
50 Amnesty International 2000. However, one UN official argued that if refugees could live in tents, criminals could, too (see Zaalberg 2006: 338).
51 Bernabéu 2007: 77; Baldwin 2006.
52 Lorenz 2000: 132.
53 Rausch 2006: 120. See also Hartmann 2003.
54 On the following, see Perito 2004: 186-187.
55 Italy's engagement in Kosovo was motivated not least by the fact that criminals used Kosovo to smuggle and traffic people and goods to Italy. UNMIK, in its fight against organized crime, relied much on the Carabinieri and the Guardia di Finanza.
56 Lutterbeck 2004: 65, footnote 17.
57 Cockell 2002: 496.
58 Perito 2004: 188.
59 Perito 2004: 221.
60 Judah 2000: 334.
61 For examples of attacks, see United Nations 2003: 5.
62 For a positive appraisal of police training in Kosovo, see Jones et al. 2005 (e.g., page 192).
63 It must be noted that corruption and cronyism are partly a legacy of Communism.
64 Perito 2004: 191.
65 Perito 2004: 219-224.
66 See Rausch 2006: 121.
67 Perito 2004: 224-227; Strazzari 2008: 162.
68 For an illustration, see Holohan 2005: 66-67.
69 Interview with a former senior UNMIK official, Southern Germany, September 2008. See also Holohan 2005.

70 Interview with EULEX official, Pristina, November 2008. See also Holohan 2005: 57; Rausch 2006: 119.

71 In turn, civilian actors, especially NGOs, were reluctant to interact with the military. See Abiew 2003: 31.

72 Rausch 2002: 27.

73 For an example, see NATO 2003.

74 Stefanova 2004: 275, footnote 10.

75 Zentrum für Internationale Friedenseinsätze 2003: 42-44. Some officials who witnessed Mini's performance in Kosovo doubt that his actions in the law enforcement realm matched his later description of these (personal communication with former KFOR officer, April 2009).

76 Stefanova 2004: 268.

77 Interview with former KFOR officer, Western Europe, January 2009. See also di Giovanni 2003: 122-123.

78 Zaalberg 2006: 332-333.

79 Interview, Southern Germany, September 2008. See also Rausch 2002: 27.

80 Dziedzic 2002: 44. UNMIK Police also often gathered unusable evidence (Dziedzic 2002: 51). It is noteworthy, too, that in May 2001 the main suspect in the bus bombing escaped from the US Army's Camp Bondsteel (International Crisis Group 2004: 23, footnote 91).

81 Interview, Belgrade, October 2008. On the problems of separate military and civilian communications equipment, see Holohan 2005: 103.

82 Interview, Pristina, December 2008.

83 Baldwin 2006: 496.

84 Perito 2004: 211-213.

85 Holt and Boucher 2009: 24.

86 Interview with KFOR officer, Pristina, December 2007.

87 Interview, Pristina, December 2008.

88 See United Nations 2004; International Crisis Group 2004.

89 On this failure, see Human Rights Watch 2004.

90 Zentrum für Internationale Friedenseinsätze 2006: 43; International Crisis Group 2004: 19.

91 Institut für Europäische Politik 2007: 38.

92 International Crisis Group 2004: 20-22. Some critics argued that the behavior of French troops in March 2004 revealed a peculiar French approach to peacekeeping (see, more generally, Tardy 2000). Some French KFOR troops were from elite units, such as the Foreign Legion, and would not have hesitated to be in harm's way if ordered to do so. But according to critics, France thought that keeping the peace in Kosovo would be easier if Kosovo was no longer an ethnic patchwork, i.e., if Kosovo Serbs moved to northern Kosovo and if Albanians left the North (interview with international security observer, Pristina, October 2008). According to this view, French decision-makers saw the March 2004 riots as an expression of an untenable status quo.

93 International Crisis Group 2004: 45-46; Zaremba 2007: Part 4.

94 Quoted in: Zaremba 2007: Part 4.

95 See Amnesty International 2005.

96 Platzer 2005.

97 International Crisis Group 2004: 20.

98 On the ambiguities of local ownership more generally, see Donais 2008.
99 Interview with former KFOR officer, Pristina, November 2008; International Crisis Group 2004: 22.
100 Ian Traynor : NATO force 'feeds Kosovo sex trade', in: The Guardian, 7 May 2004.
101 Mendelson 2005: 23-24.
102 In mid-2006, 160 places were no-go areas for 'internationals'. Interview with UNMIK Police officer, Pristina, August 2006.
103 Interviews with international and Kosovo police and social services providers, Pristina, 2006-2008.
104 See Friesendorf 2008.
105 See Scheye 2008; Arifagić and Šabović 2007; Friesendorf 2007c.
106 For an explanation for why this is the case, see Strazzari 2008: 164-165.
107 For more thorough overviews, see European Commission and Council of Europe 2007; UNODC 2008; European Commission 2008. The most detailed information can be found in two (leaked) reports produced by, respectively, a Berlin think tank (Institut für Europäische Politik 2007) and the German intelligence service (Bundesnachrichtendienst 2005).
108 Strazzari 2008: 161.
109 Bundesnachrichtendienst 2005: 4.
110 Institut für Europäische Politik 2007: 53.
111 Bundesnachrichtendienst 2005: 3.
112 Interview, Pristina, November 2008. See also European Commission 2008: 52-53.
113 European Commission and Council of Europe 2007: 16.
114 UNODC 2008: 64.
115 UNODC 2008: 65. The largest Kosovar diaspora is in Germany and Switzerland.
116 Interview with a member of the Macedonian Parliament, Skopje, December 2008.
117 Interview with security observer, Pristina, October 2008. See also Strazzari 2008: 163.
118 Interview with Director of Kosovo NGO, Pristina, October 2008.
119 Interviews with KPS officer, Pristina, October 2008, and with EULEX official, Pristina, November 2008; European Commission 2008: 51; UNODC 2008: 82.
120 European Commission 2008: 36 and 53-54.
121 Interview with journalist, Kosovo, October 2008.
122 Interview with local staff of international organization, Serbian enclave in Southern Kosovo, January 2008.
123 Krenar Gashi, EULEX Treats Kosovo War Crimes as Priority, in: BalkanInsight.com, 27 February 2009.
124 Interviews with journalist and with Kosovo ministry official, Kosovo, October 2008.
125 January 2007 edition of the report, p. 5. Some KFOR officials, when asked about the report, believe that it conflates anti-aircraft missiles with rocket-propelled grenades (RPG).
126 January 2007 edition of the report.
127 Interview with KFOR officer, November 2008; Strazzari 2008: 160; Bundesnachrichtendienst 2005: 5.
128 See Andreas 2008.
129 See Anastasijevic 2006: 5. That there has been a pax mafiosa is the near unanimous view of interviewees. According to the German Federal Intelligence Service

(Bundesnachrichtendienst 2005: 4), Serbs and ethnic Albanians cooperated in the smuggling of drugs, alcohol and cars.

130 Bundesnachrichtendienst 2005: 5.

131 UNODC 2008: 20 and 39.

132 Strazzari 2008: 161.

133 European Commission 2006: 38. See also Institut für Europäische Politik 2007; Bundesnachrichtendienst 2005.

134 Interview with UN official, United Nations Headquarters, New York City, February 2009.

135 Interview, Pristina, October 2008.

136 Quoted in UNODC 2008: 106.

137 Bundesnachrichtendienst 2005: 5.

138 Strazzari 2008: 163.

139 Bundesnachrichtendienst 2005: 6.

140 On money laundering, see UNODC 2008: 97.

141 Interview with UNMIK Police officer, Pristina, December 2008.

142 See Petrit Qollaku and Vjosa Musliu, Crime on the Rise in Kosovo, Warns Bank Chief, in BalkanInsight, 17 July 2009, available at http://www.balkaninsight.com/en/main/news/21153/ (download 11 August 2009).

143 Interview with US military officer, Camp Bondsteel, January 2008.

144 Interview with local staff of an international organisation, Serbian enclave in Southern Kosovo, January 2008. According to a former KFOR officer (personal communication, April 2009), Serbian leaders insisted on convoy protection, but only to use such protection as 'evidence' that there was no real freedom of movement.

145 Interviews with KFOR officers, various parts of Kosovo, 2007-2008.

146 Interview with KFOR MTF officer, January 2008.

147 Interview with EULEX official, Pristina, October 2008.

148 Interview with KFOR MTF officer, October 2008.

149 Interview with KFOR MTF officer, October 2008. KFOR had to treat carefully with regard to CIMIC. Seemingly innocuous activities such as laying water pipes could lead to accusations of one ethnic group cheating the other. CIMIC was thus of a highly political nature, and any errors could lead to violence.

150 Interview with KFOR MTF officer, December 2007.

151 Interview with KFOR MTF officer, October 2008.

152 Interview with KFOR MTF officers, January 2008.

153 See, more generally, de Coning 2007.

154 Interview with former UNMIK Police officer, Belgrade, October 2008.

155 Interview with KFOR officer, Kosovo, November 2008.

156 Interview with KFOR officer, Kosovo, November 2008.

157 Interview with KFOR officer, Kosovo, November 2008.

158 Interview with KFOR officer, Kosovo, December 2007.

159 Interview with KFOR MTF officer, January 2008.

160 Hardened Rubber Bullets Killed Kosovo Protesters, in: Reuters, 18 April 2007, at http://www.alertnet.org/thenews/newsdesk/L18289584.htm (download 5 April 2009); Amnesty International 2009.

161 Interview, Pristina, November 2008.

162 Interview with KFOR MTF officer, Kosovo, October 2008.

163 Interview with KFOR MTF officer, January 2008.
164 Interview with KFOR officer, Kosovo, December 2007.
165 Interview with KPS officer, Pristina, October 2008.
166 Interview with KFOR officer, Kosovo, November 2008.
167 Ceku Announces Kosovo's Armed Forces, in: B92 News, 22 November 2008.
168 Interview with KFOR officers, various parts of Kosovo, December 2007 and January 2008.
169 European Commission 2008: 51.
170 Interview with KFOR MTF officer, October 2008.
171 Interview with KFOR MTF officer, December 2007.
172 Interview with non-commissioned officer leading a patrol, Kosovo, October 2008.
173 Author observations at MSU checkpoint outside of Pristina, November 2008.
174 Interview with KFOR officer, Kosovo, November 2008.
175 Interview with KFOR officer, Kosovo, December 2007.
176 Another reason for why security sector actors have not been able to establish clearer divisions of labour has been the unresolved status question (Law 2006: 8).
177 On the travails of the CIU in the early phase, after its creation in 1999, see Dziedzic 2002: 42.
178 Rausch 2006: 120.
179 Interview, Pristina, October 2008.
180 Interview with KFOR MTF officer, November 2008.
181 Interview with KPS spokesperson, Pristina, January 2008.
182 Interview with KFOR MTF Military Police officer, January 2008.
183 Interview with KFOR officer, Kosovo, November 2008.
184 Interview with KFOR officer, January 2008.
185 It must be noted, though, that UNMIK Police was involved in KPS planning. Thus, even if the KPS did not go through official UNMIK channels when drawing on KFOR support, such requests did not completely bypass UNMIK Police. Interview with KPS spokesperson, Pristina, January 2008.
186 Interview with Kosovo journalist, Pristina, December 2007.
187 Interview with KPS spokesperson, Pristina, January 2008.
188 Interview with KFOR MTF officer, December 2008.
189 Interview with KFOR MTF officer, January 2008.
190 Interview with EULEX official, Pristina, October 2008.
191 This tendency is manifested, among other documents, in European Commission 2008.
192 Interview with KPS officer, Pristina, January 2008.
193 Interview with KFOR MTF officer, January 2008.
194 Interview with the Director of an international NGO, Pristina, December 2007.
195 Interview with KFOR MTF officer, January 2008.
196 Interview with research consultant, Pristina, October 2008.
197 Interview with staff of international organization, Serbian enclave in Southern Kosovo, January 2008.
198 See Serb leader accuses Kosovo police, in: B92 News, 7 March 2009 (http://www.b92.net/eng/news/politics-article.php?yyyy=2009&mm=03&dd=07&nav_id=57661), download 9 March 2009. See also Four Kosovo Serbs hurt in clashes with police, in: B92 News, 8 March 2009 (http://www.b92.net/eng/news/politics-article.php?yyyy=2009&mm=03&dd=08&nav_id=57672), download 9 March 2009.

199 Interview, Pristina, October 2008.
200 Interview with a Kosovo journalist and the Director of a Kosovo NGO, Pristina, December 2007.
201 Interview with EULEX official, Pristina, October 2008.
202 In one case, an investigation involved five consecutive international prosecutors. Interview with UNMIK Police officer, Pristina, December 2008.
203 For examples during the early post-conflict period, see Holohan 2005; Zaalberg 2006: 339.
204 For examples, see Zaremba 2007.
205 Interviews with domestic and international security observers and practitioners, Kosovo, 2006-2008. The tendency to regard human rights violators as stability providers goes back to the early post-war period (O'Neill 2002). On this tendency during the later period, see Institut für Europäische Politik 2007.
206 Quoted in: Zentrum für Internationale Friedenseinsätze 2003: 94.
207 For criticism and examples, see Strazzari 2008: 165; Institut für Europäische Politik 2007: 55-56.
208 See Renate Flottau and Hans Hoyng, "Welcome to Colombia", in: Spiegel Online, 18 October 2004, at http://www.spiegel.de/international/spiegel/0,1518,323632,00.html (download 18 March 2009); Institut für Europäische Politik 2007: 79 and 113. See also War Crimes Prosecutor Stunned by Relations Between Haradinaj and Chiefs of UNMIK, in: Kosovo Compromise, 11 December 2007.
209 Interview with EULEX official, Pristina, October 2008. See also Reljić 2008: 86. For examples of 'internationals' allegedly blocking prosecution efforts, see King and Mason 2006.
210 A German report convincingly deconstructs the euphemistic public relations style of UNMIK, contrasting it to a dire reality (Institut für Europäische Politik 2007).
211 Interview with the Director of a Kosovo NGO, Pristina, November 2008.
212 Human Rights Watch 2008.
213 Interview with KFOR MTF officers, January 2008.
214 Interview, northern Kosovo, January 2008.
215 Interview, Pristina, November 2008.
216 Interview with UNMIK Police officer, Pristina, November 2008.
217 Interview, Kosovo, November 2008.
218 Interview with EULEX official, Pristina, November 2008.
219 EULEX, similar to UNMIK, was endowed with executive competencies in sensitive areas, especially organized crime, civil property cases, war crimes, inter-ethnic crime, high-level corruption and witness protection.
220 This strategy was laid out in several documents: Joint Operating Procedures for Cooperation between the ESDP Mission and KFOR in Military Support to Police Operations; Joint Operating Procedures for Cooperation between the ESDP Mission and KFOR to Response in Case of Civil Disturbance Situations; Joint Operating Procedures for Cooperation between the ESDP Mission and KFOR in Border Management; and Joint Operating Procedures for Cooperation between the ESDP Mission and KFOR in Information Exchange, Including the Field of Intelligence.
221 EULEX and KFOR train at Camp Vrello, in: EULEX News, 27 February 2009, available at www.eulex-kosovo.eu/?id=8&n=72 (download 10 March 2009).
222 See International Crisis Group 2008

223 Interview, Pristina, November 2008.
224 Interview, UN Headquarters, New York City, February 2009.
225 Interviews with EULEX officials, Pristina, October and November 2008.
226 Interview with EULEX official, Pristina, October 2008. See also Institut für Europäische Politik 2007: 66-67. Some observers argued that such caution was no longer warranted since popular support for suspected criminals considered war heroes had waned over the years, with citizens growing tired of crime and corruption (interview with EULEX official, Pristina, December 2008).
227 Interview with former EULEX official, Western Europe, November 2008.
228 Interview with EULEX official, Pristina, October 2008.
229 Email communication with EULEX official, February 2009.
230 Interview with UNMIK Police officer, Pristina, November 2008.
231 The NIC also informed a number of additional capitals, as well as national contingent commanders.
232 Interview with that official (who at the time was working for EULEX), Pristina, November 2008.
233 Festnahmen im Kosovo: Opposition verlangt Aufklärung über mutmassliche BND-Leute, in: FAZ.Net, 24 November 2008, available at www.faz.net (download 24 November 2008).
234 Die traurigen Männer von 11A, in: Der Spiegel 49, 2008, 67-70.
235 Interview, Pristina, December 2008.
236 Institut für Europäische Politik 2007: 80 (see also page 117).
237 Interview, November 2008.
238 Interview, Pristina, November 2008. The problematic image of the MSU may have contributed to France's decision, in late 2008, to move most of its Gendarmes to EULEX (KFOR 2009: 24-25).
239 Interview, Pristina, December 2008.
240 Interview, Pristina, December 2007.
241 Interviews with MSU officers, Kosovo, December 2007 and November 2008.
242 Interview, Pristina, December 2008.
243 Interviews with NGO staff and security practitioners in Kosovo and neighbouring countries, 2006-2008. See also Friesendorf 2006.
244 On the many unresolved war crimes cases, see Amnesty International 2008; AI: Not Enough Done to Solve Kosovo War Crimes, in: B92 News, 20 March 2009, available at http://www.b92.net/eng/news/crimes-article.php?yyyy=2009&mm=03&dd=20&nav_id=57952 (download 2 April 2009).
245 On the distinction between output, outcome, and impact, see Schroeder and Friesendorf 2009.
246 Interview, Pristina, November 2008.
247 International Crisis Group 2006: 10.
248 Interview, Pristina, October 2008.
249 On the persistence of problems affecting KFOR, see Institut für Europäische Politik 2007: 76-77.
250 See NATO Could Withdraw from Kosovo in Four Years, in: BalkanInsight, 4 August 2009, at http://www.balkaninsight.com/en/main/news/21463/ (download 8 August 2009).
251 Interview with UNMIK official, northern Kosovo, January 2008.

252 Interview, Pristina, October 2008.
253 Interview, Pristina, December 2008.
254 Interview with MSU officials, Kosovo, November 2008.
255 Interview with former KFOR officer, Pristina, October 2008.
256 Interview, Pristina, November 2008.
257 Interview with that official, Belgrade, October 2008.
258 Interview with KFOR MTF officer, October 2008.
259 European Commission 2008: 36.
260 Interview with KFOR MTF officer, October 2008.
261 See International Crisis Group 2007b: 17.
262 Interview, Pristina, November 2008.
263 It must be noted that fuel smuggling should not be conflated with serious crime, as it involved many individuals who were not organized, made only small profits and were forced into this business by the dire economic conditions prevailing in most parts of the Balkans.
264 See EULEX Report to the UN, 17 June 2009, at http://www.eulex-kosovo.eu/?id=8&n=110 (download 8 August 2009); One Kosovo Police Officer and One Journalist Injured During Protests in Northern Kosovo, in The Kosovo Times, 5 August 2009, available at http://www.kosovotimes.net/kosovo-chronicle/941-one-kosovo-police-officer-and-one-journalist-injured-during-protests-in-northern-kosovo.html (download 11 August 2009).
265 Interview, Pristina, November 2008.
266 Zentrum für Internationale Friedenseinsätze 2003: 92.
267 Rausch 2006: 121.
268 Interview, Pristina, December 2008.
269 Human Rights Watch 2008.
270 Jones et al. 2005: 182; Wilson 2006.
271 UNODC 2008: 30.
272 Interview with UNMIK Police officer, Pristina, December 2008.
273 Hansen 2002b: 80.
274 See Zaremba 2007.
275 Interviews with members of international organizations and NGOs, various parts of Kosovo, October-November 2008. Interview with NGO staff supporting prostitutes and victims of human trafficking, Sofia (Bulgaria), July 2006.
276 For an example, see Rausch 2002: 30.
277 Interview, Pristina, December 2008.
278 On Kosovo intelligence services, see Jeta Xharra, Kosovo's Intelligence Services Come in from the Cold, in: Balkan Insight, 23 December, available at http://www.pressonline.com.mk/default-en.asp?ItemID=F8FD773BBA13794E8FFF7E47CF989AD0 (download 15 April 2009); Institut für Europäische Politik 2007: 48 and 79; Dugolli and Peci 2006; Bundesnachrichtendienst 2005: 7.
279 Interview with KFOR MTF officers, October 2008.
280 Interview, Kosovo, November 2008.
281 Interview, Pristina, November 2008.
282 Interview with KFOR MTF officer, January 2008.
283 Interview with KFOR MTF officer, October 2008.

284 Interview, Pristina, November 2008.
285 See Keohane 1984; Oye 1986.
286 Interview, Germany, September 2008.
287 Interview with UNMIK Police officer, November 2008.
288 Personal communication with security observer, April 2009.

Chapter 5

Conclusion: Improving Military Support to Law Enforcement

The end of the Cold War has transformed international politics and the nature of warfare. Since the 1990s, criminalised warfare has been on the ascendance, with civilians being the main victims of this trend. In response, peacekeeping has changed, to the effect that international intervention in war-torn countries increasingly resembles policing. Peacekeeping has, in the words of Mary Kaldor, become "cosmopolitan law-enforcement. Since the new wars are, in a sense, a mixture of war, crime and human rights violations, so the agents of cosmopolitan law-enforcement have to be a mixture of soldiers and policemen."[1]

If law enforcement is important during wars, it is even more so after war. Post-war security gaps should not open up because they undermine international stabilisation and peace-building efforts and lead to people being driven from their homes or being killed. Much has been written about how to fight serious crime after war. Recommendations include a more systematic deployment of CIVPOL, pre-deployment training for international security actors and the creation of coordination structures enabling systematic and legitimate SSG in war-torn countries.

The peculiar nature of serious crime after war, where the same person may commit different types of crime, can lead to functional overlaps between international and domestic crime-fighting actors. The militarisation of the police, the policisation of the military and covert operations by intelligence services can thus be seen as inevitable, even though these trends clash with the SSR principle of delineating functional responsibilities among security actors. The trafficking of weapons, for instance, clearly threatens a safe and secure environment, and even a recalcitrant military would have difficulties arguing that stopping this type of crime was not within its mandate. Yet the trafficking of weapons is often intertwined with other criminal activities. Counter-efforts are thus likely to push the military onto the turf occupied by the police in stable, democratic countries. Also, the arrest of dangerous criminals, including war criminals, may require military assets.

In Bosnia, Kosovo and elsewhere, military and police duties have become partly indistinguishable,[2] and divisions of labour among intelligence-led institutions have partly disappeared What Fred Schreier writes about intelligence work more generally applies to intervention in war-torn countries as well: "[E]ver more intelligence is collected by the different services on the same subjects. The traditional divisions between external, internal and also criminal intelligence are becoming increasingly blurred. Missions and objectives overlap, enhancing the opportunities for misunderstandings and rivalries."[3]

This book does not challenge these views: it confirms that international intervention in war-torn countries defies traditional distinctions between internal and external security as well as those among military, police and intelligence work. But this study takes the discussion a step further. Through an in-depth look at two empirical cases it gauges the extent to which crime-fighting in international protectorates is fraught with problems of effectiveness, efficiency and accountability. Focusing not only on the strategic level but also on the operational and tactical levels, the book reveals how difficult it is to gear the military towards a crime-fighting role. Many observers nowadays agree that the military may have to substitute for police forces up until the point when international or domestic police can take over. But in Bosnia and Kosovo, developments have not been linear. Often, the military was doing too little when it was most needed, and, from the perspective of the police and other civilian actors, was doing too much many years after the war. Observers also argue in favour of a 'surgical' approach by which the military eliminates critical nodes in illicit networks. Drawing on the lessons of Bosnia, a US report states that the objective of military operations is

> *not* to rid the country of crime and corruption. This would [...] be an endless task worthy of being labeled 'mission creep'. The objective [...] is finite, since power is concentrated in only a few hands. The aim is to marginalise and neutralise a relatively small number of hard-line leaders in order to open the political space for moderate political leaders and empower those aspiring to the openness and accountability of the rule of law. Once this is accomplished, the environment should be propitious for local public security officials to take responsibility for developing the rule of law.[4]

However, the cases of Bosnia and Kosovo show that the military may need to do things more mundane than staging operations against top targets. And even 'surgical' operations do not guarantee success. Moreover, domestic ownership, due to institutional corruption and the entrenched position of criminals in positions of power after war, is a principle that can easily hurt vulnerable individuals and groups whom SSR efforts are supposed to protect.

This concluding chapter first summarises the main findings of the two case studies. It then outlines an ideal-type strategy for military support of law enforcement in war-torn countries. Lastly, the discussion is extended to cases beyond the Balkans.

Case Study Findings

Bosnia

The case of Bosnia illustrates the travails of post-conflict stabilisation efforts. On the security governance level numerous obstacles have hindered effective, efficient and legitimate military support of the fight against serious crime. IFOR and, until the later 1990s, SFOR did not regard law enforcement support as part of their mandate and did not devise appropriate RoE. Military support of crime-fighting varied across sectors, reflecting divergences in political will as well as national caveats. Troops generally lacked the skills and equipment needed to fight serious crime. Worse, the military exacerbated crime problems, as was the case with human trafficking. Further, both NATO and EU military missions were ill-prepared and reluctant to interact closely with other international actors, especially CIVPOL (this lack of interaction reflects weakness on the part of the police as well). Last, the military gathered vast amounts of intelligence. But national contingents often failed to share intelligence and also made too few efforts to use military intelligence for supporting criminal justice efforts.

Obstacles to fighting serious crime are apparent with regard to SSG as well. NATO provided relatively little support to Bosnian police and prosecutors. The creation of the MSU and the Blue Box/Green Box concept were innovative, but in practice, SFOR largely eschewed activities that smacked of policing. When troops became involved, they did so unsystematically. Also, military involvement in crime-fighting has not decreased over time, on the contrary. The military was largely unwilling and unable to fight crime at a time when suspected war criminals had not yet built up sophisticated support networks, inter-ethnic crime was rampant and organised crime was pervasive. EUFOR tried to make a difference, yet at a time when opportunities for the military to make a difference were diminished. As Bosnian observers did not fail to observe, international actors tackled crime too late.[5]

SSR principles should also inform military involvement in crime fighting. NATO's lack of activism largely prevented the creation of grey areas between military and policing work and thus sent confusing signals to domestic actors – yet at the cost of impunity for serious crime. As the military, especially the MSU and IPU, became more active, grey zones became larger. Also, SSR principles were not properly respected. With regard to proportionality, it is questionable, for instance, whether the military should use aerial surveillance to search for marihuana plantations. With regard to subsidiarity, EUFOR counter-crime operations during the mission's first term may have signalled that the rule of law was an EU priority; but those operations may equally have undermined public faith in the ability of Bosnian institutions to guarantee the rule of law.

With regard to military involvement in police reform, the military has mainly confined itself to providing training and equipment. Close contact between the military and Bosnian police has, to some extent, (re-)militarised the latter. Most international actors in Bosnia emphasise that military training did not reach the doctrinal level; they argue that EUFOR and the US military merely used their superior capabilities to support the police technically and tactically.[6] This view underestimates socialisation effects: Simply by being around soldiers, police officers, especially those working for 'militarised' units such as SWAT teams, will think more like soldiers. However, it is unlikely that military support has changed police strategies and doctrines. In fact, by 2006, all security actors in Bosnia agreed that military involvement in law enforcement should be limited as much as possible. For instance, the EUPM official who proposed using EUFOR helicopters for border control also emphasised the need for ensuring operational dominance by the police. The more-than-residual law enforcement role of EUFOR after its activist first term was due to the weakness of the police.

Shortcomings of military involvement resulted from the partial absence of conditions influencing the prospects of fighting serious crime after war (see Table 1 in chapter 2). IFOR and, in the early stage, SFOR felt they were in a war-like environment. Yet even in the later 1990s, this cautious stance lingered on – at a time when security conditions were more conducive to law enforcement and when basic infrastructure was better and the legal framework tighter.

A major problem was that Bosnian security forces were too weak or unreliable to fight serious crime. Although the numbers of police were stunning, there was much corruption and criminal collusion. Moreover, security forces were divided along ethnic lines, and their dubious war-time record neither inspired the confidence of local citizens nor international actors.

This case study has shown that 'internationals', too, were often unable to enforce laws. There were not enough strong, international police officers, prosecutors and judges. All international institutions in Bosnia showed a lack of political will, inability to adapt to criminal challenges and a lack of institutional learning. A security gap opened up due to overly cautious military and weak civilian law enforcement institutions. Constabulary forces were deployed but not properly used. The importance of interpersonal relationships underlined the lack of institutional frameworks for, and the ad-hoc manner of, crime fighting. When proactive military officers were sent to Bosnia, when they received proper guidance from their superiors and when military and civilian representatives shared the same views, crime would be fought; if not, not.

The picture is not entirely bleak. Both SFOR and EUFOR improved their counter-crime performance over time, indicating individual and institutional learning. NATO and the EU came to perceive public security as a vital element of post-conflict stabilisation. Decision-makers understood that the military would not be able to withdraw as long as serious crime posed a significant risk and that without military support, the police would not be able to assume primacy over law enforcement. Military crime-fighting thus improved on the strategic, operational and tactical levels.[7]

One should not overstate the progress made, however. As security conditions improved and as criminals turned away from violence towards more sophisticated ways of making money or gaining power, fighting the types of serious crime discussed in this book became easier. Moreover, progress has not been linear – there have been many ups and downs in Bosnia.

Kosovo

The Kosovo case reveals the difficulties of transferring lessons from one peace operation to the next. In this war-torn province (and later country), NATO has contributed abundantly to crime-fighting efforts. Military involvement came earlier than in Bosnia, due to the late deployment and weaknesses of UNMIK, as well as the absence of statutory domestic security actors. However, KFOR involvement was haphazard. Even though NATO had a more precise mandate in Kosovo than it did in Bosnia, national caveats and diverging RoE prevented KFOR from systematically putting pressure on those committing serious crime. Moreover, troop-contributing nations sent primarily combat forces to Kosovo.

Yet the expectation of conventional warfare gave way to the reality of small-scale attacks on vulnerable groups and of organised crime. National prerogatives and interference undermined the ability of COM KFOR to ensure a harmonised approach across Kosovo. Also, troops lacked language and policing skills, as well as equipment such as CRC gear. Moreover, many soldiers had not been properly informed about typical post-war problems and thus exacerbated crimes such as human trafficking. Furthermore, military cultures and secrecy provisions impinged on civil-military interaction and information sharing.

With regard to SSG, KFOR supported civilian institutions by establishing security perimeters, dismantling illegal checkpoints, and tipping off police about crime. Yet there were also many instances in which KFOR failed to support police, prosecutors and judges. Often, the military dealt with dilemmas in problematic ways. The absence of a reliable international or domestic criminal justice system forced KFOR to improvise, leading to the neglect of basic judicial principles. Another dilemma relates to cooperation with the KPS. The riots of March 2004 revealed the danger of transferring responsibilities to domestic police forces at too early a stage (KFOR had transferred many responsibilities to the KPS around 2003). After the riots, KFOR scaled down its engagement with the KPS.[8]

Yet as independence neared, and after independence, relations between KFOR and domestic police forces were close again. Officially, UNMIK was supposed to coordinate military support provided to domestic police forces. But on the ground, KFOR forged close, direct links with domestic actors. For instance, better controls of main arteries into and out of Kosovo led smugglers to use horse and donkey caravans to cross deserted mountains. By early 2007, KFOR was therefore beginning to work more closely with Customs for off-road patrols.[9] Such involvement many years after the war reveals that military involvement in crime-fighting does not necessarily linearly diminish over time.

The 'international community' wanted to build sustainable domestic institutions in Kosovo as a precondition for withdrawing from the province/country. But the empirical analysis revealed five problems. These have undermined international SSR efforts by sending the wrong signals to the political institutions and citizens of Kosovo.

First, the military has been policised and the police have been militarised. For instance, ten years after the war, KFOR was still embroiled in CRC in Northern Kosovo.[10] Paramilitarisation has been partly necessary. However, this trend has created a large grey area not compatible with the SSR objectives of preventing the military from encroaching on internal security matters and demilitarising domestic police forces.

Second, direct KFOR involvement in law enforcement has undermined SSR norms, too. As discussed below, the military should respect principles of proportionality and subsidiarity when operating in civil-military grey zones. KFOR often improvised admirably to protect vulnerable populations and to put pressure on criminals. However, some interventions were disproportional. Moreover, KFOR's partial substitution of the police can, again, partly be justified in terms of necessity. But there are also examples of KFOR activism, such as some MSU operations. Close cooperation between KFOR and the KPS violated the norm of subsidiarity as well, which stresses police dominance over law enforcement. UNMIK Police did not create a buffer between KFOR and the KPS because UNMIK Police was stretched too thin. In Kosovo, an international military force had close, direct links with a domestic police force many years after the war. This risked installing military thinking in police work.

Third, the empirical analysis reveals cooperation problems, turf battles and blame-games. International actors have pushed Kosovo institutions to better cooperate with one another. The failure of international actors to do so themselves has harmed the credibility and legitimacy of the 'international community'. Kosovo officials and citizens, over time, have become tired of 'internationals' telling them what to do, seeing that the latter did not play by the rules that they themselves had defined.

Fourth, crime-fighting by 'internationals' in general, and KFOR in particular, lacked effectiveness. The difficulty of international missions to fight crime has damaged their credibility in the eyes of Kosovo institutions and citizens. It also allowed domestic spoilers of counter-crime efforts to point at international failures, thus obscuring their own obstructionism.

Fifth, the 'international community' has not been a very accountable community. Allegations and evidence of wrong-doing have made Kosovo institutions and citizens doubt that international rule of law efforts are more than cheap talk. In addition to a lack of political will to institutionalise better democratic checks and balances, accountability problems in Kosovo are a result of the complex security architecture. Numerous international and domestic actors have worked in what one EULEX intelligence official described as a "massive grey area" in which the military, police and intelligence agencies intermingle.[11]

KFOR's crime-fighting has been hampered by numerous adverse conditions (see table 1 in chapter 2). On the domestic level, these include a violent immediate post-war phase, as well as a lack of basic infrastructure and a sound legal framework. The fact that Kosovo did not have reliable, unbiased security forces mattered, too, as did corruption and criminal collusion by many in domestic positions of power.

However, post-war conditions and the lack of domestic capacity are insufficient for explaining inefficiency, ineffectiveness and weak accountability of counter-crime efforts. Problems pertaining to international intervention forces have to be taken into account as well. The 'international community' has not properly fought serious crime in Kosovo because of a widespread failure to muster sufficient political will, adapt to new circumstances and learn from the past. Crime-fighting has been undermined by the late deployment and unsystematic use of CIVPOL, constabulary forces and international criminal justice personnel; the failure of troop-contributing nations to equip and train KFOR troops for law enforcement tasks; divergent national practices; the failure of KFOR and other international actors to gather and share information and intelligence; and many other shortcomings.

As is the case with Bosnia, counter-crime efforts in Kosovo illustrate the difficulty of governing international protectorates and ensuring public order after war. That a security gap opened up in Kosovo, and that it was not systematically filled later on, is the responsibility of numerous international actors. These include NATO and the Alliance's member states.

Improving Military Contributions to Post-Conflict Law Enforcement

The second chapter of this book showed how security governance, SSG and SSR help to understand military contributions to post-conflict law enforcement. This section formulates a strategy for improving such contributions (see Table 2).

Security Governance

On the security governance level, countries involved in stabilising a war-torn country should make available troops most appropriate for a particular scenario. If the peace is fragile and if spoilers are well-armed, robust military capacities are needed. With regard to timing, in the absence of strong CIVPOL capacities, the military should start fighting crime immediately –

Table 2: Improving military support of crime-fighting after war

Security Governance	• Send troops able to operate in civil-military grey areas • Fight serious crime immediately after war • Formulate robust military mandates and RoE • Limit national caveats • Ensure good interoperability and command structures • Train troops in languages and basic policing skills • Inform troops about typical post-war problems • Provide adequate equipment • Prepare soldiers to cooperate closely with international civilian actors • Gather and exchange information and intelligence
Security Sector Governance	• Mitigate obstacles preventing close military-police cooperation • Support the police (through security perimeters, heavy weaponry or tip-offs) • Train troops in cooperating with criminal justice actors • Decrease military involvement over time
Security Sector Reform	• Fight crime, but delineate policing from military functions as much as possible • Limit damage by respecting principles of proportionality and subsidiarity • Avoid military primacy over SSR activities • Circumscribe the role of PMSC

whether a country can be stabilised depends not least on the conduct of the military during the first months after the end of major combat operations.[12]

Also, proper military mandates, and broad interpretations of mandates, are needed.[13] Military mandates should be robust and, if necessary, include the fight against serious crime as a military task in order to avoid later misunderstandings. All governments want to retain maximum leverage over 'their' troops. As a consequence, mandates tend to treat tasks on the civil-military interface vaguely. Whether or not supporting the fight against serious crime is part of ensuring a 'safe and secure environment' is thus open to interpretation by military commanders and their civilian superiors. If including the fight against serious crime in military mandates is politically not palatable, it is crucial to flexibly interpret military responsibilities. Robust military mandates and flexible interpretations should be complemented by robust RoE allowing soldiers to stop rioters, looters, traffickers and others who benefit from chaos.[14] All too often, RoE in peacekeeping and humanitarian operations do not include public security functions.[15]

Governments should not impose caveats significantly curtailing the power of national commanders and the multinational force commander. Parallel reporting and command structures, and the 'call-home syndrome', will not simply go away. Nevertheless, governments can reinforce the position of the multinational force commander by narrowing the gap between RoE of national contingents and RoE of the military mission as a whole.[16] Governments, especially defence ministries, should avoid micromanaging 'their' troops.

Practically, to fight serious crime, troop-contributing countries and international organisations must ensure interoperability. Also, in contrast to conventional warfare, counter-insurgency relies on the ability of non-commissioned officers and junior officers to take quick decisions on their own – small wars are 'corporals' wars'. The same holds true for law enforcement, where there is often no time to wait for commands from higher up in the hierarchy. Significant decision-making powers must therefore be devolved to companies, platoons and squads.

Much depends on training, which ideally should be provided before deployment. Troops must possess the language skills needed for operating in a multinational environment and to conduct tasks such as CRC. They also need to be familiar with basic policing skills such as crime scene preservation and filing crime reports. Some such skills can be taught in a day.[17] Knowledge about more difficult issues such as interviewing witnesses, forensics and collecting evidence and criminal intelligence is desirable, too, yet more time-consuming to acquire. Soldiers also need to know about typical problems in war-torn countries. Knowledge on human trafficking, for example, facilitates the identification of victims at checkpoints and reduces the number of peacekeepers using the services of trafficked persons. Adequate equipment is important, too – tanks are less suitable for stopping a riot than batons, shields and light vehicles.

Training should enable and promote close cooperation between the military and civilian institutions, especially CIVPOL, international prosecutors and international judges. Team-building exercises before deployment may reduce later friction between military and police missions.[18] It is also crucial to cooperate with NGOs, private businesses and other actors who do not share the coercive outlook of the military, yet whose relief and peacebuilding activities address root causes of crime. For example, close cooperation between the military and NGOs is required when only the military has the means to investigate complaints about human rights abuses reported to NGOs. Coordination is particularly relevant with regard to intelligence. Military intelligence-gathering can pose risks to civilians cooperating with the military. Yet CIMIC projects do provide ample insights into security problems on the local level. While the military should avoid situations that would taint their civilian collaborators as spies, it should also not deprive itself of the opportunity to gather intelligence in order to fight serious crime.

Another challenge is that intelligence collected by the military is often of little use in court.[19] This may be because soldiers are unfamiliar with police procedures. But more importantly, the military may resort to covert, and outright illegal, means when collecting intelligence. Military and policing aims differ. The military needs intelligence to achieve victory, which does not necessarily require following 'proper' procedures. The same applies to intelligence agencies whose aim is to shape policy by predicting and forestalling emerging risks and threats.[20] The military and intelligence services are unwilling to disclose their sources and modi operandi and thus risk becoming part of the chain of evidence. Moreover, the military and intelligence services may decide not to tip off the police about crime at an early stage in order to get to the core nodes of criminal, terrorist or insurgent networks. The police, in contrast, seek tips leading to the apprehension of criminals. It depends on intelligence to build cases; intelligence must be collected according to the books to be usable in court.

These problems will continue to hamper cooperation among the military, the intelligence community and law enforcement agencies. Forcing the military and intelligence services to disclose sources and means would reduce incentives to gather intelligence. But the military should shed its distrust of non-military actors. More trust will lead the military, among other advantages, to tip off the police more often. Training the military to collect information and intelligence in a way that enables successful prosecution is crucial, too. While the difference between patrols and HUMINT teams should be maintained, training soldiers about overt information collection such as questioning techniques and the use of interpreters would support prosecution.[21] Constabulary forces (as well as military police) are good at collecting criminal intelligence. Their deployment, while posing questions regarding the delineation of military and policing functions, therefore makes the fight against serious crime more effective and efficient.

The concept of security governance thus provides a framework for structuring military support of post-conflict law enforcement on an international level. The most crucial parameter for whether the military can systematically address serious crime is the political will of troop-contributing countries, especially powerful ones, to let 'their' troops enforce the law.

Security Sector Governance

SSG guides military support of post-conflict law enforcement, too. As shown above, SSG pertains to security arrangements on a domestic level, in this case in post-conflict countries, and linkages between the various security sector actors. Ideally, a counter-crime SSG system relies on civilian law enforcement agencies. But when these are not present or too weak, the military has to step in.

Forging viable police-military networks is not easy. Networking is facilitated by similar worldviews and institutional cultures. Both the police and military tend to focus on the perpetrators of violent acts more than on the victims, and are less prone to taking into account root causes of violence and crime than human rights and development experts tend to do. However, the military and police are different enough to ensure disputes over tactics and strategies. The military has stricter secrecy provisions than the police and is better at employing overwhelming force than defusing tension. Moreover, soldiers tend to hold police work in low esteem.[22] Such incongruities can result in red tape, information exchange failures and turf battles. Mitigating these networking obstacles is a main challenge of SSG.

Relations between the military and police vary considerably. Soldiers may support CIVPOL and domestic police by creating a security perimeter, reinforcing police efforts to dismantle illegal checkpoints by sending a tank, or tipping off police on the whereabouts of a wanted person. The Green Box/Blue Box concept developed in Bosnia in the late 1990s distinguishes between areas where the military (Green Box) and the police (Blue Box) have primacy. Military involvement may be direct as well, by arresting suspected war criminals, raiding brothels, detaining arsonists, or seizing criminal assets.

To ensure that suspects are tried, the military needs to cooperate with international or, if available, domestic prosecutors and judges. This requires knowing how to secure a chain of evidence and how the criminal justice system works. Soldiers may need to be familiar with differences between common and civil law, the role of investigative judges and local laws for seizing assets. Pre-deployment training can provide soldiers with some of these skills.

The structure of an SSG system should evolve parallel to the post-conflict security situation. In the immediate post-conflict phase (the 'garrison phase'), military involvement in law enforcement is particularly deep and thus joint or streamlined civil-military command structures are particularly needed. One option is to place civilian agencies under military command. However, for political and normative reasons, governments are reluctant to do so. Alternatively, the military can be put under the command of a civilian administrator. However, troop-contributing nations, especially the US, have been unwilling to do so.[23] In the absence of unified command (on the strategic, operational and tactical levels), close CIMIC is essential. It may also be possible to have civilian command on the strategic level and coordinate joint operational and tactical military-police activities in advance.[24]

A second post-conflict stage is reached as the number of CIVPOL increases, domestic crime fighters get better and conditions become less dangerous. In this phase, the military should transfer responsibilities to the police and criminal justice sector in the areas of criminal investigation, CRC and general public order.[25] To promote the transfer of competencies without sacrificing public order, smooth military-police networks are essential. These networks should be flexible enough to adapt to changes in the external environment and the internal composition of the governance system (which requires decentralisation), and be guided by common objectives and efficiency (which requires centralisation).

Yet soldiers should not withdraw too quickly, in case peace falters. Contingency measures can be enshrined in Memoranda of Understanding signed by the military and civilian decision-makers. International actors should maintain a balance between ensuring security (through a pro-active military) and respect for the norm of civilian leadership over law enforcement (through military restraint). Already in 2000, the UN recommended developing "methodologies and standard operating procedures of the transition from the provision of security by international military to international police and finally to local police."[26] Since then there has been no lack of appeals for clear division of labour for actors engaged in various types of international intervention.[27] But in practice, this remains a challenge.

A third phase is reached when security risks have become minimal. The military has now transferred law enforcement responsibilities to civilian institutions. It may still arrest suspected war criminals or collect intelligence. The military may also hold over-the-horizon forces ready to intervene in case of emergencies. But now, the military has become a means of last resort.

Security Sector Reform

International military forces can contribute to stability by engaging in SSR-related activities such as DDR, the control of SALW and demining. These activities enable the implementation of SSR initiatives.[28] Direct military law enforcement is problematic. There is friction between the need to fight serious crime after war and the need to reform the domestic security sector. As discussed above, SSR envisages a separation of military and policing functions. 'Locals' are told to avoid grey zones. To the extent that 'internationals' militarise law enforcement, they clash with their own principles.[29] However, the human and political costs of an inactive military under the condition of weak civilian law enforcement outweigh the disadvantage of weakening the norm of civilian primacy over law enforcement.

Problems of military law enforcement can be limited. When soldiers arrest people or face rioters, they should avoid excessive use of force. Proportionality (the use of force commensurate with security needs) should guide military involvement.[30] The military is trained and equipped to use overwhelming force against organised enemies for reasons of force protection and to send a signal of determination.[31] But such a stance is counterproductive in law enforcement because it may make the military appear like an occupation army, capable of violating human rights and setting in motion a spiral of violence. The military thus needs to know how to calibrate the use of force and to apply force discriminately. These are well-know counter-insurgency principles that equally apply to law enforcement.

The military must also avoid arbitrary action so as not to lose legitimacy. Soldiers may need to detain culprits, but should do so in accordance with basic judicial procedures. As stated in the OSCE Code of Conduct: "If recourse to force cannot be avoided in performing internal security missions, each participating State will ensure that its use must be commensurate with the needs for law enforcement. The armed forces will take due care to avoid injury to civilians or their property."[32]

Whether damage to SSR efforts can be limited hinges on proper military pre-deployment training and coordination on the security governance level (see above). Moreover, the military should support the transfer of law enforcement responsibilities to the police once such transfer is feasible. Thus, in addition to proportionality, subsidiarity is the second principle that should guide civil-military relations in post-conflict law enforcement: armed forces should be confined to supporting civilian authorities and should be subordinated to civilian authorities.[33] If military support of law enforcement after the immediate post-conflict phase is still needed, mechanisms should be devised to pitch CIVPOL in between the military and domestic law enforcement agencies. This would reduce the risk of militarising domestic police forces.

International military forces may also drive the reform of domestic security actors. However, this is problematic from an SSR perspective. The military should not be the lead actor in defence reform, so as not to weaken democratic control. Military support provided to police reform is equally problematic; the UN recommends abstention.[34] The absence of CIVPOL may warrant such training. The US military has trained the Afghan National Police (ANP) primarily because CIVPOL are too thinly spread over this vast country.[35]

However, SSR aims at demilitarising domestic police forces. Providing police forces with military training, equipment and intelligence may militarise domestic police, send the wrong signal to post-conflict countries and undermine efforts to create police forces guided by democratic norms. Citizens in post-conflict countries have usually suffered from abusive, corrupt and militarised security forces. Fostering public trust in civilian policing thus depends on limiting the role of the military in internal security.[36]

Military training may be justified as long as the military does not shape police doctrines, but merely provides specialised knowledge and equipment. Police officers specialised in hostage situations, for example, may receive sniper training from the military. But direct and deep relationships between international military forces and the domestic police in post-conflict countries are unhealthy. Militarising police forces may undermine their democratic control, and, by fixating on coercive strategies, may distort the security priorities of citizens and hold back human development.[37]

Similarly controversial, and increasingly common, is the training of law enforcement institutions, especially police who work in conflict, post-conflict and transition states, by PMSCs. Employees of PMSCs are often former soldiers. This poses the risk of instilling a military spirit into civilian institutions. Bolstering the credibility and sustainability of SSR requires circumscribing and regulating the role of PMSCs.

Beyond the Balkans

The cases of Bosnia and Kosovo showed that the ideal-type strategy for military support of law enforcement could not be entirely implemented. After all, the conditions facilitating the pursuit of the strategy (see table 1 in the second chapter) were partially absent. Elsewhere, these conditions were even more absent. While this study focuses on the Balkans, it is important to note that military efforts against serious crime pose problems anywhere. In fact, law enforcement in Balkan peace operations has been relatively successful in comparison to other parts of the world where international actors have intervened. This study underscores that crime-fighting should be one of the objectives of military transformation. The concept of the Responsibility to Protect has gained much traction among scholars and policy practitioners.[38] Serious crime victimises people in many countries. By contributing to crime-fighting, international military forces help to protect vulnerable people. Yet military crime-fighting is unsystematic, reflecting insufficient preparation for law enforcement, divergent interpretations of mandates, competition among military actors and between them and civilian institutions and other vagaries of international intervention.

Iraq is the most notorious recent case in which international actors – with the US in a hegemonic position – have neglected crime-fighting after the presumed end of major combat operations. The invasion of Iraq was a military success, but its aftermath was a policing disaster. Public order broke down for various reasons, including the US decision to disband Iraqi security forces and the inability of Coalition forces to expand their activities beyond a narrowly defined military remit.[39] Iraq quickly transformed into a quagmire marked by fighting between, and alliances of convenience among, Coalition and government forces, local insurgents, government-sponsored militias, foreign terrorists and organised crime groups.[40] More attention paid to law enforcement in the crucial immediate post-war period could have saved tens of thousands of lives.

Afghanistan provides another example of unsystematic crime-fighting by 'internationals'. Following the successful ouster of the Taliban in late 2001, the UN, due to the Bush administration's abhorrence of nation-building, adopted a 'light footprint' strategy. The aim was to let Afghan security forces secure Afghanistan. But creating a well-functioning security sector representing the various ethnic and political domestic groups proved difficult, not least because international investment into Afghanistan has been negligible when compared to the vast financial and personnel resources invested into Bosnia and Kosovo. As analysts of the RAND Corporation write, Bosnia, on a per capita basis,

> had received 50 times more international military personnel and 16 times more economic assistance than did Afghanistan over the first couple of years of reconstruction. In Afghanistan, the [US] administration refused to use U.S. troops for peacekeeping and opposed the deployment of international forces outside the capital for the same purpose. Security was to remain a responsibility of the Afghans, despite the fact that the country had neither army nor police forces. Nor surprisingly, Afghanistan became more – not less – dependent on external assistance as the years went by.[41]

Domestic institutions have been too weak to prevent a motley of insurgents, terrorists and criminals of various sorts (commonly oversimplified under the label 'Taliban') to control large swaths of Afghanistan. To make things worse, the government has been part of the problem, with corruption hampering effective law enforcement. For instance, the ANP is seen by most Afghans as predatory and unreliable.[42] Since the end of a deceptively calm period lasting until around 2007, NATO's International Security Assistance Force and troops operating under the US-led Operation Enduring Freedom have been facing a fierce insurgency that has been thriving on revenues from the heroin trade and that had spilled over into Pakistan. By summer 2009, the new US administration of Barack Obama was facing the possibility of having to invest billions of dollars into a very fragile and very poor country each year over a very long period of time.[43] Rectifying the mistakes made in the years after 9/11 seemed an insurmountable task.

If international actors had invested more into state and nation-building in Afghanistan, at a time when most Afghans would have welcomed international security forces opposing local strongmen, this catastrophic situation might have been averted. A major element in such a strategy would have been to task military forces to ensure public security, as a precondition for enabling Afghans and international agencies to rebuild the economy. Moreover, international actors should have put more pressure on suspected criminals. As in Bosnia and Kosovo, spoilers have largely acted with impunity. Reasons include the fixation of the Bush administration on hunting down members of Al-Qaeda, which led the CIA and other agencies to support warlords, some of whom assumed crucial positions in government.[44] More generally, foreign governments and their representatives in Afghanistan have been concerned about causing instability by uprooting Afghan power structures. The fact that in early 2009 a heated debate erupted over whether NATO should target the thriving heroin industry is evidence of the continuing confusion over how to cope with serious crime after war.[45]

Instead of better coordinating international assistance to Afghanistan, sending more CIVPOL and taking other steps against spoilers of security, international actors have improvised. For instance, in the absence of sufficient numbers of international police officers (mainly the fault of European states, especially Germany[46]), Military Policy officers and employees of PMSCs such as DynCorp became crucial for training the ANP.[47] Also, the US, eager to put more boots on the ground in the fight against insurgents, has trained and equipped auxiliary police forces. Such strategies exacerbate the militia problem in Afghanistan and hamper efforts by European and other donor countries to delineate military from policing tasks.

Haiti is another case illustrating the merger between crime and war, as well as between crime-fighting and war-fighting. International stabilisation missions deployed to Haiti in the 1990s failed to dismantle rampaging militias and criminal gangs, which were instruments of political and economic elites, and to create effective and accountable security forces. Police forces were overwhelmed by the firepower, ruthlessness and organisation of the gangs.[48] An approach that included the military was therefore warranted. By 2006, UN forces found themselves fighting well-armed gangs, the largest of which operated in the slums of Port-au-Prince. Only combined, intelligence-led operations by UN soldiers, formed police units and SWAT teams succeeded in defeating the gangs.[49]

Counter-gang operations in Haiti are a positive example of military engagement in law enforcement. However, it took foreign actors a long time to face the reality of gangs governing entire neighbourhoods and to devise proper police-military coordination mechanisms. Moreover, there are doubts as to whether the success of the international war on gangs in Haiti has been strategic, given that root causes enabling the rise of violent para-state and non-state actors continue to haunt the country.[50]

Final Thoughts

International interventions in the Balkans and beyond prove that establishing public security after war is needed for building states and nations. This study leans towards a 'security first' approach.[51] Certainly, security is necessary, but not sufficient by itself, for stabilising war-torn countries and for protecting people – a 'security only' approach would be self-defeating. Security comes first because without it development agencies, private companies, NGOs, the media and other actors promoting human development and state accountability cannot enter a country, are forced to leave it, give up, or are eliminated by those pursuing private interests with violent means.

Internal security should be the prerogative of the police. But due to conditions in war-torn countries and the absence of domestic or international policing, foreign military forces should more systematically target those committing serious crime and protect those vulnerable to attack. While adapting the military towards crime-fighting is problematic in many ways, the costs of not doing so are greater.

It is unclear, however, whether governments deploying personnel to war-torn countries will move in this direction. Not only is there a continuing lack of political will to send more and better CIVPOL forces to places that need them. There is also a lack of political will to rethink the role of the military and translate this rethinking into practice. Better muddling through therefore seems all one can realistically hope for.

Notes

1. Kaldor 2005: 11.
2. This is emphasized, among others, by Rausch (2006: 134).
3. Schreier 2009: 217.
4. U.S. Army Peacekeeping and Stability Operations Institute 2000: 21.
5. See, for example, an op-ed by Zija Dizdarević in Oslobođenje, 25 November 2007.
6. Interview with EU official, Sarajevo, July 2008; interview with German military official, Sarajevo, July 2008.

7 For instance, constabulary commanders stress that regular military forces have, over time, come to better understand constabularies and their advantages (interview with a EUFOR officer, Sarajevo, July 2008).

8 Phone interview with former KFOR officer, October 2008.

9 Confidential international intelligence report, January 2007.

10 EULEX/KFOR Fire Shock Bombs, Rubber Bullets and Tear Gas to Disperse Serbs, in: KosovoCompromise, 30 April 2009, at www.kosovocompromise.com/cms/item/latestnews/en.html?view=story&id=1945&sectionId=1 (download 30 April 2009).

11 Interview, Pristina, November 2008.

12 Rees 2006: 10.

13 See also Kaldor and Salmon 2006: 31.

14 International Commission 2001: 62.

15 Call and Stanley 2001.

16 Stephens 2005.

17 Kaldor and Salmon 2006: 31.

18 See Zentrum für Internationale Friedenseinsätze 2006: 31.

19 This and the following paragraph draws on interviews with a senior North American police officer and with a former member of a Western European intelligence service (Western Europe, May and September 2008), as well as on Zentrum für Internationale Friedenseinsätze 2003: 44, 99; Zentrum für Internationale Friedenseinsätze 2006: 106; Treverton 2003: 167.

20 On cooperation problems between intelligence and law enforcement agencies, see Baker 1994/1995.

21 Mintz 2007.

22 Janowitz 1960: 419.

23 On different command structure options, see Dziedzic and Perito 2008: 12.

24 Zentrum für Internationale Friedenseinsätze 2006: 43.

25 International Commission 2001: 64.

26 United Nations 2000: Paragraph 96f.

27 See, for example, Gowan and Johnstone 2007: 17.

28 See Hänggi and Scherrer 2008: 15, Table 1.4.

29 Wilton Park 2004: 7.

30 Venice Commission 2008: 26; Franken 2006.

31 On military organization, see Haltiner 2001.

32 OSCE 1994: Paragraph 36. See also OECD 2007: 164.

33 Venice Commission 2008: 26.

34 United Nations 2003b: 88.

35 See Zentrum für Internationale Friedenseinsätze 2006: 103; Wilder 2007.

36 Mobekk 2005: 5-6.

37 UNDP 2002: 6.

38 See http://www.responsibilitytoprotect.org. See also Wheeler and Egerton 2009.

39 Perito 2008: 60-63.

40 On the criminalized side of the Iraq war, see Williams 2009.

41 Dobbins et al. 2008: xx.

42 Interviews with security observers and practitioners, Kabul and Jalalabad, July 2009.

43 Walter Pincus: Analysts Expect Long-Term, Costly U.S. Campaign in Afghanistan, in: Washington Post, 9 August 2009.

[44] See Rashid 2009: Parts 3 and 4.

[45] Judy Dempsey: NATO allows strikes on Afghan drug sites, in: International Herald Tribune, 11-12 October 2008, p. 3; Martin Winter: NATO streitet über Jagd auf Drogenhändler, in: Süddeutsche Zeitung, 29 January 2009. See also Karp and Ponzio 2007: 226.

[46] See Sedra 2006: 97.

[47] See Der Discount-Krieg, in: Der Spiegel 41/2007, 32-38; Wilder 2007. See also, more generally, Murray 2007. PMSCs have increasingly been training police forces, not only in Afghanistan but also in West African countries and elsewhere. From an SSR point of view, this trend is problematic. PMSCs are weakly regulated, and both these companies and the governments paying them often refuse to disclose details about the exact work of PMSCs. Moreover, many PMSC employees are former soldiers, which risks to imbue police forces trained by such companies with a military spirit.

[48] Mendelson-Forman 2006: 23.

[49] Dziedzic and Perito 2008. See also Mobekk 2008.

[50] See Cockayne 2009.

[51] For a recent treatment, see Etzioni 2007.

References

Abiew, Francis Kofi 2003: NGO-Military Relations in Peace Operations, in: *International Peacekeeping* 10: 1, 24-39.

Ahić, Jasmin 2007: Reconstruction of BiH Police, in: Philipp Fluri and George Katsirdakis (eds.): *Security Sector Reform in the New Partnership for Peace Members: Bosnia-Herzegovina, Montenegro, Serbia* (Brussels: DCAF and NATO), 10-27.

Allred, Keith J. 2006: Peacekeepers and Prostitutes: How Deployed Forces Fuel the Demand for Trafficked Women and New Hope for Stopping It, in: *Armed Forces & Society* 33: 1, 5-23.

Amnesty International 2000: *Setting the Standard? UNMIK and KFOR's Response to the Violence in Mitrovica, March.*

Amnesty International 2005: *Kosovo/Kosova (Serbia and Montenegro): The March Violence – One Year On*, Public Statement, AI Index EUR 70/006/2005, 17 March.

Amnesty International 2008: *Serbia (Kosovo): The Challenge to Fix a Failed UN Justice Mission*, AI Index EUR 70/001/2008, 29 January.

Amnesty International 2009: Kosovo: *No Justice for the February 2007 Killings*, Public Statement, AI Index EUR 70/001/2009, 9 February.

Anastasijevic, Dejan 2006: *Organized Crime in the Western Balkans*, Paper presented at the HUMSEC Conference, Ljubljana, November.

Andreas, Peter 2000: *Border Games: Policing the U.S.-Mexico Divide* (Ithaca, N.Y.: Cornell University Press).

Andreas, Peter 2004: The Clandestine Political Economy of War and Peace in Bosnia, in: *International Studies Quarterly* 58: 1, 29-51.

Andreas, Peter 2005: Criminalizing Consequences of Sanctions: Embargo Busting and its Legacy, in: *International Studies Quarterly* 49: 2, 335-360.

Andreas, Peter 2008: *Blue Helmets and Black Markets: The Business of Survival in the Siege of Sarajevo* (Ithaca, NY: Cornell University Press).

Andreas, Peter and Ethan Nadelmann 2006, *Policing the Globe: Criminalization and Crime Control in International Relations* (Oxford: Oxford University Press).

Andreas, Peter and Richard Price 2001, *From War Fighting to Crime Fighting: Transforming the American National Security State*, in: International Studies Review 3: 3, pp.31–52.

Ank, Christopher (ed.) 2007: *Civil-Military Cooperation in Post-Conflict Operations: Emerging Theory and Practice* (London and New York: Routledge).

Aoi, Chiyuki, Cedric de Coning and Ramesh Thakur 2007: Unintended Consequences, Complex Peace Operations and Peacebuilding Systems, in: Chiyuki Aoi, Cedric de Coning and Ramesh Thakur (eds.): *Unintended Consequences of Peacekeeping Operations* (Tokyo: United Nations University Press), pp. 3-19.

Arifagić, Edis and Senad Šabović 2007: A Human Security Assessment of EU Engagement in Kosovo, in: *Südosteuropa Mitteilungen* 47: 1, 34-49.

Armitage, David T. Jr. and Anne M. Moisan 2005: *Constabulary Forces and Postconflict Transition: the Euro-Atlantic Dimension*, Strategic Forum No. 218, Institute for National Strategic Studies, National Defense University, November.

Arquilla, John and David Ronfeldt (eds.) 2001: *Networks and Netwars: The Future of Terror, Crime, and Militancy* (Santa Monica, CA.: RAND).

Arsovska, Jana 2008: Decline, Change or Denial: Human Trafficking and EU Responses in the Balkan Triangle, in: *Policing* 2: 1, 50-62.

Arsovska, Jana and Phillippe Verduyn 2008: Globalization, Conduct Norms and "Culture Conflict": Perceptions of Violence and Crime in an Ethnic Albanian Context, in: *British Journal of Criminology* 48: 2, 226-46.

Ashdown, Paddy 2007: *Swords and Ploughshares: Bringing Peace to the 21st Century* (London: Weidenfeld and Nicolson).

Ba, Alice D. and Matthew J. Hoffmann (eds.) 2005: *Contending Perspectives on Global Governance: Coherence, Contestation and World Order* (London and New York: Routledge).

Baer, Robert 2003: *See No Evil: The True Story of a Ground Soldier in the CIA's War on Terrorism* (New York: Three Rivers Press).

Baillie, Robbie 2005: *Saving the Future*, in: EUFOR Forum No. 5, June, Sarajevo, page 5.

Baker, Steward A. 1994/1995: Should Spies be Cops?, in: *Foreign Policy* No. 97 (Winter), pp. 36-52.

Baldwin, Clive 2006: Implementation Through Cooperation? Human Rights Officers and the Military in Kosovo, 1999-2002, in: *International Peacekeeping* 13: 4, 489-501.

Bellamy, Alex J. 2002, The Great Beyond: Rethinking Military Responses to New Wars and Complex Emergencies, in: *Journal of Defence Studies* 2: 1, 25-50.

Belloni, Roberto 2005: Peacebuilding at the Local Level: Refugee Return to Prijedor, in: *International Peacekeeping* 12: 3, 434-447.

Berman, Jacqueline and Cornelius Friesendorf 2008: Coercive Governance as Crime Control: EU Foreign Policy and the Fight Against Human Trafficking, in: *European Foreign Affairs Review* 13: 2, 189-209.

Bernabéu, Irene 2007: Laying the Foundations of Democracy? Reconsidering Security Sector Reform Under UN Auspices in Kosovo, in: *Security Dialogue* 38: 1, 71-92.

Bigo, Didier 2001, Internal and External Security(ies), the Möbius Ribbon, in Mathias Albert, Didier Bigo, Martin Heisler, Fritz Kratochwil, David Jacobson, Yosef Lapid: *Identities, Borders and Orders: Rethinking International Relations Theory* (Minneapolis, University of Minnesotta Press).

Born, Hans (ed.) 2003, *IPU-DCAF Handbook on Parliamentary Oversight of the Security Sector: Principles, Mechanisms and Practices*, Geneva.

Born, Hans and Ian Leigh 2008: *Handbook on Human Rights and Fundamental Freedoms of Armed Forces Personnel*, Vienna: OSCE/ODIHR.

Born, Hans, Karl W. Haltiner and Marjan Malešič 2004: Democratic Control of Armed Forces: Renaissance of an Old Issue, in: Hans Born, Karl W. Haltiner and Marjan Malešič: *Renaissance of Democratic Control of Armed Forces in Contemporary Societies* (Baden-Baden: Nomos), pp. 13-21.

Bose, Sumantra 2002: *Bosnia After Dayton: National Partition and International Intervention* (Oxford: Oxford University Press).

Bronson, Rachel 2002: When Soldiers Become Cops, in: *Foreign Affairs* 81: 6, 122-132.

Bryden, Alan and Heiner Hänggi (eds.) 2005, *Security Governance in Post-Conflict Peacebuilding* (Geneva: Geneva Centre for the Democratic Control of Armed Forces).

Bryden, Alan, Timothy Donais and Heiner Hänggi 2005: *Shaping a Security Governance Agenda in Post-Conflict Peacebuilding*, Policy Paper No. 11, Geneva: Geneva Centre for the Democratic Control of Armed Forces, November.

Brzoska, Michael and Andreas Heinemann-Grüder 2004: Security Sector Reform and Post-Conflict Reconstruction Under International Auspices, in: Alan Bryden and Heiner Hänggi (eds.): *Reform and Reconstruction of the Security Sector* (Geneva: LIT and Geneva Centre for the Democratic Control of Armed Forces), 121-143.

Bundesnachrichtendienst 2005: *Organized Crime in Kosovo*, BND Analyse 22 February.

Buzan, Barry, Ole Waever and Jaap de Wilde 1998: *Security: A New Framework for Analysis* (Boulder: Lynne Rienner).

Caddick-Adams, Peter 1998: Civil Affairs Operations by IFOR and SFOR in Bosnia, 1995-97, in: *International Peacekeeping* 5: 3, 142-154.

Call, Charles T. and William Stanley 2001: Protecting the People: Public Security Choices After Civil Wars, in: *Global Governance* 7: 2, 151-172.

Caparini, Marina 2006: Applying a Security Governance Perspective to the Privatisation of Security, in: Alan Bryden & Marina Caparini, eds., *Private Actors and Security Governance* (Vienna and Berlin: DCAF and LIT), 264-282.

Caplan, Richard 2004: International Authority and State Building: The Case of Bosnia and Herzegovina, in: *Global Governance* 10: 1, 53-65.

Carothers, Thomas (ed.) 2006, *Promoting the Rule of Law Abroad: In Search of Knowledge* (Washington D.C.: Carnegie Endowment for International Peace).

Center for Democracy in Vienna 1998: *Bosnia After SFOR?* Conference Proceedings, 21-23 January 1998.

Cerone, John 2001: Minding the Gap: Outlining KFOR Accountability in Post-Conflict Kosovo, in: *European Journal of International Law* 12: 3, 469-488.

Chandler, David 2002: Anti-Corruption Strategies and Democratization in Bosnia-Herzegovina, in: *Democratization* 9: 2, 101-20.

Chandler, David 2004: The Problems of 'Nation-Building': Imposing Bureaucratic 'Rule from Above', in: *Cambridge Review of International Affairs* 17: 3, 577-591.

Chandler, David 2005: From Dayton to Europe, in: *International Peacekeeping* 12: 3, 336-349.

Clark, Wesley K. 2001, *Waging Modern War: Bosnia, Kosovo, and the Future of Combat* (New York: PublicAffairs).

Clarke, John L. (ed.) 2006, *Armies in Homeland Security: American and European Perspectives* (Washington DC: National Defense University Press).

Cockayne, James 2009: Winning Haiti's Protection Competition: Organized Crime and Peace Operations Past, Present and Future, in: *International Peacekeeping* 16: 1, 77-99.

Cockayne, James and Daniel Pfister 2008, *Peace Operations and Organised Crime*, Geneva Papers No. 2 (Geneva: Geneva Centre for Security Policy).

Cockell, John C. 2002: Civil-Military Responses to Security Challenges in Peace Operations: Ten Lessons from Kosovo, in: *Global Governance* 4: 8, 483-402.

Collier, Paul, V.L. Elliott, Håvard Hegre, Anke Hoeffler, Marta Reynal-Querol, and Nicholas Sambanis 2003, *Breaking the Conflict Trap: Civil War and Development Policy* (New York: Oxford University Press and World Bank).

Council of Europe 2006: *Alleged Secret Detentions in Council of Europe Member States, Information Memorandum II*, Committee on Legal Affairs and Human Rights, Rapporteur: Dick Marty, AS/Jur (2006) 03 rev, 22 January, Strasbourg.

Cousens, Richard P. 1998: Providing Military Security in Peace-Maintenance, in: *Global Governance* 4: 1, 97-105.

Crane, Conrad C. 2005: Phase IV Operations: When Wars Are Really Won, in: *Military Review* 85: 3, 1 May.

Currie, Robert J. 2007: Abducted Fugitives Before the International Criminal Court: Problems and Prospects, in: *Criminal Law Forum* 18: 349-393.

Czempiel, Ernst-Otto and James N. Rosenau (eds.) 1992: *Governance Without Government: Order and Change in World Politics* (Cambridge: Cambridge University Press).

Daalder, Ivo H. 2000: *Getting to Dayton: The Making of America's Bosnia Policy* (Washington D.C.: Brookings Institution Press).

Daase, Christopher 2002: Internationale Risikopolitik: Ein Forschungsprogramm für den sicherheitspolitischen Paradigmenwechsel, in: Christopher Daase, Susanne Feske and Ingo Peters (eds.): *Internationale Risikopolitik: Der Umgang mit neuen Herausforderungen in den internationalen Beziehungen* (Baden-Baden: Nomos), 9-35.

Daase, Christopher and Stefan Engert 2008: Global Security Governance: Zur Effektivität und Legitimität neuer Formen des Regierens in der internationalen Sicherheitspolitik, in: *Politische Vierteljahresschrift*, Sonderheft 1/2008.

De Coning, Cedric 2007: Civil-Military Coordination Practices and Approaches Within United Nations Peace Operations, in: *Journal of Military and Strategic Studies* 10: 1.

De Graaf, Bob 2005: The Wars in Former Yugoslavia in the 1990s: Bringing the State Back in, in: Duyvesteyn, Isabelle and Jan Angstrom (eds.) 2005: *Rethinking the Nature of War* (London and New York: Frank Cass), 159-176.

Di Giovanni, Janine 2003: *Madness Visible: A Memoir of War* (New York: Vintage Books).

Dimitrios, Chousianitis 2006: *Military Police Platoon of Multinational Task Force North*, in: EUFOR Forum No. 14, April, Sarajevo, p. 9.

Dobbins, James, Michele A. Poole, Austin Long and Benjamin Runkle 2008: *After the War: Nation-Building From FDR to George W. Bush* (Santa Monica, CA.: RAND Corporation).

Donais, Timothy (ed.) 2008: *Local Ownership and Security Sector Reform* (Vienna and Berlin: DCAF and LIT).

Donais, Timothy 2003: The Political Economy of Stalemate: Organised Crime, Corruption and Economic Deformation in Post-Dayton Bosnia, in: *Conflict, Security and Development* 3: 3, 359-82.

Dugolli, Ilir and Lulzim Peci 2006: *Intelligence Agencies of Kosovo: Dismantling, Osmosis, or Integration?*, May, Pristina: Kosovar Institute for Policy Research and Development (KIPRED).

Duyvesteyn, Isabelle and Jan Angstrom (eds.) 2005: *Rethinking the Nature of War* (London and New York: Frank Cass).

Dziedzic, Michael J. 2002: Policing From Above: Executive Policing and Peace Implementation in Kosovo, in: Renata Dwan (ed.): *Executive Policing: Enforcing the Law in Peace Operations*, SIPRI Research Report No. 16 (Oxford: Oxford University Press), 39-51.

Dziedzic, Michael J. and Andrew Bair 1998: Bosnia and the International Police Task Force, in: Robert B. Oakley, Michael J. Dziedzic and Eliot M. Goldberg (eds.): *Policing the New World Disorder: Peace Operations and Public Security* (Washington DC: National Defense University Press).

Dziedzic, Michael J. and Robert M. Perito 2008: *Haiti: Confronting the Gangs of Port-au-Prince*, Special Report 208, September, Washington D.C.: United States Institute of Peace.

Ehrhart, Hans-Georg 2007: *Civil-Military Co-Operation and Co-Ordination in the EU and in Selected Member States*, D.G. External Policies of the Union, Policy Department External Relations, Brussels, 2007.

Ehrhart, Hans-Georg and Albrecht Schnabel 2004: Changing International Relations and the Role of the Military in Post-Conflict Peacebuilding Operations, in: S+ F, *Sicherheit und Frieden* 22: 1, 7-12.

Eilstrup-Sangiovanni, Mette 2005: Transnational Networks and New Security Threats, in: *Cambridge Review of International Affairs* 18: 1, 7-13.

Etzioni, Amitai 2007: *Security First: For A Muscular, Moral Foreign Policy* (New Haven, Conn.: Yale University Press).

European Commission 2006: *Kosovo (under UNSCR 1244) 2006 Progress Report*, Brussels, SEC (2006) 1386, 8 November.

European Commission 2008: *Kosovo (Under UNSCR 1244/99) 2008 Progress Report*, Commission Staff Working Document, COM(2008) 674, 5 November, Brussels.

European Commission and Council of Europe 2007: *CARPO Regional Project: Update of the 2006 Situation Report on Organized and Economic Crime in South-Eastern Europe*, Strasbourg, June.

European Stability Initiative 2007: *On Mount Olympus: How the UN Violated Human Rights in Bosnia and Herzegovina, and Why Nothing Has Been Done to Correct It*, 10 February, ESI: Berlin, Brussels, Istanbul.

European Stability Initiative 2007b: *The Worst in Class: How the International Protectorate Hurts the European Future of Bosnia and Herzegovina*, 8 November, ESI: Berlin, Brussels, Istanbul.

European Union 2005: *Seven Principles and Guidelines for Increasing Co-operation between EUPM-EUFOR and EUSR*, Brussels: PSC Conclusion, 13 September.

European Union 2006: *Common Operational Guidelines for EUPM-EUFOR Support to the Fight Against Organized Crime*, Sarajevo, 11 May.

Fagan, Adam 2005: Civil Society in Bosnia Ten Years After Dayton, in: *International Peacekeeping* 12: 3, 406-419.

Fako, Amel 2007: *The Role of External Actors in the Fight Against Trafficking in Persons in Bosnia and Herzegovina*, Paper presented at the HUMSEC conference, 4-6 October, Sarajevo.

Farrell, Theo and Terry Terriff 2002: *The Sources of Military Change: Culture, Politics, Technology* (Boulder, CO: Lynne Rienner).

Forster, Anthony 2006: *Armed Forces and Society in Europe* (Basingstoke: Palgrave).

Franken, Mark 2006: *Welche Polizeiaufgaben kann Militär übernehmen?, Interne Information zur Sicherheitspolitik*, Februar, Wien: Büro für Sicherheitspolitik des Bundesministeriums für Landesverteidigung.

Friesendorf, Cornelius 2005: Squeezing the Balloon? United States Air Interdiction and the Restructuring of the South American Cocaine Industry in the 1990s, in *Crime, Law & Social Change* 44: 1, 35-78.

Friesendorf, Cornelius 2006: Zuwenig Prävention, Opferschutz und Zusammenarbeit: Strategien gegen den Menschenhandel in Südosteuropa, in: *Südosteuropa-Mitteilungen* 46: 5-6, 22-35.

Friesendorf, Cornelius 2007, *US Foreign Policy and the War on Drugs: Displacing the Cocaine and Heroin Industry* (London and New York: Routledge).

Friesendorf, Cornelius 2007b: Pathologies of Security Governance: Efforts Against Human Trafficking in Europe, in: *Security Dialogue* 38: 3, 379-402.

Friesendorf, Cornelius 2007c: *Ahead of the Status Decision: Kosovo Between New Violence and Volatile Peace*, CSS Analyses in Security Policy 2: 9 (Center for Security Studies, ETH Zurich).

Friesendorf, Cornelius 2008: *Kosovo's Controversial Independence*, CSS Analyses in Security 3: 29, Center for Security Studies, ETH Zurich.

Friesendorf, Cornelius and Susan E. Penksa 2008: Militarized Law Enforcement in Peace Operations: EUFOR in Bosnia & Herzegovina, in: *International Peacekeeping* 15: 5, 677-694.

Friesendorf, Cornelius, Ursula C. Schroeder and Irma Deljkić (forthcoming): Bosnia and the Art of Policy Implementation: Obstacles to International Counter-Crime Strategies, in: Wolfgang Benedek, Petrus van Duyne, Christopher Daase, and Vojin Dimitrejevic (eds.): *Transnational Terrorism, Organized Crime, and Peace-Building: The State of the Art in Human Security in the Western Balkans* (Basingstoke: Palgrave Macmillan).

Fukuyama, Francis 2006: Guidelines for Future Nation-Builders, in: Francis Fukuyama (ed.): *Nation-Building: Beyond Afghanistan and Iraq* (Baltimore: The Johns Hopkins University Press), 231-244.

Gates, Robert M. 2009: A Balanced Strategy: Reprogramming the Pentagon for a New Age, in: *Foreign Affairs* 88: 1 (January/February), 28-40.

George, Alexander L. 2000: The Role of Force in Diplomacy: A Continuing Dilemma for U.S. Foreign Policy, in: Brands, William H. (ed.): *The Use of Force After the Cold War* (College Station: Texas A & M University Press), 59-92.

Gill, Lesley 2004: *The School of the Americas: Military Training and Political Violence in the Americas* (Durham, NC, and London: Duke University Press).

Glenny, Misha 1999: The Balkans 1804-1999: *Nationalism, War and the Great Powers* (London: Granta Books).

Gordon, Stuart 2007: Unintended Consequences of Civil-Military Cooperation in Peace Operation, in: Chiyuki Aoi, Cedric de Coning and Ramesh Thakur (eds.): *Unintended Consequences of Peacekeeping Operations* (Tokyo: United Nations University Press), pp. 109-130.

Gowan, Richard and Ian Johnstone 2007: *New Challenges for Peackeeping: Protection, Peacebuilding and the "War on Terror"*, Working Paper, New York: International Peace Academy, March.

Hall, Rodney Bruce and Thomas J. Biersteker (eds.) 2002: *The Emergence of Private Authority in Global Governance* (Cambridge: Cambridge University Press).

Haltiner, Karl W. 2001: Policemen or Soldiers? Organizational Dilemmas of Armed Forces in Peace Support Operations, in: Gerhard Kümmel (ed.): *The Challenging Continuity of Change and the Military: Female Soldiers, Conflict Resolution, South Africa* (Strausberg: Sozialwissenschaftliches Institut der Bundeswehr), 359-384.

Haltiner, Karl W. and Gerhard Kümmel 2008: Staat und Militär: Erosion einer Symbiose? Einige Fragen zum Funktionswandel von Streitkräften, in: Karl W. Haltiner and Gerhard Kümmel (eds.): *Wozu Armeen? Europas Streitkräfte vor neuen Aufgaben* (Baden-Baden: Nomos), 11-16.

Hänggi, Heiner 2003, Making Sense of Security Sector Governance, in: Heiner Hänggi and Theodor H. Winkler (eds.): *Challenges of Security Sector Governance* (Vienna and Berlin: DCAF and LIT), 3-23.

Hänggi, Heiner 2009: Security Sector Reform, in: Vincent Chetail (ed.): *Post-Conflict Peacebuilding: A Lexicon* (Oxford: Oxford University Press), 337-349.

Hänggi, Heiner and Vincenza Scherrer 2008: Recent Experience of UN Integrated Missions in Security Sector Reform, in: Heiner Hänggi and Vincenza Scherrer (eds.): *Security Sector Reform and UN Integrated Missions: Experience from Burundi, The Democratic Republic of Congo, Haiti and Kosovo* (Vienna and Berlin: DCAF and LIT), 3-25.

Hansen, Annika S. 2002: *From Congo to Kosovo: Civilian Police in Peace Operations* (New York: Oxford University Press for the International Institute for Strategic Studies).

Hansen, Annika S. 2002b: Civil-Military Cooperation: The Military, Paramilitaries and Civilian Police in Executive Policing, in: Renata Dwan (ed.): *Executive Policing: Enforcing the Law in Peace Operations*, SIPRI Research Report No. 16 (Oxford: Oxford University Press), 67-84.

Hartmann, Michael E. 2003: *International Judges and Prosecutors in Kosovo: A New Model for Postconflict Peacekeeping*, Special Report No. 112 (Washington, DC: U.S. Institute of Peace).

Hazen, Jennifer 2007: Can Peacekeepers Be Peacebuilders?, in: *International Peacekeeping* 14: 3, 323-338.

Heimerl, Daniela 2005: The Return of Refugees and Internally Displaced Persons: From Coercion to Sustainability?, in: *International Peacekeeping* 12: 3, 377-390.

Hills, Alice 1998: International Peace Support Operations and CIVPOL: Should There Be a Permanent Global Gendarmerie?, in: *International Peacekeeping* 5: 3, 26-41.

Hills, Alice 2001: The Inherent Limits of Military Forces in Policing Peace Operations, in: *International Peacekeeping* 8: 3, 79–98.

Holbrooke, Richard 1998: *To End a War* (New York: Random House).

Holohan, Anne 2005: *Networks of Democracy: Lessons from Kosovo for Afghanistan, Iraq, and Beyond* (Stanford: Stanford University Press).

Holt, Victoria and Alix J. Boucher 2009: Framing the Issue: UN Responses to Corruption and Criminal Networks in Post-Conflict Settings, in: *International Peacekeeping* 16: 1, 20-32.

Holt, Victoria K. and Tobias C. Berkman 2006, *The Impossible Mandate? Military Preparedness, the Responsibility to Protect and Modern Peace Operations* (Washington, DC: The Henry L. Stimson Center).

Hozic, Aida A. 2007: *Crime and Sovereignty in the Balkans*, Paper presented at the Annual Meeting of the International Studies Association, March 2007, Chicago, Il.

Human Rights Watch 2002: *Hopes Betrayed: Trafficking of Women and Girls to Post-Conflict Bosnia and Herzegovina for Forced Prostitution*, Vol. 14, No. 9.

Human Rights Watch 2004: *Failure to Protect: UNMIK and KFOR's Inability to Protect Serbs and Other Minorities*, 25 July.

Human Rights Watch 2008: *Kosovo Criminal Justice Scorecard*, March 27.

Innes, Michael A. 2005: Terrorist Sanctuaries and Bosnia-Herzegovina: Challenging Conventional Assumptions, in: *Studies in Conflict & Terrorism* 28: 4, 295-305.

Institut für Europäische Politik 2007: *Operationalisierung von Security Sector Reform (SSR) auf dem Westlichen Balkan (Operationalizing SSR in the Western Balkans)*, Report for the German Bundeswehr, Berlin, 9 January.

International Commission 2001, *Report of the International Commission on Intervention and State Sovereignty: The Responsibility to Protect*, December.

International Crisis Group 1997: *Grave Situation in Mostar: Robust Response Required*, ICG Bosnia Report No. 19, 13 February, Sarajevo.

International Crisis Group 1999: *Is Dayton Failing? Bosnia Four Years After the Peace Agreement*, ICG Balkans Report No. 80, 28 October, Sarajevo.

International Crisis Group 1999b: *Rule over Law: Obstacles to the Development of an Independent Judiciary in BiH*, ICG Report No. 72, 5 July, Sarajevo.

International Crisis Group 1999c: *Kosovo: Let's Learn from Bosnia – Models and Methods of International Administration*, Balkans Report No. 66, 17 May.

International Crisis Group 1999d: *The Policing Gap: Law and Order in the New Kosovo*, ICG Balkans Report No. 74, 6 August.

International Crisis Group 2000: *War Criminals in Bosnia's Republika Srpska: Who Are the People in Your Neighbourhood?*, ICG Balkans Report No. 103, 2 November, Sarajevo/Washington/Brussels.

International Crisis Group 2000b: *Reunifying Mostar: Opportunities for Progress*, ICG Balkans Report No. 90, 19 April, Sarajevo/Washington/Brussels.

International Crisis Group 2000c: *Kosovo Report Card*, Balkans Report No. 100, 28 August.

International Crisis Group 2001: *No Early Exit: NATO's Continuing Challenge in Bosnia*, ICG Balkans Report No. 110, 22 May, Sarajevo/Brussels.

International Crisis Group 2001b: *Bosnia's Precarious Economy: Still not Open for Business*, ICG Balkans Report No. 115, 7 August, Sarajevo/Brussels.

International Crisis Group 2001c: *Bosnia: Reshaping the International Machinery*, ICG Balkans Report No. 121, 29 November, Sarajevo/Brussels.

International Crisis Group 2002: *Policing the Police in Bosnia: A Further Reform Agenda*, Balkans Report No. 130, 10 May, Sarajevo/Brussels.

International Crisis Group 2002b: *Courting Disaster: The Misrule of Law in Bosnia & Herzegovina*, Balkans Report No. 127, 22 March, Sarajevo/Brussels.

International Crisis Group 2002c: *Arming Saddam: The Yugoslav Connection*, ICG Europe Report No. 136, 3 December, Brussels.

International Crisis Group 2004: *Collapse in Kosovo*, ICG Europe Report No. 155, 22 April.

International Crisis Group 2006: *An Army for Kosovo?*, Europe Report No. 174, 28 July.

International Crisis Group 2007: *Ensuring Bosnia's Future: A New International Engagement Strategy*, Europe Report No. 180, 15 February, Brussels.

International Crisis Group 2007b: *Kosovo Countdown: A Blueprint for Transition*, Europe Report No. 188, 6 December.

International Crisis Group 2008: *Kosovo's Fragile Transition*, Europe Report No. 196, 25 September.

International Crisis Group 2009: *Bosnia's Incomplete Transition: Between Dayton and Europe*, Europe Report No. 198, 9 March.

Janowitz, Morris 1960: *The Professional Soldier: A Social and Political Portrait* (Glencoe, Ill.: The Free Press).

JISB Interview 2007: The European Union and Statebuilding in the Western Balkans, Interview with Lord Paddy Ashdown, in: *Journal of Intervention and Statebuilding* 1: 1, 107-118.

Jones, Seth G., Jeremy M. Wilson, Andrew Rathmell and K. Jack Riley 2005: *Establishing Law and Order After Conflict* (Santa Monica, CA: RAND).

Judah, Tim 2000: *The Serbs: History, Myth & the Destruction of Yugoslavia*, 2nd Edition (New Haven and London: Yale University Press).

Kaldor, Mary 2005: *New & Old Wars: Organized Violence in a Global Era* (Cambridge: Polity).

Kaldor, Mary and Andrew Salmon 2006: Military Force and European Strategy, in: *Survival* 48: 1, 19-34.

Kaplan, Robert D. 2005: *Imperial Grunts: On the Ground with the American Military, from Mongolia to the Philippines to Iraq and Beyond* (New York: Vintage Books).

Karp, Candace and Richard Ponzio 2007: NATO, SSR and Afghanistan, in: David M. Law (ed.): *Intergovernmental Organisations and Security Sector Reform* (Vienna and Berlin: DCAF and LIT), 219-235.

Kenney, Michael 2007: From Pablo to Osama: *Trafficking and Terrorist Networks, Government Bureaucracies, and Competitive Adaptation* (University Park, Pennsylvania: Pennsylvania State University Press).

Keohane, Robert 1984: *After Hegemony: Cooperation and Discord in the World Political Economy* (Princeton, NJ: Princeton University Press, 1984).

KFOR 2009: *Gendarmerie National de la France and Its Role in Kosovo*, in: KFOR Chronicle, 3rd Edition, 28 March.

King, Iain and Whit Mason 2006: *Peace at any Price: How the World Failed Kosovo* (Ithaca, NY: Cornell University Press).

Knaus, Gerald and Felix Martin 2003: Travails of the European Raj, in: *Journal of Democracy* 14: 3, 60-74.

Krahmann, Elke 2003: Conceptualizing Security Governance, in: *Cooperation and Conflict* 38: 1: 5-26.

Krahmann, Elke 2005: Security Governance and Networks: New Theoretical Perspectives in Transatlantic Security, in: *Cambridge Review of International Affairs* 18: 1, 15-30.

Kraska, Peter B. (ed.) 2001: *Militarizing the American Criminal Justice System: The Changing Roles of the Armed Forces and the Police* (Boston: Northeastern University Press).

Krause, Keith 2007: *Towards a Practical Human Security Agenda*, Policy Paper No. 26, Geneva: Geneva Centre for the Democratic Control of Armed Forces.

Larsen, Josefine Ingela 2002: *Police Forces with Military Status in International Peace Operations: Preliminary Findings*, 28 October, Norwegian Defence Research Establishment Report FFISYS/4153, Kjeller.

Law, David M. 2006: *The Post-Conflict Security Sector*, Policy Paper No. 14, June, Geneva: Geneva Centre for the Democratic Control of Armed Forces (DCAF).

Leakey, David 2006: ESDP and Civil-Military Cooperation: Bosnia and Herzegovina, 2005, in: Anne Deighton with Victor Mauer (eds.), *Securing Europe? Implementing the European Security Strategy*, Zürcher Beiträge zur Sicherheitspolitik No. 77 (Zurich: Center for Security Studies, Swiss Federal Institute of Technology), 59-68.

Limanowska, Barbara 2002: *Trafficking in Human Beings in Southeastern Europe*, Sarajevo: UNICEF, UNOHCHR, OSCE.

Limanowska, Barbara 2005: *Trafficking in Human Beings in South Eastern Europe*, Sarajevo: UNICEF, OHCHR, OSCE.

Limanowska, Barbara and AnnJanette Rosga 2004: The Bar Raid as "Outcome Space" of Anti-Trafficking Initiatives in the Balkans, in: Elizabeth Dunn, Daniel Dor, Caroline Baillie, and Yi Zheng (eds.): *Traveling Facts* (Berlin: Campus), 154-176.

London Statement 2002: *Defeating Organized Crime in South Eastern Europe*, Lancaster House Ministerial Conference, 25 November, available at http://www.stabilitypact.org/org-crime/london-statement.pdf (20 October 2008).

Lorenz, Roger F. M. 2000: The Rule of Law in Kosovo: Problems and Prospects, in: *Criminal Law Forum* 11: 2, 127-142.

Lutterbeck, Derek 2004: Between Police and Military: The New Security Agenda and the Rise of Gendarmeries, in: *Cooperation and Conflict* 39: 1, 45–68.

Lutterbeck, Derek 2005: Blurring the Dividing Line: The Convergence of Internal and External Security in Western Europe, in: *European Security* 14: 2, 231-253.

Lyck, Majbritt 2008: *Peace Operations and International Criminal Justice: Building Peace After Mass Atrocities* (London and New York: Routledge, 2008).

Malcolm, Noel 2002: *Bosnia: A Short History* (London: Pan Books).

Mandel, Robert 2007: Reassessing Victory in Warfare, in: *Armed Forces & Society* 33: 4, 461-495.

Mani, Rama 1998: Conflict Resolution, Justice and the Law: Rebuilding the Rule of Law in the Aftermath of Complex Political Emergencies, in: *International Peacekeeping* 5: 3, 1-25.

Mappes-Niediek, Norbert 2003: *Balkan-Mafia: Staaten in der Hand des Verbrechens – Eine Gefahr für Europa*, 2. aktualisierte und erweiterte Auflage (Berlin: Ch. Links Verlag).

Marenin, Otwin 2005: *Restoring Policing Systems in Conflict Torn Nations: Process, Problems, Prospects*, Occasional Paper No. 7, Geneva: Geneva Centre for the Democratic Control of Armed Forces, June.

Marten, Kimberly 2007, Statebuilding and Force: The Proper Role of Foreign Militaries, in: *Journal of Intervention and Statebuilding* 1: 2, 231-247.

Marucelj, Irv 2005: *Mature Peacekeeping Operations as Facilitators of Organized Crime*, IRPP Working Paper Series No. 2005-01, Montréal: Institute for Research on Public Policy, March.

Mendelson, Sarah E. 2005: *Barracks and Brothels: Peacekeepers and Human Trafficking in the Balkans*, Washington DC: Center for Strategic and International Studies.

Mendelson-Forman, Johanna 2006: Security Sector Reform in Haiti, in: *International Peacekeeping* 13: 1, 14-27.

Merlingen, Michael and Rasa Ostrauskaite 2005: ESDP Police Missions: Meaning, Context and Operational Challenges, in: *European Foreign Affairs Review* 10: 2, 215-235.

Merlingen, Michael and Rasa Ostrauskaite 2005b: Power/Knowledge in International Peacebuilding: The Case of the EU Police Mission in Bosnia, in: *Alternatives* 30: 3, 297-323.

Miettinen, Juha 2005: *MNTF(N) and Local Authorities Bear down on Organized Crime*, in: EUFOR Forum No. 5, June, Sarajevo, page 6.

Miettinen, Juha 2005b: *Operation "Deep River 1": Enhancing Cooperation on the Border"*, in: EUFOR Forum No. 10, November, Sarajevo, page 5.

Mintz, Oliver 2007: Focused Operations against Organized Crime in a Mature Peace Operations Environment, in: *Infantry Magazine* 96: 1, 38-45.

Mobekk, Eirin 2005: *Identifying Lessons In United Nations International Policing Missions*, Policy Paper No. 9, Geneva: Geneva Centre for the Democratic Control of Armed Forces, November.

Mobekk, Eirin 2006: *Transitional Justice and Security Sector Reform: Enabling Sustainable Peace*, Occasional Paper No. 13, Geneva: Geneva Centre for the Democratic Control of Armed Forces, November.

Mobekk, Eirin 2008: MINUSTAH and the Need for a Context-Specific Strategy: The Case of Haiti, in: Heiner Hänggi and Vincenza Scherrer (eds.): *Security Sector Reform and UN Integrated Missions: Experience from Burundi, The Democratic Republic of Congo, Haiti and Kosovo* (Vienna and Berlin: DCAF and LIT), 113-168.

Mockaitis, Thomas R. 2004: *Civil-Military Cooperation in Peace Operations: The Case of Kosovo, October*, Strategic Studies Institute, U.S. Army War College.

Montanaro-Jankovski, Lucia 2005: *Good Cops, Bad Mops? EU Policies to Fight Transnational Organized Crime in the Western Balkans*, EPC Issue Paper No. 40, 10 October, Brussels: European Policy Center.

Moon, Katharine H. 1997: *Sex Among Allies: Military Prostitution in U.S.-Korea Relations* (New York: Columbia University Press).

Moskos, Charles C., John Allen Williams and David R. Segal 2000: Armed Forces after the Cold War, in: Charles C. Moskos, John Allan Williams and David R. Segal (eds.): *The Postmodern Military: Armed Forces after the Cold War* (New York: Oxford University Press), 1–13.

Mueller, John 2004, *The Remnants of War* (Ithaca: Cornell University Press).

Münkler, Herfried 2005: *Die Neuen Kriege* (Hamburg: Rowohlt Taschenbuch Verlag).

Murphy, Colum 2004: *"Aza Beast": Attacking the Roots of War – A Bosnian War Journal* (Bursinel: Pandora/Smisao).

Murray, Tonita: Police-Building in Afghanistan: A Case Study of Civil Security Reform, in: *International Peacekeeping* 14: 1, 108-126.

Naarden, Gregory L. and Jeffrey B. Locke 2004: Peacekeeping and Prosecutorial Policy: Lessons from Kosovo, in: *The American Journal of International Law* 98: 4, 727-743.

Nadelmann, Ethan A. 1993: *Cops Across Borders: The Internationalization of U.S. Criminal Law Enforcement* (University Park: Pennsylvania State University Press).

NATO 2003: *KFOR's Detention of Indicted War Criminals Haradin Bala (Aka Shala), Isak Musliu (Aka Qerqiz) and Agim Murtezi (Aka Murrizi)*, Press Release, 17 February.

Nordstrom, Carolyn 2004: *Shadows of War: Violence, Power, and International Profiteering in the Twenty-First Century* (Berkeley: University of California Press).

O'Neill, William G. 2002: *Kosovo: An Unfinished Peace* (Boulder: Lynne Rienner).

Oakley, Robert B., Michael Dziedzic and Eliot M. Goldberg (eds.) *1998: Policing the New World Disorder: Peace Operations and Public Security* (Washington DC: National Defense University Press).

Organisation for Economic Co-Operation and Development (OECD) 2007, *The OECD DAC Handbook on Security System Reform (SSR): Supporting Security and Justice*, Paris.

Organization for Security and Co-operation in Europe 1994, Code of Conduct on Politico-Military Aspects of Security, Paris, adopted in Budapest on 3 December.

Osland, Kari M. 2004: The EU Police Mission in Bosnia and Herzegovina, in: *International Peacekeeping* 11: 3, 544-560.

Oye, Kenneth A. (ed.) 1986: *Cooperation under Anarchy* (Princeton, NJ: Princeton University Press).

Packett, Virgil L. II, James F. Smith, Edwin P. Woods and Edward C. Guilford Jr. 2005: Bosnia and Herzegovina: Coalition Doctrine and LOT Houses, in: *Military Review*, March-April, 70-74.

Palmer, Laura and Cristina Posa 1999: The Best-Laid Plans: Implementation of the Dayton Peace Accords in the Courtroom and on the Ground, in: *Harvard Human Rights Journal*, Vol. 12, Spring, 361-383.

Paris, Roland 2004: *At War's End: Building Peace After Civil Conflict* (Cambridge: Cambridge University Press).

Parish, Matthew T. 2007: The Demise of the Dayton Protectorate, in: *Journal of Intervention and State Building*, Vol. 1, Special Supplement, 1 December, 11-23.

Peake, Gordon and Otwin Marenin 2008: Their Reports Are Not Read and Their Recommendations Are Resisted: The Challenge for the Global Police Policy Community, in: *Police Practice and Research* 9: 1, 59-69.

Peavie, Barrett K. 2001: *Intelligence Sharing in Bosnia* (Fort Leavenworth, Kansas: US Army Command and General Staff College, 2001).

Penksa, Susan E. 2006: *Policing Bosnia and Herzegovina (2003–2005): Issues of Mandates and Management in ESDP Missions*, CEPS Working Document No. 255, December (Brussels: Centre for European Policy Studies).

Penksa, Susan E. forthcoming: Security Governance, Complex Peace Support Operations and the Blurring of Civil-Military Tasks, in: Christopher Daase and Cornelius Friesendorf (eds.): *Rethinking Security Governance. The Problem of Unintended Consequences* (London and New York: Routledge).

Percival, Chris 2005: Operation Spring Clean, in: *EUFOR Forum* No. 2, March, Sarajevo, p. 8.

Perdan, Slobodan 2006: Security Sector Reform: The Building of Security in Bosnia and Herzegovina, in: *Conflict, Security & Development* 6: 2, 179-209.

Perdan, Slobodan 2008: Bosnia: SSR under International Tutelage, in: Timothy Donais (ed.): *Local Ownership and Security Sector Reform* (Vienna and Berlin: DCAF and LIT), 253-272.

Perito, Robert 2004: *Where is the Lone Ranger When We Need Him? America's Role for a Postconflict Stability Force* (Washington DC: United States Institute of Peace Press).

Perito, Robert 2008: Police in Peace and Stability Operations, in: *International Peacekeeping* 15: 1, 51-66.

Platzer, Christian 2005: Taktik im Kosovo: Konsequenzen nach den Märzunruhen, in: *Truppendienst* 282: 2.

Pugh, Michael 1998: Military Intervention and Humanitarian Action: Trends and Issues, in: *Disasters* 22: 4, 339-351.

Pugh, Michael 2000: Civil-Military Relations in the Kosovo Crisis: An Emerging Hegemony?, in: *Security Dialogue* 31: 2, 229-242.

Pugh, Michael 2001: The Challenge of Civil-Military Relations in International Peace Operations, in: *Disasters* 25: 4, 345-357.

Pugh, Michael 2002: Postwar Political Economy in Bosnia and Herzegovina: The Spoils of Peace, in: *Global Governance* 8: 4, 467-482.

Pugh, Michael 2005: Transformation in the Political Economy of Bosnia Since Dayton, in: *International Peacekeeping* 12: 3, 448-462.

Pugh, Michael 2007: *A Political Economy Perspective of How Corruption Happens in Conflict and Peacebuilding*, Paper presented at The Fletcher School, Tufts University, 13 April, available at http://www.brad.ac.uk/acad/twe/publications/working_papers/How_corruption_happens.pdf (download 29 July 2008).

Pugh, Michael and Neil Cooper (with Jonathan Goodhand) 2004: *War Economies in a Regional Context: Challenges of Transformation* (Boulder, Co.: Lynne Rienner).

Raab, Jörg and Brinton H. Milward 2003: Dark Networks as Problems, in: *Journal of Public Administration Research & Theory* 13: 4, 413-439.

Rashid, Ahmed 2009: *Descent Into Chaos: The U.S. and the Disaster in Pakistan, Afghanistan, and Central Asia* (New York: Penguin Books).

Rausch, Colette (ed.) 2006: *Combating Serious Crimes in Postconflict Societies: A Handbook for Policymakers and Practitioners* (Washington: United States Institute of Peace Press).

Rausch, Colette 2002: The Assumption of Authority in Kosovo and East Timor: Legal and Practical Implications, in: Renata Dwan (ed.): *Executive Policing: Enforcing the Law in Peace Operations*, SIPRI Research Report No. 16 (Oxford: Oxford University Press), 11-32.

Rees, Edward 2006: *Security Sector Reform (SSR) and Peace Operations: "Improvisation and Confusion" from the Field*, at http://www.ssrnetwork.net/doc_library/document_detail.php?id=3998.

Refugee Policy Group 1998: *Civilian and Military Means of Providing and Supporting Humanitarian Assistance During Conflict: A Comparative Analysis* (Paris: Organisation for Economic Co-operation and Development).

Reljić, Dušan 2008: Der Staat der Mafia: Organisierte Kriminalität im Kosovo, in: *Blätter für deutsche und internationale Politik*, No. 4, 83-93.

Ritscher, Allison 2005: Democratization in Bosnia: A More Effective Role for SFOR, in: Albrecht Schnabel and Hans-Georg Ehrhart (ed.): *Security Sector Reform and Post-Conflict Peacebuilding* (New York: United Nations University), 114-132.

Rose, Gideon 1998: The Exit Strategy Delusion, in: *Foreign Affairs*, January/February.

Rumiz, Paolo 2000: *Masken für ein Massaker: Der manipulierte Krieg – Spurensuche auf dem Balkan* (München: Kunstmann).

Šabić, Senada Šelo 2005: *State Building Under Foreign Supervision: Intervention in Bosnia-Herzegovina 1996-2003*, Bureau for Security Policy at the Austrian Ministry of Defence, National Defence Academy (Vienna), and Institute for International Relations (Zagreb), May (Vienna: Akademie Landesverteidigungsademie).

Scharf, Michael P. 1998: The Prosecutor v. Slavko Dokmanović: Irregular Rendition and the ICTY, in: *Leiden Journal of International Law* 11, 369-382.

Scheye, Eric 2008: UNMIK and the Significance of Effective Programme Management: The Case of Kosovo, in: Heiner Hänggi and Vincenza Scherrer (eds.): *Security Sector Reform and UN Integrated Missions: Experience from Burundi, The Democratic Republic of Congo, Haiti and Kosovo* (Vienna and Berlin: DCAF and LIT), 169-219.

Schnabel, Albrecht 2002: Post-Conflict Peacebuilding and Second-Generation Preventive Action, in: *International Peacekeeping* 9: 2, 7-30.

Schnabel, Albrecht 2006: Insurgencies, Security Governance and the International Community, in: Alan Bryden and Marina Caparini (eds.), *Private Actors and Security Governance* (Vienna: LIT), 65-85.

Schnabel, Albrecht and Hans-Georg Ehrhart (eds.) 2005: *Security Sector Reform and Post-Conflict Peacebuilding* (Tokyo: United Nations University Press).

Schnabel, Albrecht and Hans-Georg Ehrhart 2005: Post-conflict Societies and the Military: Challenges and Problems of Security Sector Reform, in: Albrecht Schnabel and Hans-Georg Ehrhart (eds): *Security Sector Reform and Post-Conflict Peacebuilding* (Tokyo: United Nations University Press), 1–16.

Schneckener, Ulrich 2006: Fragile Statehood, Armed Non-State Actors and Security Governance, in: Alan Bryden & Marina Caparini (eds.): *Private Actors and Security Governance* (Vienna and Berlin: LIT), pp. 23-40.

Schreier, Fred 2009: Human Trafficking, Organised Crime and Intelligence, in: Cornelius Friesendorf (ed.): *Strategies Against Human Trafficking: The Role of the Security Sector* (Geneva and Vienna: DCAF and Austrian National Defence Academy, 2009), 213-259.

Schroeder, Ursula C. and Cornelius Friesendorf 2009: Statebuilding and Organized Crime: Implementing the International Law Enforcement Agenda in Bosnia, in: *Journal of International Relations and Development* 12: 2, 137-167.

Sedra, Mark 2005: *Civil-Military Relations in Afghanistan: The Provincial Reconstruction Team Debate*, Canadian Institute of Strategic Studies Strategic Datalink, No. 126, March.

Sedra, Mark 2006: Security Sector Reform in Afghanistan: The Slide Towards Expediency, in: *International Peacekeeping* 13: 1, 94-110.

Sele, Richard K. 1999: Civil-Military Operations in the Post-War Sarajevo Region, in: *Low Intensity Conflict and Law Enforcement* 8: 1, 87-118.

Sharp, Jane M. O. 1997/1998: Dayton Report Card, in: *International Security* 22: 3, 101-137.

Siegel, Adam B. 2001: Associating Development Projects with Military Operations: Lessons from NATO's First Year in BiH, in: *International Peacekeeping* 8: 3, 99-114.

Sion, Liora 2006: "Too Sweet and Innocent for War"? Dutch Peacekeepers and the Use of Violence, in: *Armed Forces & Society* 32: 3, 454-474.

Slaughter, Anne-Marie 2004: *A New World Order* (Princeton and Oxford: Princeton University Press).

Sloan, James 2003: Prosecutor v. Todorović: Illegal Capture as an Obstacle to the Exercise of International Criminal Jurisdiction, in: *Leiden Journal of International Law* 16: 85-113.

Small Arms Survey 2005: *'Gun Culture' in Kosovo: Questioning the Origins of Conflict* (Oxford: Oxford University Press), 205-227.

Smith, Joshua G., Victoria K. Holt and William J. Durch 2007: *Enhancing United Nations Capacity to Support Post-Conflict Policing and Rule of Law*, Stimson Center Report No. 63, Washington D.C.: The Henry L. Stimson Center, November.

Smith, Rupert 2006: *The Utility of Force: The Art of War in the Modern World* (London: Penguin Books).

Sowers, Thomas S. 2005: Beyond the Soldier and the State: Contemporary Operations and Variance in Principal-Agent Relationships, in: *Armed Forces & Society* 31: 3, 385-409.

Stanchev, Krassen 2005: Economic Perspectives on Organized Crime, in: Ekavi Athanassopoulou (ed.): *Fighting Organized Crime in Southeast Europe* (London and New York: Routledge), 25-33.

Stark, Christine A. 2004: *The Rule of Law in Peace Keeping Operations*, Strategy Research Project U.S. Army War College, Carlisle Barracks, Pennsylvania, 19 March.

Stedman, Stephen John 1997: Spoiler Problems in Peace Processes, in: *International Security* 22: 2, 5-53.

Stefanova, Radoslava 2004: Fighting Organized Crime in a UN Protectorate: Difficult, Possible, Necessary, in: *Southeast European and Black Sea Studies* 4: 2, 257-279.

Stephens, Dale 2005: The Lawful Use of Force by Peacekeeping Forces: the Tactical Imperative, in: *International Peacekeeping* 12: 2, 157-172.

Strazzari, Francesco 2008: L'Oeuvre au Noir: The Shadow Economy of Kosovo's Independence, in: *International Peacekeeping* 15: 2, 155-170.

Sudetic, Chuck 2000: The Reluctant Gendarme: Why Is France Protecting Indicted War Criminals in the Sector of Bosnia It Controls?, in: *The Atlantic Monthly* 284: 4 (April), 91-98.

Tardy, Thierry 2000: *La Problématique de la Maîtrise des Troubles à l'Ordre Public dans le Cadre des Opérations de Maintien de la Paix* (Paris: Fondation Pour la Recherche Stratégique).

Teran, Nika Stražišar 2007: *Peacebuilding and Organized Crime: The Cases of Kosovo and Liberia*, Working Paper No. 1, Bern: Swisspeace.

Tilly, Charles 1985: War Making and State Making as Organized Crime, in: Peter B. Evans, Dietrich Rueschemeyer and Theda Skocpol (eds.): *Bringing the State Back In* (Cambridge: Cambridge University Press), 169-191.

Todorova, Maria 1997: *Imagining the Balkans* (Oxford: Oxford University Press).

Treverton, Gregory F. 2003: *Reshaping National Intelligence for an Age of Information* (Cambridge: Cambridge University Press).

U.S. Army Peacekeeping and Stability Operations Institute 2000: *SFOR Lessons Learned in Creating a Secure Environment with Respect for the Rule of Law*, May.

U.S. Army 2007: *The U.S. Army Marine Corps Counterinsurgency Field Manual* (Chicago and London: The University of Chicago Press).

Ulfkotte, Udo 2005: *Grenzenlos Kriminell: Die Risiken der EU-Osterweiterung –Was Politiker verschweigen* (München: Goldmann).

UNDP 2002: *Human Development Report 2002: Deepening Democracy in a Fragmented World* (New York and Oxford: Oxford University Press for the United Nations Development Programme).

UNHCR and OSCE 1999: *Preliminary Assessment of the Situation of Ethnic Minorities in Kosovo*, 26 July.

United Nations 2000: *Report of the Secretary-General on the Implementation of the Report of the Panel on United Nations Peace Operations*, 20 October, available at http://www.un.org/peace/reports/peace_operations/docs/55_502e.pdf (download 19 January 2009).

United Nations 2003: *Report of the Secretary-General on the United Nations Interim Administration in Kosovo*, 15 October.

United Nations 2003b: *Handbook on UN Multidimensional Peacekeeping Operations* (New York: United Nations Best Practices Unit).

United Nations 2004: *Report of the Secretary-General on the United Nations Interim Administration in Kosovo*, S/2004/348, 30 April.

UNODC 2008: *Crime and its Impact on the Balkans and Affected Countries*, March (Vienna: United Nations Office on Drugs and Crime).

Vacca, Alfredo 2005: Operation Spring Clean 2, in: *EUFOR Forum* No. 3, April, Sarajevo, page 8.

Van Creveld, Martin 1991: *The Transformation of War* (New York: Free Press).

Van Dijk, Jan 2007: Mafia Markers: Assessing Organized Crime and Its Impact Upon Societies, in: *Trends in Organized Crime* 10: 4, 39-56.

Van Duyne, Petrus C., Matjaz Jager, Klaus von Lampe and James L. Newell (eds.) 2004: *Threats and Phantoms of Organised Crime, Corruption and Terrorism: Critical European Perspectives* (Nijmegen: Wolf Legal Publishers).

Vandenberg, Martina E. 2007: Peacekeeping and Rule Breaking: United Nations Anti-Trafficking Policy in Bosnia and Herzegovina, in: H. Richard Friman and Simon Reich (eds.): *Human Trafficking, Human Security, and the Balkans* (Pittsburgh: University of Pittsburgh Press), 81-95.

Venice Commission 2008: *Report of the Democratic Control of the Armed Forces*, Adopted by the European Commission for Democracy Through Law (Venice Commission) at its 74th Plenary Session, Venice, 14-15 March, Strasbourg: Council of Europe, CDL-AD(2008)004, 27 March.

Vetschera, Heinz and Matthieu Damian 2006: Security Sector Reform in Bosnia and Herzegovina: The Role of the International Community, in: *International Peacekeeping* 13: 1, 28-42.

Vetter, Stephen M. 1995: *Military Intelligence Support to Civilian Law Enforcement Agencies: Rethinking the Way Defense Intelligence Combats Emerging Perils*, United States Army Command & Staff College, 17 April, available at http://www.globalsecurity.org/intell/library/reports/1995/VSM.htm (download 26 September 2008).

Weiss, Thomas G. 1995: Military-Civilian Humanitarianism: The 'Age of Innocence' Is Over, in: *International Peacekeeping* 2: 2, 157-174

Weiss, Thomas G. 1999, *Military-Civilian Interactions: Intervening in Humanitarian Crises* (Lanham, MA: Rowman & Littlefield).

Wheeler, Nicolas J. and Frazer Egerton 2009: The Responsibility to Protect: 'Precious Commitment' or a Promise Unfulfilled?, in: *Global Responsibility to Protect* 1: 1, 114-132.

Wilder, Andrew 2007: *Cops or Robbers? The Struggle to Reform the Afghan National Police* (Kabul: Afghanistan Research and Evaluation Unit, July).

Williams, Phil 2009: Organized Crime and Corruption in Iraq, in: *International Peacekeeping* 16: 1, 115-135.

Williams, Phil and Gregory Baudin-O'Hayon 2003: Global Governance, Transnational Organized Crime and Money Laundering, in David Held and Anthony McGrew (eds.): *Governing Globalization: Power Authority and Global Governance* (Cambridge: Polity), 127-144.

Wilson, Jeremy M. 2006: Law and Order in an Emerging Democracy: Lessons from the Reconstruction of Kosovo's Police and Justice Systems, in: *The Annals of the American Academy of Political and Social Science* 605: 1, 152-177.

Wilton Park 2004: *International Post-Conflict Policing Operations: Enhancing Co-Ordination and Effectiveness*, Wilton Park Conference Organised in Cooperation with the Foreign and Commonwealth Office and the University of Bradford, 26–30 January.

Wisler, Dominique 2007: The International Civilian Police Mission in Bosnia and Herzegovina: From Democratization to Nation-Building, in: *Police Practice and Research* 8: 3, 253-268.

Woodward, Susan L. 2004: Enhancing Cooperation Against Transborder Crime in Southeast Europe: Is There An Emerging Epistemic Community?, in *Journal of Southeast European and Black Sea Studies* 4: 2, 223-240.

Wulf, Herbert 2007: Reconstructing the Public Monopoly of Legitimate Force, in: Alan Bryden and Marina Caparini (eds.): *Private Actors and Security Governance* (Vienna and Berlin: DCAF and LIT), 87-106.

Zaalberg, Thijs W. Brocades 2006, *Soldiers and Civil Power: Supporting or Substituting Civil Authorities in Modern Peace Operations* (Amsterdam: Amsterdam University Press).

Zaremba, Maciej 2007: *Series on Kosovo*, in: Dagens Nyheter, 25 June 2007, available at http://www.dn.se/koloni-kosovo-av-maciej-zaremba-1.703822 (download 25 March 2009).

Zentrum für Internationale Friedenseinsätze 2003: *Organized Crime as an Obstacle to Successful Peacebuilding*, Report, 7th International Berlin Workshop, 11-13 December.

Zentrum für Internationale Friedenseinsätze 2006: *International and Local Policing in Peace Operations: Lessons Learned and the Way Forward to Integrated Approaches*, Report, 8th International Berlin Workshop, 14-16 December 2006.

Zirnite, Peter 1997: *Reluctant Recruits: The U.S. Military and the War on Drugs* (Washington: Washington Office on Latin America).

Zürn, Michael 1998 : *Regieren jenseits des Nationalstaates: Globalisierung und Denationalisierung als Chance* (Frankfurt am Main: Suhrkamp).

About the Author

Cornelius FRIESENDORF is a lecturer at the University of Frankfurt and a research fellow at the Peace Research Institute Frankfurt (PRIF/HSFK). His work focuses on Security Sector Reform, civil-military relations in peace operations and strategies against organised crime. He holds a doctorate in political science from the University of Zurich as well as degrees from the London School of Economics and the Free University Berlin. Between 2007 and 2009 he was a fellow at DCAF. He has conducted fieldwork in South America, North Africa, the Balkans, South Asia, and most recently, Afghanistan. Contact: friesendorf@hsfk.de

About DCAF

The Geneva Centre for the Democratic Control of Armed Forces (DCAF) is one of the world's leading institutions in the areas of security sector reform and security sector governance.

DCAF provides in-country advisory support and practical assistance programmes, develops and promotes appropriate democratic norms at the international and national levels, advocates good practices and conducts policy-related research to ensure effective democratic governance of the security sector.

Detailed information is available at www.dcaf.ch

Geneva Centre for the Democratic Control of Armed Forces (DCAF)
Rue de Chantepoulet 11, PO Box 1360, CH-1211 Geneva 1, Switzerland
Tel: ++41 22 741 7700; fax: ++41 22 741 7705; e-mail: info@dcaf.ch

Geneva Centre for the Democratic Control of Armed Forces (DCAF)

Alan Bryden; Boubacar N'Diaye; Funmi Olonisakin (Eds.)
Challenges of Security Sector Governance in West Africa
This book is intended to contribute to confidence and peace-building through developing a better understanding of the challenges of security sector governance and generating practical policy recommendations based on work conducted by West African experts. It analyses the nature of security sector governance in each of the 16 West African states, provides an assessment of the effectiveness of governance mechanisms, in particular relating to democratic oversight of the security sector, and takes into account the regional and international dimensions to the issue.
2008, 432 S., 29,90 €, br., ISBN 978-3-8258-8681-3

Heiner Hänggi; Vincenza Scherrer (Eds.)
Security Sector Reform and UN Integrated Missions
Experience from Burundi, the Democratic Republic of Congo, Haiti and Kosovo
This volume examines the experience of UN integrated missions in supporting SSR in Burundi, the Democratic Republic of Congo, Haiti and Kosovo. Based on the lessons drawn from these case studies, the volume develops a set of recommendations for future UN engagement in post-conflict SSR.
2008, 272 S., 29,90 €, br., ISBN 978-3-8258-1126-6

Alexandre Lambert
Democratic Civilian Control of Armed Forces in the Post-Cold War Era
This volume systematically analyses both the framework and criteria of democratic civilian control of armed forces and security sector governance in their dynamic evolution in the post-Cold War era. Based on an inter-disciplinary and holistic analytical approach, it critically assesses the normative and functional value and importance of the principle of democratic civilian control within contemporary security architectures.
2009, 440 S., 29,90 €, br., ISBN 978-3-8258-1127-3

David Nosworthy (Ed.)
Seen, but not Heard
Placing Children and Youth on the Security Governance Agenda
2009, 336 S., 29,90 €, br., ISBN 978-3-8258-1398-7

Timothy Donais (Ed.)
Local Ownership and Security Sector Reform
2008, 312 S., 29,90 €, br., ISBN 978-3-8258-1652-0

Hans Born; Albrecht Schnabel (Eds.)
Security Sector Reform in Challenging Environments
More often than not Security Sector Reform (SSR) takes place against many odds, in barely enabling political, security, economic and social environments. Such difficult contexts may be characterised by widespread corruption, ongoing violence, imprecise, open-ended or non-inclusive peace agreements and post-conflict architectures, lack of resources, ''stolen'' or impending elections or referenda – all circumstances that stand in the way of full-fledged, holistic and sustainable SSR efforts. Following an overview of ''ideal'' SSR requirements, contrasted with typical obstacles inhibiting SSR efforts, the main body of this volume offers evidence-based analyses of positive and negative SSR records in barely enabling environments.
2009, 288 S., 29,90 €, br., ISBN 978-3-643-80013-8

LIT Verlag Berlin – Münster – Wien – Zürich – London
Auslieferung Deutschland / Österreich / Schweiz: siehe Impressumsseite